THE TROJAN WALRUS

An unsigned copy is worth a lot of money!

(ooops...)

THE
TROJAN
WALRUS

The Misadventures of an
English Stowaway on the Aegean Sea

Julian Blatchley

Matador
9 Priory Business Park,
Wistow Road, Kibworth Beauchamp,
Leicestershire. LE8 0RX
Tel: 0116 279 2299
Email: books@troubador.co.uk
Web: www.troubador.co.uk/matador
Twitter: @matadorbooks

ISBN 978 1784624 842

British Library Cataloguing in Publication Data.
A catalogue record for this book is available from the British Library.

Printed and bound by CPI Group (UK) Ltd, Croydon, CR0 4YY
Typeset in 11pt Aldine401 BT Roman by Troubador Publishing Ltd, Leicester, UK

Matador is an imprint of Troubador Publishing Ltd

This book is dedicated to
Renate and Nerissa
Two ladies who love Greece and, inexplicably, me!

CONTENTS

CHAPTER ONE

A SERENDIPITOUS SAUSAGE

In which we hear an alarming allegation concerning a sausage... Piraeus in winter... the critical avoidance of okra... second mates, an irrelevant but heartfelt digression... yearnings... rapt by an historic shore... nationality, musings and angst with regard to... a change of plan... lamentations on the decline of the British Merchant Navy... the deteriorating prospects of British seaman in general with one in particular... ashore but feeling adrift... we meet the portentous sausage at a critical juncture and clear it of all suspicion... a lemming leaps.

This is a tale about a radical change in my life. It was an event occasioned by unquiet times and a coincidence of circumstances which had led me, at the opening of the narrative, to the brink of an abyss. There I teetered for a while, by turns pulled forward by a lemming-like compulsion to jump and drawn back by the instinct of self-preservation; and then, at the crucial instant, a sausage pushed me over the edge.

Later in this account you will become accustomed to my convoluted taste in metaphors... a-simile-ation, if you will... but for those readers who assume that I have unleashed imagery in the opening paragraph, I must be quite clear: this was no sausage of the mind but rather a real, gleaming, engorged skin straining under the pressure of savoury contents; a sausage sensible to feeling as to sight, which marshalled me along the way that I was going in an entirely corporeal manner; and I encountered it as I lugged my kit-bag through Piraeus docks in search of a ferry-boat one mad March afternoon.

It was a blazing, brilliant and bitter day, delicately balanced somewhere on the cusp of winter and spring; the sort of day which can often be found in the

Mediterranean in the early months of the year. The ice-blue heavens cascaded such radiance upon the drab waterfront that even the grimy concrete of Greece's utilitarian port-city seemed tinged with the nobility of a greater age, but the coruscating light was accompanied by a wind that sliced like a scalpel.

The air temperature, driven by a brisk, northerly breeze, was as crisp as a wind off the tundra, yet, if you got out of the air-stream and into the sunshine, it was suddenly as warm as the finest of English summer days. The direct sunlight baked like a blow-torch, causing my scalp to perspire a little under the burden of the great canvas sea-bag on my shoulder, so that when a small bead of moisture escaped the hair-line the wind pounced on it, transformed it to ice, and sent it skittering down my cringing neck. Passing through the shadows of awnings and kiosks was like walking from a boiler-room into a fridge. The Greeks call such conditions '*ilio meh dontia*'... 'sun with teeth': schizophrenic weather, but so beautiful that even the strident, stinking, savage traffic and the dry, dilapidated, dirty fountains failed to give their customary offence in the effulgence.

I generally don't like cities much, and Piraeus is not a beautiful one in any case. My aim had been to get onto a ferry to an island with all possible despatch. However, the distance to the required terminal was uncertain and breakfast had been at oh-six-hundred; it was now after three in the afternoon and the combination of an empty belly, a shoulder complaining under the awkward weight of the sea-bag and the cosmetic effect of the light on the grimy city was sufficient to divert my steps into a taverna.

The restaurant was a typical down-town Piraeus eatery; a narrow, echoing, indifferently-lit hall behind jaded metal-framed windows. A counter ran along most of one side of the room, and a single row of square tables stretched down the other side. There was a strong suspicion of cobwebs lurking up in the gloomy rafters; the furniture was painted a jaded grey and covered with check tablecloths from which all joy had long ago been washed out; the swarthy cook leaned his tattooed and hairy forearms on the counter and peered expressionlessly around the dog-end of his cigarette. What light there was emanated from un-shaded fluorescent tubes. Heating was something which happened elsewhere, and the clients retained their coats.

In most places in the civilised world I would have hurried past with a shudder, but from previous experience in Greece I knew that the appearance of urban restaurants is often in complete contradiction to the quality of their food.* Peering into the sombre depths I noted that this one was well-stocked with obviously local clientele... nuggety, bronzed men in sailor's pea-jackets and fisherman's caps... and decided it was worth taking a chance on. Selecting a table behind the door to avoid the worst of the cool draft, I ordered something called '*loukaniko*', which sounded familiar; I thought it was probably meatballs, but it didn't really matter as at least I knew that it wasn't tripe or bloody okra.†

Having ordered I addressed myself to a beer, and, gazing out of the lack-lustre window at the contrasts of sun and shadow outside, I reflected back over the previous week and the events which had brought me to this smoky, chilly, Spartan, echoing and irretrievably foreign establishment.

* * *

"What the hell's up with you this morning, Two-Oh?" scowled Captain Andy. "You're simpering like a tart in a rugby club shower!"

'Two-Oh' was me, the second mate, and the Two-Oh of a commercial ship is expected to be a reliable, stoical sort of chap. A fully proficient and experienced navigator, only two promotions away from commanding the vessel, the second mate is a man trusted to be the master's principle confidant in planning and controlling navigation, and the chief mate's first resource in handling cargo. Perhaps most tellingly of all, he is entrusted with navigating the ship in the dead of the graveyard watch, when all others sleep soundly under the aegis of his skill and judgement. A proficient second mate, in a nutshell, is ideally a creature of worth, deserving of the world's approbation.

The world in general, however, rarely concerns itself with second mates. They exist largely below the conscious horizon, or at best as a vague, misconstrued entity, in the same way that swan's wings are only ever associated

---

* Decrepit caverns are frequently concealed gems, laying on their down-market, plastic table-covers fresh food and decent local barrel-wines for a very modest price. Anything with a linen table cloth, or laid place settings, however, is as often as not an over-priced, pig-processing plant equipped with a bank of microwaves which serves box-wine and last week's moussaka 'a la ping'.

† I detest okra; the taste has nothing to recommend it, and the texture nauseates me. If I went out with a double-barrelled shotgun and met Heinrich Himmler, Pol Pot and an okra farmer, I'd give the okra farmer both barrels.

with fractured arms. The popular perception seems to be that ships ply the oceans at the behest of omniscient or alcoholic (there is no middle ground) captains, and are manned by superhuman bo'suns, ingenious ship's boys, deranged cooks, villainous amputees and misanthropic, incomprehensible Glaswegian chief engineers. No second mates. As a shining proof that this is no idle assertion, ask yourself: 'How many crew does the Love Boat have?' I think I counted six, and definitely nothing resembling a second mate. In fact, I challenge anyone to tell me the name of a famous second mate in fiction or history... even I can only think of Charles Lightoller and Arthur Hawkins.*

The universal invisibility of second mates, I suggest, is greatly to their credit, because one thing we may be quite clear about is that something is rarely invisible if it is unreliable... the common consciousness never dwells upon the brake that functioned, the parachute that opened or the rhinoceros repellent that worked. By and large, I was comfortable with this anonymity, and contented myself with the smug conceit that, if the world ever *did* concern itself with second mates, then adjectives such as 'capable' and 'dependable' would be what it would hear, along with metaphorical links to pillars, rocks, and other images connected with permanence, composure and competence. I found Captain Andy's accusation hurtful, but only briefly unjustified.

On our port side, between a gently-undulating sheet of silver-spangled azure sea and a sky of flawless sapphire, a hazy olive-grey coastline was hardening and developing detail with every mile the ship advanced. On the starboard bow a long line of cliffs, high and rocky, brightly yellowish-white in the brilliant winter sunlight, rose steadily out of the sea; and beyond them a great, grey hump began to take form on the shimmering horizon. It looked as if the ship was steaming into an enormous closed bay, but a glance at the chart showed that the closest point to port was Cape Tainaron, the cliffs to

---

* Lightoller was the senior surviving officer of the Titanic, a skilled, stolid, courageous man to whom many survivors owed their lives.

Hawkins was the second mate of the gasoline-carrying tanker San Demetrio which was abandoned by her crew after she was hit and set on fire by eleven-inch shells from a German pocket-battleship. Finding the tanker still on fire but afloat a day later, Hawkins re-boarded her with the chief engineer and half the crew. They successfully fought the fires and restored power, then Hawkins, without charts or instruments and steering with a spanner, navigated her safely to the Clyde. I make no claim to be this sort of second mate.

starboard were the east side of the island of Kythera, and the hump dead ahead none other than the fabled Cape Malea, nemesis of Odysseus. *Seatank York* was in Greek waters, steaming across the south coast of the Peloponnese, through waters fabled in legend and history from the dawn of memory to the Second World War, and would shortly round Malea to enter the Aegean Sea. And I was becoming more euphoric with every mile, because I was coming home.

* * *

Now, anyone who knows me will cry out at this point that I am spouting complete and utter hogwash. I am a stout (few stouter!) son of the northern English mountains; the issue of a Yorkshire father and a Westmerian mother, weaned on Cumberland sausage and raised on Stilton, beef, Yorkshire pud and Hartley's bitter from infancy to adultery. I was educated in Shakespeare, Waterloo and cricket at a draughty and venerable pile on a moorland hillside, where blood-sports were played between the inmates and shorts were *de rigueur* until the Third Form, even in three feet of snow. I have known the words of all five verses of Rule Britannia since the age of ten. If you cut me in half, I would bleed gravy and the words 'A present from Windermere' would be found inscribed in my midriff. I am as English as Stratford-upon-Avon, a hundred per cent more English than Winston Churchill and, until October 1984, I would have dealt with anyone who dared to even think otherwise according to the Marquess of Queensbury's rules. And yet, by the end of February 1985 I was feeling homesick at the sight of a country which, barely half a year previously, I had thought of only as the haunt of dancing waiters, soldiers in ballet-dresses and Anthony Quinn.

What a change a few months can make. It was not even five months previously that three staunchly English chappies… Rex, Malcolm and I… had loaded our somewhat jaundiced preconceptions of Mediterranean mores, means and morals onto an ageing sailing boat called *Nissos* and sailed out of Alimos Marina for a two-week yacht-charter holiday; fourteen days in which we became Goldsmith's 'fools who came to mock and remained to pray.'* We developed a strangely intense fascination with the country and all fell to some

---

* See 'Adjacent to the Argonauts'.

degree under its spell: in my case, the allure was so strong that I had made a last minute decision to stay 'for a while longer'.

Having formed a very chummy relationship with Spiros Thallasodoros, the agent who had provided our yacht *Nissos,* I had spent almost a month bringing his boats back to Alimos from all over Greece for the winter; a magical experience, rough on occasion, but deeply satisfying and one which had given me a passing acquaintance with a surprising number of the Greek islands, coasts and waters in so short a time. Then, as the season died completely and Greece succumbed to winter torpor, I had taken up residence on the island of Poros for a few weeks. Here I spent my time in studious pursuits. I familiarised myself with the year's new wine and the winter cuisine, tried out the results of my two-cassette language course on the tolerant locals, poked around a few of the local antiquities and took the master-class in relaxation which the islands in winter can offer *par excellence*.

Even in mid-December, when the brightly changeable weather of autumn finally gave way to the duller cloud and rain of winter, my new love affair with the Hellenic lifestyle did not cool and I had little thought of leaving; but beer-vouchers do not grow on trees… not unless you own the trees, at any rate… and when the unwelcome summons back to another world inevitably came just before Christmas, I decided that it ought to be heeded. I went complacently, signing on the *SeatankYork* in Singapore for a six month voyage. Fair enough, I thought… even allowing for the inevitable 'Sorry, your relief got mauled by a rogue gerbil, could you remain on board another month?' telex from the Human Remains department, I could still be back in Greece by the end of June with three months off to enjoy the summer. I intended to make a few delivery trips for Spiros, to look for some like-minded female company, and keep an eye out for an affordable small boat of my own on which to spend my leaves.

But, you know, the darned place had got further under my skin than I had realised. As the *SeatankYork* ploughed westwards across the Bay of Bengal with a cargo of Indonesian crude oil for Fos in the south of France I became wistful, and spent the long ocean watches reprising the ports of the Argo-Saronic.

When off-watch, I bored anyone who would listen with tales of the Aegean. As I laid-off the courses from Suez across the Mediterranean I experienced an elevation of my emotions which I unaccountably made no attempt to repress; indeed, I indulged my feelings by edging the parallel rulers as far north as I dared without arousing comment from the Old Man, just to pass that little bit closer to Homer's islands. I spent long hours perusing the chart catalogue and charts of the Aegean, reading the pilot-books for the area, memorising weather patterns, making lists and planning cruising itineraries. I scrounged any out-of-date Mediterranean charts and pilot-books, and photocopied that which I could not purloin.

Once we passed though Suez and into the Mediterranean, proximity intensified my feelings. I fell into a bizarre humour which I might describe as euphoric melancholia; elated at the mere proximity of Greece barely over our northern horizon, and saddened by its inaccessibility. Then we got to Fos, and towards the end of the discharge Andy came into the control room to announce that our next loading port would be Novorossiysk, on the Black Sea coast of the Soviet Union. We had to pass the length of the Aegean, through the Dardanelles and the Bosphorus… the prospect of merely seeing the islands of the Wine-Dark Sea made me feel as if I had won the lottery.

* * *

So thus it was that I came to be accused of simpering like a tart in a rugby club shower as we entered the Aegean on a cloudless, brilliant, almost warm day at the end of February. Although not on watch until midday, I had been around the bridge most of the morning, seeing in my mind's eye a cavalcade of historic landmarks as they passed by just out of sight to the north.

With nothing in sight but sea and other occasional ships, I greedily eyed the chart as we passed Pylos, the Navarino of antiquity where I knew Admiral Sir Edward Codrington and his fleet had sunk eighty-odd Turkish and Egyptian ships to settle the course of the Greek revolution.* Just east of Pylos lay the great Venetian renaissance fortresses of Methoni and Koroni. A little further north was Kalamata, scene of the Commonwealth evacuation of Greece during the Second World War, and north of that lay ancient Olympia, where the Games were born.

Next we passed the Mani, fastness of the revolutionary Petrobey Mavromichaelis and, some claim, the home of the Buonapartes. We sailed

---

* He said it was an accident.

through the 1941 battleground off Cape Matapan, and in my imagination I saw the hellish blossoms of battleship broadsides flowering out of the inky night, and the shattered hulls of the Italian cruisers plunging to the seabed beneath us.

Shortly after passing Matapan (now called by its Greek name, Tainaron) I took over the watch as we entered the Kythera channel... ancient Sparta now lay just northwards and the lands of those ferocious Lacedaemons reached its southernmost point at the massive, sheer, barren cliffs of Cape Malea, just ahead. This, of course, was the legendary Akra Malea, Cape of Storms, where the Aegean met the Mediterranean and Odysseus took the definitive wrong turn.

Just beyond this celebrated Rubicon, however, waited an enticement even more enthralling than all the history and legend which had inspired me through the morning; for on the east side of Malea lies Monemvasia, a preserved Byzantine walled town clinging to the flank of a towering column of rock known as the Gibraltar of the East. From there northwards I didn't care a fig for anything Odysseus or anyone else in history might have done, because my own feet had walked those ancient, cobbled alleyways, and my own lungs had collapsed at the top of those cliffs. Monemvasia had been our most southerly port on the cruise of the *Nissos*. I was now entering familiar territory.

There is deep, deep water off Akra Malea and, in the gaiety of our hearts, the weather being fine and the traffic light, we passed it less than a mile off. With the aid of binoculars we were able to make out a seal gravely watching us as we went massively by, and we were very much taken with a precipitous flight of whitewashed steps which wound half the height of the cliff from a monastery near the summit to a tiny chapel close to the sea.

"Must be the monk's karzi,"* offered the highly unromantic Andy. "I'll bet *they* don't eat prunes before going to bed!" (It was no very great surprise to find our bold leader immune to the natural, cultural and historical charms of Greece... he was, and remains, a man of narrow academic interests, acknowledging the superiority of the Complete Oxford English Dictionary over the concise version only because you can see further when standing on top of it.)

As the colossal cape passed astern, the great, square-topped rock of Monemvasia, whose summit I had laboriously ascended a few months before, came into view. I swung the ship to port, the gyro-compass ticking like a cricket

---

* Lavatory

as the great, reddish rock slid smoothly around the horizon until it sat broad on our port bow. From that moment, I considered myself upon home ground.

All afternoon I watched the landmarks (which, on the basis of one brief acquaintance, I unhesitatingly dubbed 'familiar') pass by, boring anyone foolish enough to come within earshot with my commentary. Monemvasia stood out proudly, its towering cliffs and even the walls of the citadel visible. Gerakas and Kiparissi were mere smudges on the horizon. Leonidhion I could not make out at all, but I knew they were there... and so did anyone else who came within ten yards of me!

We passed between the islands of Falconera and Parapola, which we had seen only distantly from *Nissos;* but then the imperious, precipitous flanks of familiar Hydra began to come into view close to port ahead, and to the west of it the cone of Trikeri. Behind that I could just make out Spetsae. As I handed over the watch to the chief mate at four in the afternoon, the picturesque and well-remembered lighthouse on Akra Zourva at the east end of Hydra was plainly in view. Beyond Tselevinia I could see Poros.

So near and yet so far... a scant few miles over that short stretch of sea Pan ruled the anarchic Hydra harbour, and Petros served out drinks and sardonic wit in his Poros cafe. A Flying Dolphin hydrofoil carved through the Tselevinia gap on her way to Spetsae, and coming the other way I could clearly see the old day-cruise ship *Hermes* chugging back to Athens... I instantly recognised her silhouette, knew her name. There were even a couple of sails in sight. Abruptly the proximity of this other world hit me with an almost physical shock; I felt such a pang, such an urgency to be back in these peaceful, pristine surroundings, that all of a sudden the remaining four months of my contract stretched before me like a life-sentence at hard labour. To my consternation, I found myself surreptitiously removing the merest hint of moisture from the corner of a treacherous eye.

I tried to take a nap after my watch but was too enthused to sleep long, and soon found myself back around the bridge just as dark was falling to see the Temple of Sounion. In the fading light I was just able to make out its tall, slender pillars, and then we slid between Makronisi and the western Cycladic island of Kea. The island loomed, black against the indigo of the eastern sky, crowned with a speckle of lights which marked the position of the *chora*, or central village, high up on the mountain above the harbour. Possibly due to rose-tinted spectacles, possibly due to the lethargic nature of Greek electricity, the lights had an unusually warming amber tone which radiated hospitality. It was one of those images of a lifetime; land coal-face dark either side of us, the sky still orange over Sounion to the west with the mountains starkly silhouetted, the purple dark overwhelming the east, and the cluster of welcoming lights high on the hill. My mind teemed with images of safe returns... Odysseus patting his dog, *HMS Centurion* creeping into Spithead, Robinson Crusoe rescued, Apollo XIII splashing down... and the desire to continue my exploration of this enchanting sea waxed into a compulsion, almost into an obsession.

* * *

That night we passed through the Cavo Doro strait and up through the Sporades. The next day brought new marvels as we transited the Dardanelles, passing between the almost-modern battlefield of Gallipoli on the port side and the most ancient one of Troy on the starboard.

We crept through the Sea of Marmara, around the Hagia Sofia and the Blue Mosque and into Istanbul itself. The Haliç, the Topkapi Palace and the Bosphorus Bridge slid past our port bridge wing as we picked our way gingerly though a stampede of ancient, suicidal ferryboats into a strait so narrow that even the sounds and smells of Istanbul reached us distinctly... the ululations of the muezzins, ship's whistles, the drone and honking of traffic, exhaust fumes, spices, pine resin. A train of heavily laden ships passed us, coming the opposite way. As daylight faded we finally entered the Black Sea, exhausted by a day of professional challenge and sensory overload.

Three days later, as we started loading at a buoy in Novorossiysk under the stern, suspicious eyes of a battalion or so of Soviet officials, I was still preoccupied with the strength of my attachment to a country I hardly knew. I was a little uneasy about it, if the truth be told... I was an Englishman, after all. Objective self-scrutiny... I'll try anything once... told me that this had to be a passing fondness. There was no diminution in my regard for England. How could I suddenly become so infatuated with a land so utterly, uncompromisingly foreign as Greece? I was hitherto an instinctively patriotic Brit, and I could not quite come to terms with such strength of feeling for another country. The suggestion that my loyalties might be susceptible of division was as unexpected as being hit by a custard pie during a papal audience.

Then there was the question of lifestyles... I had become greatly enamoured of the way that Greeks lived, granted; but my tastes were English to the point of caricature. I loved bitter beer, roast beef, English mustard, field mushrooms, baked York ham. Sausages. Back bacon. Black pudding. Cheddar and Stilton. Cricket. Pubs. I already knew that these things were all completely unobtainable in Greece. How long could I survive without these staples, the basic essentials of civilised life?

As I inconclusively ruminated over these incongruities, Captain Andy marched into the control room, looking rather more official than was his wont. At first I assumed this was due to the presence of two Russian functionaries, uniformed men of nameless purpose who were conscientiously kippering themselves in the smoke of extorted cigarettes at the far end of the cargo office; but drawing up a chair, he ran a hand through his hair and gave me a weary look.

"It looks like I've got a bit of bad news, Blatch," he said; and then, seeing some alarm on my face, he hastily added, "Don't worry... it's nothing bad at home, nothing personal. But it looks like they may be selling the ship."

"Oh ho!" I replied.

This, in the eighties, was a constant threat for British seamen... the British Merchant Navy was imploding, crumbling in the face of cut-price competition, and the number of companies willing to pay adequate salaries to British officers was decreasing every day. The advent of satellite navigation had made our vaunted astro-navigation skills worthless almost overnight; our highly practical training was a long-term asset which showed in the condition of a ship after many years, but the new breed of ship-managers, who were replacing the traditional ship-owners, had little interest in anything beyond the budget at the end of the current working day. British officers were suddenly having to compete for work with people from developing economies, most of whose training was much more cursory, but who could live like kings on a fraction of our salaries.

I took a look around the old control room, with its chipped instrument panel, ancient hydraulic actuators and long defunct draft-gauges; I took in the massive, antiquarian inert gas cabinet, which worked only for those Gnostics who possessed the combination of occult knowledge and the virtuoso fingers of a concert pianist; I gazed at the familiar, scarred linoleum and abused furniture; my eye lingered on the tatty, much-amended pipeline diagram, spattered with cryptic reminders and annotations in mismatched dymo-tape and permanent marker. 'Take the bloody thing and welcome!' would have been the immediate response in a happier age, but not in these uncertain times.

The prospect of losing yet another ship… any ship… hit straight to the gut, and most especially for junior officers and ratings. The *modus operandi* of the new breed of ship-'managers' was to retain a 'top four' to hold the hands of the new officers; many of the masters, chief mates, chief and second engineers were being retained to lead foreign crews, but no-one wanted to pay a junior officer or seaman a European wage, and in the stampede to reduce costs no-one had the slightest interest in where the next tranche of senior officers was going to come from. This was a particularly bitter pill for me, as I had already sailed as chief mate in another company, but that company had replaced all its European officers and I had been forced to revert to second mate again to get a start with a different outfit. There was a serious chance that this was the scrap-heap for me.

"How long have we got?" I asked. Andy shrugged.

"Not long, by the looks of it. They've changed the dis-port. We're to discharge at…" he frowned at a telex slip, "Ag-ee-os Theo-dorros, in Greece…"

"Áyios Theóthoros." My correction was quite involuntary and equally unappreciated, because Andy fixed me with a baleful eye and repeated firmly, "No, it says here Ag-ee-os Theo-dorros. And then we have to go to the anchorage at Piraeus for surveys. And we've got the new owner's superintendent coming on board in Istanbul, to travel down with us."

Piraeus! My heart, moments before on the floor at the news of our impending severance, rebounded joyously and whacked me under the chin. To Andy's mystification, and to the consternation of the suspicious Soviets, I gave a great bellow of delighted laughter.

* * *

A week or so later I was leaning on the bridge wing in the spring sunshine when Andy came out of the chartroom to join me, a foolscap pad in one hand and a mug of coffee in the other. For a moment we stood together, taking in the scene… the sterile rock of Salamis Island to port, the concrete mass of Piraeus and Athens to starboard, and astern of us the fertile slopes and olive-scrub peaks of Aegina.

Within this natural amphitheatre bustled the thriving anchorage of Piraeus. Ships of all types and sizes swung to their anchors or churned in and out; tugs, bunker barges, provisions- and crew-boats milled; the edge of the anchorage was a perfect chain of ferries headed for the islands; the VHF radio crackled with staccato exchanges as pilots, agents and service-boats sought their clients. We took it all in somewhat grimly... a mere five years before, a good proportion of the ships and voices in any major port of the world would have been British. Now flags-of-convenience and Asian or east European accents held sway, and I won't pretend it didn't hurt. Greeks, who had previously bought up all our old ships, were now the proud incumbents of modern, newly-built vessels whilst we ran the clunkers; and the teeming Piraeus anchorage had all the indicators of a global maritime empire coming into its own as ours sank into the mists of history.

Eventually, Andy broke the silence.

"You've seen the telex from Human Remains, I take it?"

I nodded. John, the chief mate, had brought a copy up after lunch. The crewing agency had given the junior officers one month's pay, exclusive of guaranteed overtime, in lieu of notice, and told us that they would 'retain us on their files in case of future requirements: however, at the present time...' Tra la, etcetera.

"I'm sorry. I did what I could, and I reminded them you've already done a trip as mate. But you know how it is."

"Are you staying on?" I asked him.

He nodded. "Aye, just for a while. Me and Chiefy are going to do a month's handover with the new crowd. Then they've offered me a bulk-carrier." He grimaced. "A ruddy bulkie. Eight months on, four off, paid in US dollars, the ship's twenty years old and only two Brits on board. I don't think I'll bother."

"Well, good luck with that I.G. panel!" I grinned. He grimaced back, and brandished his writing pad.

"You'll be going off on Tuesday. I need to know where you want to fly to... Manchester, is it?"

I shook my head. Down our starboard side foamed a Flying Dolphin hydrofoil, a dashing gold and blue cylinder at the tip of an arrowhead of champagne bubbles as it roared past on its way to Aegina, Methana and Poros. I gestured towards it with my coffee mug and told him, "Don't worry, I'll take the bus."

* * *

So that was how I came to be sitting in the restaurant in Piraeus, but the view through the grimy window wasn't quite so bright as it had been from the anchorage. At breakfast I had been employed on a ship, in very familiar surroundings and hierarchy, with colleagues and countrymen. Now I was a jobless itinerant on land, alone and surrounded by indifferent strangers… and however friendly I had found rural Greeks, I was quickly learning that the urban species can redefine indifference. My couple of attempts to use the Greek I thought I had learned had failed rather abysmally, directions had been harder to extract than dragon tonsils, and I had a strong suspicion I had been swindled at the currency exchange. I suddenly had none of the sense of belonging here that had been so manifest on the ship. It dawned on me that breakfast belonged in another world entirely, and despite my recent euphoria I suddenly had a fluttering in my guts, a touch of nervousness, and a strong sense that I was in a very foreign country indeed. I began for the first time to vacillate about my decision to stay, and to wonder how much a ticket home would cost. Then, just at the nadir of my thoughts, just as I began to succumb to doubt, the waiter sidled up and deposited in front of me a plate containing a mound of chips and two gleaming, turgid, glorious sausages.

The relief of meeting, at this point of crisis, so familiar an old staple, delivered a relief similar to the first swallow of cool beer after a day's hiking; for here were no effete European sausages, no pale, boiled *würstchen* or lumpy *andouilles*, but rather good, honest, gently-curved bangers of recognisable form, hue and magnitude. The skin crackled and yielded under my knife just like an English snag and I bit into a moist, savoury filling. It was like finding air on Mars, like turning over the examination paper and finding that you've already answered the first question six times in revision, like the 'snap' of the parachute opening. It was a lifeline, a life support system, it was confirmation that I could exist in this environment. With renewed confidence overflowing from my breast, and juice dribbling out of the corner of my mouth, I embraced my destiny.

That sausage was, you might say, a link between worlds.

CHAPTER TWO

DRAMATIS PERSONAE

A gentleman's lodging... Poros in winter... how to snare a sailor... Société très Anonyme... Spiros impartially considered... anatomy of a flotilla... Dramatis Personae... Dramatis Naviae... the Armada assembles... scratch appointments... taking it advisedly.

On leaving the ship I decided to base... and debase... myself in Poros, a brilliantly white, terracotta-roofed town. It lay on the lovely, pine-wooded island of the same name, positioned hard against the Peloponnesian shore of the Saronic Gulf, and possessed almost everything a young, single adventurer with a nautical bent and a tendency to worship his belly could desire... a beautiful natural harbour, beaches, excellent restaurants and bars, nightlife, and a plentiful supply of lady visitors.

Poros was really two islands; the large, forested island of Kalavria, which had resort developments around the beaches on its south side, and the much smaller, boot-shaped Sphaeria, where the town of Poros was situated. They sat so close to the coast of the Peloponnese that they formed a large, almost totally enclosed bay which provided excellent shelter. The town lay at the closest point to the mainland... indeed, the word 'Poros' actually means a ford or crossing-point... and was bordered on three sides by an enormously long quay with good depths of water alongside. The various crenulations of the two islands offered a number of other delightful anchorages besides, and all this was situated an easy day's sail from Athens in a strategic position at the junction of the Saronic and Argolic gulfs. The happy combination of location, characteristics and charm made it an ideal hub for cruising the islands.

Poros was not only a yachtsman's haunt but also a thriving tourist destination. The charming warren of lanes between the close-packed traditional houses were richly endowed with splendid eateries offering tasty grills, the best fish the Mediterranean could offer, and every variety of traditional Greek cookery. There were beaches, night-spots and water sports centres. Over the narrow channel on the Peloponnesian shore lay the more agrarian and rather less picturesque mainland town of Galatas, and between there and Navplion were many sunny slopes covered with vineyards, which maintained a copious supply of fresh, young wine. In addition to these perfections, at the time I arrived, Greece as a whole was ridiculously cheap for a Northern European and also attracted a startlingly high proportion of female tourists.

Nothing could have been better suited for my purposes. Poros was a hive of maritime activity and a place from which I could easily keep a keen ear to the ground for opportunities to do some sailing. It was a vibrant and beautiful place to live, and well connected… a very easy commute to Piraeus, from where I could catch ferries, visit Athens or get to the airport if required, and, lying just a five-minute boat-ride across the narrow strait from the Peloponnese mainland, the island also boasted easy access by road or sea to Navplion and Corinth, Epidavros and Ermioni.

* * *

I took lodgings in a guest-house high up in the main town of Poros, very close to the clock tower and sitting on the spine of the hill where it afforded a view of both the Bay of Poros and the *Stenon Porou*, the narrow but navigable passage between the town and the mainland.

My landlady, *Kyria** Fotini, utterly enchanted to have a long-term, cash paying and apparently solvent guest in her house so early in the year, was an enormous floral bundle of motherly solicitude with a taste for scents so powerful as to eclipse the loo-cleaner and so indiscriminate as to embrace, on occasion, her husband's after-shave. She installed me in her best room, a cavernous, elegant, high-ceilinged affair on the second floor with classical

---

*   Mrs

plaster cornices, a split-level, stripped wooden floor, shuttered windows on three sides and small balconies facing the bay and the channel.

The room boasted what would now be called a 'futon,' but was then known as 'a mattress on the floor.' There was a curtain to close-off the raised section where this elegant sleeping arrangement lay, one rush-seated wooden chair and one extruded plastic one, a tin table, a rickety set of three drawers with a cracked mirror, a clothes-rail with a plastic cover, and a tiny fireplace. This latter did very little to heat the room but contributed enormously to the ambience of an evening. It also seemed to give warmth and cheer to the seagulls, which flocked to the chimney and iced the roof terrace around it like a wedding-cake.

Downstairs via an exterior staircase was a small communal kitchen shared with two other rented rooms, which tended to be occupied only at weekends. It contained a marble sink with cold water, a fridge which sounded as if it was powered by a diesel engine, a single-plate electric hob, a small camping gas burner, a briquette, a knife, a few mismatched plates, two forks and some drinking-vessels which had started life as mustard-jars. The gas burner was an essential asset; when it rained even slightly seriously, the electricity was more often off than on. I soon learned to kept candles and a gas-lamp in the room.

Adjoining the kitchen was the toilet and shower, so close together that one could- and in fact had to- use them simultaneously. The strident acoustics in this oubliette transmitted every horrible intimacy through the whole house. The water pipes rattled like the terminal breath of a lung-shot rhinoceros, the toilet flush crowed like a cockerel and the shower-drain slurped like the child of a Titan draining his milk-shake… there really was no need for a lock on the door. Which was probably why there wasn't one.

As far as I was concerned, all of the above were features, not shortcomings; I was a young bachelor of no detectable sophistication, conditioned to sailing boats and elderly tramp-ships, and I would probably have been happy in a Gulag, so long as it was co-ed and had a bar. My lodging was amazingly cheap, Kyria Fotini and her rambunctious family made me palpably welcome, and the views from the room and the terrace compensated a thousand-fold for any discomfort. I had a panorama of mountains, sea and islands extending about three hundred degrees, from the naval base right around the whole bay of Poros, with its stunning backdrop of a mountain-range resembling a sleeping woman, to the narrow straits between the island

and the mainland. I was as happy as a pig in shit... and thanks to the seagulls, I had plenty of shit!

* * *

Thus comfortably installed, I let Spiros and a couple of other contacts know that I was available for boat deliveries, and contentedly fell into a lazy routine as I waited indolently for some work to stray in my direction. My great confederate was Petros, the sardonic, cynical and golden-hearted owner of the Square Cafe, and there I would go each morning for my coffee and to catch up on developments.

The Square Cafe is so named because it is set in a square, but it works both ways as the building is one of those charmless concrete cubes which, although sadly common in Greece, are refreshingly rare in Poros. Despite its lack of aesthetic qualities, however, the cafe was delightfully set amidst orange trees a little back from the road and right next to the museum, so its architectural shortcomings were mitigated by the greenery and the more elegant adjacent buildings. All along one side of the little square lay an amazing number of artefacts too big or too numerous to fit into the museum; ancient capitals, bits of columns, mill-stones, grinding-tables and even a great stone anchor.* The buildings sheltered the square from the wind and made a wonderful sun-trap in the cooler seasons; the noise of the road was kept at a respectable distance, and the scent of the oranges pervaded. I loved to sit there, to chew the fat with Petros and his clients, to cogitate on the aeons of history represented by the museum pieces, and to marvel at the historical wealth of a place which has so much of this stuff that it leaves it out in the rain.

After my morning coffee, I would betake myself to something vaguely resembling activity. I rarely had a plan before I sat down for coffee, but Petros' terrace was so strangely conducive to creative thought that I generally arose slavering with anticipation for some enterprise. Often I went over to the boatyard on the mainland and chatted with people readying their boats for the season. Sometimes I strode out, full of purpose and vigour, bent on a hike. I rented bikes or scooters and explored, and occasionally I hopped on a ferry and spent the day on another island. Whenever I heard of boats for sale I went

---

* They're still there.

off to look at them, but mostly I just patrolled the waterfront, mingling with yachties and watching young ladies getting off the ferry until it was time for a long, lazy lunch.

I was fortunate with regard to the weather in Greece at the beginning of March. It can be an unkind month of temperatures in single figures and overcast skies which leak badly, but that year the firmament remained very largely clear, bathing the land in light and clarity. The north wind, dry and still cool, swept the air of all impurities, and, when I ventured forth, I enjoyed breath-taking views. I would go often to the Paradise Taverna, close to the Temple of Poseidon up on the northern slopes of Kalavria, to marvel at the view of the Saronic.

In weather like this, one can see a hundred miles if one gets high enough, and looking northwards to Aegina and north-west past the jagged crater of Methana towards Corinth every minute detail seemed crisp in the transparent air. The clarity foreshortened the scenery, so that I felt that I could lean forward and touch the islands across the brilliant blue of the sea. Fruit-blossom and wild flowers rioted on every hand, and rebirth was in my eye and in my soul. I was delighted to be back in Greece, and as far as I was concerned, it was unquestionably spring. The foreigners readying their boats for the season thought so too; Poros, however, was under no such illusion.

Orthodox Easter was still some weeks off when I returned to the island, and the European Easter* (which would bring the first real ingress of tourists) was even later. A few visitors were already in evidence, but the combination of Lent and a paucity of punters meant that most of the restaurants were still closed. Despite the sunshine, and a riot of spring blooms, the *Poriotes*, as the indigenes were known, were mostly visible only as shadows in darkened cafes. A few, hunched in their *boufan* jackets and steering single-handed with one hand in their pocket, buzzed along the front on the ubiquitous step-through motorbikes. Poros was still deep in winter mentality.

This somnolence was broken occasionally by the arrival of ferries and hydrofoils, which brought a few people onto the streets and briefly rippled the

---

* The Orthodox church – with, I must say, commendable discernment – observes the old Julian calendar, whilst the johnny-come-lately religions follow the Gregorian one. Consequently, the date of the Orthodox Easter only occasionally aligns with other faiths.

placid atmosphere, but even this disruption was a fleeting thing. Most of the ferries were the old open types called by the locals a *pantouffle*. This means 'slipper', and refers to the shape of the ship, with a ramp forward, a low, open car-deck, and a passenger section cantilevered high up over the back end, but the word also has connotations of grandfatherly inactivity which is appropriate too. They rumbled across the bay, through the strait and over to Galatas in a suitably leisurely manner. At this time of year their clients were all locals, highly familiar with boarding and disembarking, so there was none of the frantic shouting and blowing of port policeman's whistles which the herding of a summer payload involved, and the venerable argosies were quickly and smoothly on their way again. The only real animation on the winter *paralia** came with the daily visit of the *Hermes,* the *Aegean Glory* or the *City of Poros*, ships which did a three-island day-cruise from Athens to Hydra, Poros and Aegina.

As the arriving ship's whistle boomed across the bay, mopeds erupted from alleyways and converged on the main quay. The gift shops threw open their doors and vomited their wares onto the pavement just as the first mooring-lines landed on the dock, and then a couple of hundred Japanese and Americans would perform a re-enactment of D-Day. Some remained aboard, spraying the waterfront with video-cameras. Others, telephoto lenses at the high port, rampaged down the gangways and advanced in short dashes interspersed with momentary pauses when they unleashed rapid bursts of shutter-noise from their 35mms. Then, having duly recorded every cat, flower-pot and child, it was summer for sixty minutes as they porpoised through the gift shops, burned up a few miles of ASA 400 and milled outside the ouzeries whilst waiting to have their photographs taken with an air-drying octopus.

At another imperious hoot the tourists re-embarked and, as their ship churned away from the quayside, the gift shops did not so much close as implode; clothing-racks and postcard stands were sucked back into shop interiors like a pair of skimpy knickers going up a vacuum-cleaner, lights blinked out, doors slammed, keys rattled and the proprietors sprang onto motorbikes as smoothly as gymnasts mounting a vaulting-horse. It all happened with the speed and silky ease of an umbrella folding, so that before the ship had turned the corner out of the bay, the town was contentedly back

---

* Waterfront, or coastal road.

in its midwinter torpor, somnolence so tangible on the air that one breathed it in and exhaled it in a yawn.

The simple fact was that, regardless of flowers or weather, all Poros was still curled up in its hibernatory cave. All Poros, that is, apart from the sailing community.

* * *

One charmingly sunny morning in mid-March, with a genuine harbinger of summer present in the air temperature, Spiros erupted out of a Flying Dolphin like a hen in front of a fox and didn't touch the ground until he was almost the other side of the road. Then he appeared to go in seven directions at once. With the energy and deportment of a ninja on ecstasy, he began rousing sailors from hibernation. Shergar, Xanthos and The Pretty Panzer were ripped untimely out of their winter lethargy, and within moments an electric activity bordering on panic raced headlessly up and down the waterfront.

Within a remarkably short time for so restful a place, all was bustle. People scurried to-and-fro with arms-full of boat gear; hoses snaked across yachts; laundry piled up on cabin-tops; mops, brooms and vacuum-cleaners were plied with gusto. Engines ran, and the fuel truck lumbered from boat to boat. Even O Geros and Megali, the Grand Old Men of the Poros yachting scene, were pottering on their boats with a methodical edge to their stately indolence that bordered on activity. The Grave-Robbers Flotilla was imminent, and the whole winter, which had once been available to prepare for it, had inexplicably disappeared.

As I smiled at the antics of the scurrying dock-rats I had not the least premonition that I was about to become one of them, but when Spiros exploded out of the hydrofoil on that fine morning he had a Grave-Robber to organise and a scant twenty-four hours to do it in… and the solution to one of his problems had my name written all over it.

"My dear boy!" he cried, his customary conversational bellow gently agitating the window-panes behind me with as he rounded the corner of the square twenty yards away, "How are you? How are you?"

I started to tell him that I was in the pink and then stopped, because he hadn't.

"And what are you doing this week? Nothing, I suppose… too early in the season… but we *might* have a little job, just five days… it doesn't pay much, I'm afraid. " At this point his face registered anguish equal to that of Juliet holding Romeo's corpse, "Just students, they don't have much money, but I like to try to help them out."

I grinned inwardly as I remembered first meeting Spiros, when we started our charter the previous autumn; on that occasion too he had given us to believe that he was virtually a charitable organisation.

"Still, it will pay your keep for a few days, and it will be a lot of fun. Lots of girls, you know. About fifty of them." He winked massively. It looked like a car-crusher closing on one of those little Fiats.

This proposition surprised and delighted me. It had not so far occurred that Spiros would want me for any charters; I assumed he had plenty of skippers whose local knowledge was much greater than mine, guys who wanted to sail at a holiday pace, schmooze with passengers and earn tips. That sounded pretty idyllic to me, but I had no expectation of getting that sort of work yet; I expected to serve my apprenticeship doing boat deliveries, which were less popular. Deliveries had deadlines, and being predominantly against the wind they often required hard sailing; there were no perks either… no tips, no half-full bottles of Talisker left in the galley, no bikinied crew to delight the manly senses.

"I thought all the local lads were queuing up for this job, Spiro?" I asked, and indeed that was what I had heard… everyone wanted in on the Grave-Robber. But Spiros's smile took on a shark-like width, and with one avuncular hand on my shoulder and another one, more opportunistic, on my last ham-and-cheese toastie, he dropped his voice to a confidential roar.

"Well, they are, they are… but Julian, to be quite honest, I have a small problem. I have a large boat on this charter… she's forty-eight feet. I need her because she has a lot of beds, but none of the skippers here want to take her… she's too big for them. And also, she uses a lot of fuel, so I want her to sail as much as possible… I need a *real* skipper."

That was the genius of Spiros in a nutshell; in a few words he had employed me, fed my ego, tempted me with carnal delights, manoeuvred me into a position from which I could not retreat without losing face, told me he wasn't going to pay me the going rate whilst still casting himself in the light of a benefactor, and had a free breakfast.

Well, I wouldn't have taken much persuading anyway… I was happy doing any sailing at any time, quite apart from being avidly heterosexual… so I took his explanation at face value, and accordingly hoisted my self-esteem a notch higher up the flag-pole. Oh, boy, I still had a lot to learn! If my own invitation to participate in a Grave-Robber came as a complete surprise… well, that was only because I was new in Greece and had not yet learned see things through the eyes of the locals.

* * *

So I was roped in for my first charter, and quite a charter it was too. The Grave-Robber's Flotilla was, in the mid-eighties, already a tradition in the local yachting industry. A certain international archaeological school (hence the 'Grave-Robber' title) naturally spent a lot of time in Italy, Greece and Turkey, and their students were young people whom the necessity of travel made even more impoverished than your average undergraduate. They toured the Mediterranean in the off-season, partly to have better access to the archaeological sites and museums when they were less crowded, and partly to save money. They also came from pretty much everywhere in the world, so by the time they got to the Mediterranean many had travelled a very long way. It therefore made sense to get the most out of their long-distance travelling and combine their field-trips with a bit of a holiday; since Italy was expensive and Turkey lacked economical airline connections, Greece was where they dallied.

Sometime in the early eighties a lecturer involved in organising these tours- an American at one of the numerous archaeological institutes to be found in Athens- had taken a sailing holiday in the Saronic and hit upon the idea that penurious young folk, who did not mind roughing it a little to save some money, could have a memorable vacation at quite moderate expense by hiring a few sailing boats and some skippers to drive them.

Fortune, fate or ferocious business acumen (my money would be on the latter) had then led this lecturer, his scheme still embryonic in his mind, to stray into the path of Spiros, the charismatic, fabulously plausible proprietor of Saronic Sea Charters, and a man whose mind was so fertile that his body never had a chance of keeping pace with his cerebral output. From the moment of that meeting, the Grave-Robbers Flotilla was not only conceived, it was also hand-cuffed to the midwife, frog-marched through pre-natal classes and booked in for a Caesarean section.

To describe the Grave-Robbers Flotilla, it is probably best to start with a brief sketch of Saronic Sea Charters and its enigmatic proprietor, and so I digress.

* * *

Saronic Sea Charters was an entity of no substance whatsoever, due principally to the fact that Spiros couldn't afford a boat. It also employed no permanent staff, possessed no capital that anyone had ever located, and its office was essentially a tatty leather satchel generally to be found in the back of a sand-coloured Lada Jeep; anyone wanting to sue the company would need to serve a writ at forty kilometres an hour (although certainly no more) to a car which blended into the concrete around it, travelled in its own personal smoke-screen and boasted a single, deeply ambiguous registration plate. The only real assets the business possessed consisted of a ream of headed stationery, a portable typewriter and what might have been termed a 'compound intellectual property' - the confidence, imagination, language skills and sheer brass neck of the proprietor. To these you might, if you had a *very* generous interpretation of the term 'asset,' have added the Jeep.

The company chose to do business largely in the field of renting out sailing yachts, with or without skippers, but could, in fact, have done almost anything at all... and when opportunity arose, it did. It certainly did not operate a 'walk-in' style of business- it was the sort of firm that you would have expected to have a double lock and a spy-hole in its door, if only it had possessed a door- and preferred to come to its clients rather than the other way about. For a few weeks of the year it could be reliably located at the London, Paris and Dusseldorf Boat Shows, but apart from that it existed with nomadic elusiveness, visible only in the form of adverts in the classified section of various yachting magazines.

Spiros was the company's only regular employee. During my first voyage in Greece, I had been surprised by his receptionist's unfamiliarity with nautical matters... I now knew the reason. In those days before mobile phones arrived in Greece, all the company's calls and faxes were received by a barmaid at a hotel near Alimos Marina. The 'after-hours emergency number' on the stationery was Lefteris's souvlaki joint in Amfitheas Street. If Spiros himself wasn't available, there was generally someone there prepared to do him a favour by sorting out a cock-up.

In those days most of the charter yachts in Greece were owned by private owners, and Spiros made it his business to know everything possible about every boat and proprietor on the Attic shore. His basic operating methodology was to contract for absolutely any requirement whatsoever, and then, but not until the deposit was received, go looking for the boats, skippers or hostesses to fulfil the particular needs of the client. In the high season, when late bookings came in and boats were scarce, or when they were broken down, late back due to bad weather or otherwise unavailable at the last minute, this led to some splendidly farcical eleventh-hour situations which would have destroyed the nerves of anyone with a conventional approach to business in a week; but Spiros was a man with a true genius for improvisation and the energy of a gibbon on adrenaline supplements. He thrived like a vampire in a blood-bank.

Spiros himself was as extrovert and flamboyant as his company was reclusive. Somewhat over average height, of coffee-olive complexion and evidently jolly fond of his food, he was not so much hirsute as shag-pile carpeted. Ringlets of coal-black hair sprang out half a foot in all directions from his head, as if at loggerheads with his scalp. His jowl was eternally blue with growth, a Zapata moustache drooped limply over his upper lip and his eyebrows resembled sea-urchins clinging to a rock. At his throat was a straight line where his razor daily demarcated between the cultivated and feral parts of his body, and from every gap in the buttons of his straining shirt-front erupted anarchic, wiry curls. What little could be seen of his face through the undergrowth was tanned to cinnamon, and when he pointed at something his fore-arm looked like a dachshund with no legs. Yet, if I have given the impression that Spiros's predominating characteristic was hair, I must instantly correct myself: all his yak-like shagginess was merely the backdrop for his smile. For when Spiros smiled normally (which was pretty much at any time when he was awake with his wallet closed) the world about him grew brighter; when he made a special effort, which he did readily, the very sun of Greece acknowledged the competition, let out a grunt and upped its game.

A Spiros smile gave his whole head a workout. His hair-line shot up about two inches, his eyes retreated into fleshy fissures, his back-teeth popped round the corner for a word with his earlobes and his pupils blazed like the birth of a star. There was no doubting the sincerity of a Spiros smile; not because it wasn't a calculated act-it very, very often was- but rather because you simply knew that he couldn't be feigning it. He was merely revealing his true nature, albeit when it suited him to do so. Ambrose Bierce would have conceded the sincerity of a Spiros smile.

Spiros's other dominant trait was his ability to talk both hind legs and the bum off a whole cavalry regiment. As equally at home in English as in Greek, he also possessed a deep confidence in his abilities in French, Italian and German (an opinion which his French, Italian and German clients would have been happy to contradict, had they ever been able to get a word in edgeways). When merely being sociable, he could comfortably occupy ninety per cent of any conversation… and not unpleasantly either. His entertaining fund of stories and jokes, delivered with natural timing and a sumptuous vocabulary, made a willing audience of most people. But when faced with the need to divert attention from something, or to talk down a complaint, he went into filibuster mode. Then, an ocean-liner's foghorn couldn't have got the better of him.

Spiros was a mighty believer in Hamlet's maxim: 'There is nothing either good or bad but thinking makes it so.' It was a measure of the psychology of the man, for instance, that he never saw his position as owner of a charter firm without a boat as either absurd or disadvantageous, but rather took the view that it allowed him freedom in the market.

Spiros oiled his way past anything negative and could find a positive aspect to anything short of disembowelling… had he ever taken it into his head to defend Hitler, you'd have ended up giving the brute a Nobel prize for infrastructure. It wasn't Tony Blair who invented 'spin', believe me… all he did was give it a bad name. The genius of Spiros's spin was that after you'd been spun you queued up to pay for another ride.

* * *

When the Chief Executive (and only) Officer of Saronic Sea Charters fortuitously met with the archaeology lecturer he had immediately recognised several key points. First and foremost, the students didn't have a lot of money, but there were a lot of them. Spiros instantly comprehended that this was a 'stack 'em high and sell 'em cheap' opportunity (which appealed to him not only commercially but also at an emotional level) and he identified that his product was perfect for the market… cut-price yachts for undiscerning clients was a niche he was ideally positioned to exploit.

Operating out of the high season was another feature which suited Spiros's business model. In the low season he could have his pick of boats; he could match them exactly to his requirements, take or amend bookings at the last minute with confidence that whatever he needed would be available, and he could drive a devilish bargain with owners keen for some off-season income. Then he could cram each boat full of bodies paying on a 'per head' (but not necessarily 'per bed') basis, and his returns would be excellent. The condition of the boat was not critical… if a boat looked a bit ropey this was simply a tool for driving the price down a bit further, and if it broke down, well, it was a flotilla… another boat could tow the damn thing. But perhaps the most charming aspect of working in the off-season, particularly in spring when most of the Grave-Robbers took place, was the very decent chunk of loot it brought in early in the year… a most desirable state of affairs after a long winter.

It is often said that the three most important things about a business are the location, the location, and the location. As we have seen, Spiros's business was based (in so far as it was based anywhere) at Alimos Marina in the Athenian suburb of Kalamaki; but Alimos houses half the charter boats in Greece and that Sherwood Forest of aluminium masts is stalked by many Sheriffs of Nottingham… wits are keen, secrets are badly-kept, and ethics is a county east of London. Spiros originally moved the Grave-Robber to Poros, thirty miles south-west of Kalamaki on the opposite side of the Saronic Gulf, purely to keep the enterprise away from the competition of the Alimos vultures; however, it quickly turned out to be a brilliant tactical move in many other respects.

Poros was and is a simply beautiful place to start and end your voyage. The island is not only an ideal terminus, it is also a fully-fledged destination, and the holiday starts the moment one arrives. Whatever your needs, tucked away somewhere between the Sleeping Lady in the west and the castellated island of Bourtzi in the east, you can find pretty much everything required for an island holiday… character, azure water, rural peace, stunning vistas, beaches, secluded bays, discos, restaurants, bars, cafes, excursions, antiquities, water sports… and for a sailor, there are so many bays and anchorages that one could, in fact, have a perfectly good sailing holiday without leaving the island at all.

For the Grave-Robber, Poros was perfect. It had reasonable connections to Athens by road or ferry. The kids could visit the archaeological sites at Corinth, Mycenae or Epidavros by road en route. Ancient Troezen lay only a couple of miles away, and the remains of the Temple of Poseidon were on the island itself. As far as sailing was concerned, Poros provided a safe harbour centrally placed between the Saronic and Argolic gulfs, giving a range of short cruising options depending on weather and time. The sailing was almost always decent, and the journeys a good duration to fit in with other aspects of the holiday.

So Spiros had a product, but he was also possessed of a vision which not all his countrymen can boast… he was willing to play a long game. In favourable circumstances he was prepared to give patience, and even modest investment, a try. He realised that if he played his cards right, this was not a windfall but rather an annual crop, one which could be nurtured, cultivated and harvested so long as archaeologists retained an interest in… arches, presumably, or whatever it was they liked so much. He skimped and saved on the boats, but only to a point… his outrageous brinkmanship had a line beyond which he knew that his charisma would not prevail, and that point he only ever crossed accidentally.

Not content with the sailing action, Spiros managed to involve himself in the entire tour, making hotel and restaurant bookings, organising bus rentals and airport transfers, and helping himself to a slice of the airline reservations action. He organised discounted visits to water sports schools, dinners with Greek dancing entertainments, disco-evenings, sailing races and barbeques; he even had the gall to get involved in the educational itinerary as well, booking site-visits, museum tours, lectures and presentations. In fact, in a very short time, he had made himself so much a part of the local archaeological community that he became a habitué of the archaeological social scene in Athens… without anyone thinking to question where he came from, and despite the fact that he thought an Ionic column was a list of things he had borrowed from someone called Nicholas.

Thus Spiros advanced in the world by wit, adaptation and brazen opportunism. With the charm of Terry Wogan, the cunning of Richelieu and the tenacity of boarding-school porridge on flock wallpaper he refined his creation and wooed his client. By the time I arrived on the scene, he was bringing home the bacon by the sty-full.

The charter was a four or five day event with a loose itinerary to allow the best to be made of the prevailing winds, and it had a well-set format; short voyages with swimming-stops, arrivals early enough to enjoy the town or beach, and two or three group meals or entertainments. Spiros always skippered one boat himself, to be ever-present with his Hollywood smile and blast-furnace personality to put the best and most creative interpretation on any difficulty or deficiency.

A few lecturers would attend, and these Spiros took care to accommodate separately from the students, in a small, new boat, with a sober skipper and strict allocation of one bed per person. Everyone else was lodged rather less formally; people slept in the bunk or boat most conveniently to hand when their stamina failed them, with the more determined socialisers generally ending up on the floor.

It swiftly became apparent that girls predominated over boys by a ratio of about three or even four to one. Apart from a tendency to use more water than the boys, this caused no problems… the girls, possibly because they were accustomed to fairly basic conditions on archaeological sites, were not disconcerted by the basic accommodation, and they were a worldly-wise species well capable of surviving in the robust arena of Greek courtship. Spiros soon found that, on balance, the girls were a positive asset, as a preponderance of female clients made it easier for him to find skippers at reasonable rates. In fact, rural society in Greece in the eighties still took such proprietary care of its unattached womenfolk that, at the end of a long winter barren of tourist girls, there were rumours that several of the Grave-Robber skippers actually paid Spiros for the privilege of working for him.

* * *

So this was the Grave-Robbers Flotilla, and I was a very happy chappie to be involved, especially as I was to be the captain of the flag-ship, as it were.

My boat was *Iraklis*, which means 'Hercules' and is pronounced 'Irra-kleeyse', with the stress on the last syllable. She was a Jeanneau Trinidad forty-eight footer, a boat with a good sailing reputation and a distinctive look deriving from having a curved deck-house over the saloon. Ketch-rigged* with a capacious but shapely hull, she had a large, comfortable cockpit, two good-sized double cabins, two cabins with bunk-beds and a large saloon. In the French style, she had spare bunks absolutely everywhere†... the backs of settees swung up and hung from straps, whilst coffin-like affairs could be created out of short seats by the use of 'trotter-boxes', recesses which extended leg room into wardrobes and adjoining cabins. There were so many permutations, with seats which slid-out to make double beds, hanging contraptions and extra pipe-cots in the bunk cabins that I never did manage to come to a final conclusion about how many bunks she possessed. The designers of slave-ships, however, could have taken useful notes.

Iraklis was definitely a well-used vessel. The whiteness of her hull had lost its lustre; her sails were as soft as linen with use and goose-grey with age; her interior, faintly musty and distressed with prickly, slightly threadbare upholstery, had that shabbiness one finds in the carriages of preserved steam-trains; and years of replacing losses and breakages had left her with barely one fork or glass which matched another.

Despite *Iraklis'* world-weary appearance, I rather liked her. The skipper's bunk was a pilot-berth, a cosy little glorified shelf in a niche by the chart table, which also boasted a splendidly comfortable curved wooden seat, and I took great delight in my personal 'space.' My approval radiated outwards from there. Despite wear and age the boat had pleasing lines, and the class had an excellent reputation. I tried not to be smug about having the largest sailing boat in the harbour and failed complacently; I felt rather grand surveying the world from the unusually imperious height of her helmsman's seat.

Finally overcoming my smugness, I began to prepare *Iraklis* for sea. I loaded her up with bedding from the laundry, filled the fuel tank, ran-up the engine and did an oil-change, washed her down and got contentedly to work

---

* For the non-nautical, I have attached a glossary at the end of this book. It is the same as the one in my first book, but several additional terms which occur for the first time here are included in italics.

† The French often like to do their charter-sailing in large groups. A French boat will commonly arrive in harbour with about ten people milling about on deck, tie up, and everyone will go ashore for the 'Apero'. Another ten will then emerge from below and take a shower on deck.

finding out about her water-tanks, fuel system, and rig. All appeared very orthodox, except that, buried deep in the depths of the forward locker, I found a rather wonderful thing. She had a spinnaker! Oh, how I longed to try that spinnaker... but forget it for this trip. One only flies a spinnaker with experienced crews, especially a kite this size. It looked gargantuan. With grieving heart, I re-interred it in the locker.

* * *

At lunchtime, we all went to George's Cafe where Spiros performed any necessary introductions and made his dispositions for the charter. The flotilla, we were informed, was to be comprised of eight boats.

Spiros would skipper a Gin-Fizz, an attractive, beamy, thirty-six foot centre-cockpit boat with a reputation for decent sailing qualities but rather 'wet' going to windward. Spiros himself, and anyone who wished to study extreme trichology at close hand, could share the aft cabin. The forward end included the galley, heads, and another capacious, ingenious French accommodation.

A blonde-haired Athenian of Apollon good looks called Xanthos had brought a very odd looking box-shaped thing made of flat steel plates with two masts of equal height, lots of wires, and a centre-cockpit. It looked rather more like an amateur radio enthusiast's shed than a yacht, but obviously had a capacious interior.

Yeorgaki was new to me, a stout, black haired chap with wonderfully soft eyes, an infectious grin and a little Gib-Sea 106, a pretty boat with a sweet sheer and (you guessed it) lots of beds!

A curly-haired bean-pole called Karrottos was the proud seneschal of a bright blue 'double-ender' which was obviously built of ferro-concrete, a boat with a stern as sharp as its bow. This was also roomy, and a most attractive boat in a very solid, deep-in-the-water way. It looked like he'd need half a hurricane to move it and the platoon of people it could accommodate.

O Geros and Megali were local men and both were older gents of great experience with very attractive vessels. O Geros had a traditional keel-boat, and Megali, who had a famous name as a racing man, had a sleek, lean, hungry-looking one-design of about forty feet. Both had racing interiors, which means very little trim, thin upholstery, toilet curtains rather than doors and lots of beds arranged like supermarket shelving.

That left me, with *Iraklis,* and the final boat was *Molto Allegro.* I had no idea who was going to skipper her, but I didn't envy him! On her insurance papers she was called a sailing yacht, but not since *Titanic* was dubbed 'unsinkable'* has a boat been so inaccurately described.

Molto Allegro was generally acknowledged to be one of the strongest hulls afloat, and one of the least aqua-dynamic. Almost as wide as she was long, she was very strongly constructed, fitted out inside like the seraglio of Suleiman the Promiscuous and equipped with an enormous six-cylinder engine. As a result of this lavish outfitting, she was far too heavy. To move her stocky, hefty, overloaded hull she had been given a small ketch rig, with tiny sails which could not move her in anything much short of a typhoon. She had no such reticence under motor, however. Her enormous engine could drive her along at a very respectable eight knots through almost any weather; but, being as deep in the water as a post-prandial crocodile, she was also a tsunami-generator… the wake she left behind her was out of all proportion to her size. In harbours she had to be handled very slowly to prevent damaging other boats with her wash, and at sea, since moving water takes a lot of energy, she could empty her fuel tank in half the time of most boats.

Despite her unattractive qualities, however, Spiros had a use for *Molto* on the Grave-Robber. He could hire her in very cheap, and her sumptuous interior made her attractive for accommodating the group of lecturers who were accompanying the flotilla. But who could skipper her? I could immediately see that no-one wanted the job… she was such a difficult boat. Spiros evidently didn't have a solution to this problem, because even his confidence wavered as he named Shergar for the job. I couldn't believe it, and by the look on his face, neither did Spiros. Shergar certainly didn't.

* * *

Since Shergar is to become a regular visitor to these pages, I will beg the reader to forgive another digression at this point as I sketch his character.

---

*   Actually, I don't believe she ever was, until after she sank. That's newspapers for you.

Shergar came originally from Wiltshire, almost as far from the sea as you can get in England, and his curriculum vitae prior to his debut in the Mediterranean yachting industry had included motorbike racing, go-karting, scrap-metal recovery and herding helicopters. He also did periodical work in the film industry, making cars do unusual things, and in the winter he sometimes betook himself to the French Alps, where he repaired skis and provided sympathy and support for ladies who had fallen off them. Tall, chunky, bespectacled and never seen in anything other than a T-shirt, he entirely failed to comprehend the purpose of barbers or combs. He had the freest, most infectious laughter I think I have ever heard, a bubbling, chuckling anthem of joy which rose in his throat like the cry of a hungry chick in a nest, and he could find humour in almost any situation. He wallowed luxuriously in irony and was a master raconteur with a rich fund of wonderful stories which regularly creased his audience up with laughter… in fact, shortly after I first met him, I described him in a letter as a man who could come to break the news to you that your own mother had been fatally mauled by a leopard, and have you in fits of mirth at how funny she had looked trying to hit it with her handbag.

Exiled from Britain by a misjudgement and a misfortune (the misjudgement was that a paint-job would disguise the fact that the car had been created by welding together the opposite ends of two wrecks; the misfortune was selling it to the wife of the Assistant Chief Constable) he had more or less settled in Greece, and Spiros periodically employed him as a mechanic. To call Shergar a mechanic, however, is a bit like calling Ghengis Khan a traveller… it doesn't quite give the whole picture. He was actually a barmy genius, a mad professor, an improviser, an optimist, and a lateral thinker of startling originality.

Whenever Shergar succeeded in something, he was disarmingly modest; when he failed, (and his penchant for innovation ensured that he often did, spectacularly) he roared with laughter and took the mickey out of himself at full volume before hatching a new scheme and diving headlong back into the fray.

Both in looks and nature he resembled a youthful Einstein, and he was equally at home with a ship's diesel engine or a go-kart buzz box. Despite having left school (to the mutual satisfaction of all concerned) at the age of fourteen, his powers of self-education and a practical, analytical mind meant that what he didn't know he could reason out with instinctive and crystal-clear logic.

He loved films, eagerly watching anything from shoot-'em-ups to Shakespeare, he listened religiously to the most avant-garde music available, and his idea of formal dress was a T-shirt with no swear-words on it. Frequently covered in oil, perennially late and capable of assimilating beer like a blue whale ingesting krill, he was nevertheless one of the completest ladies-men I ever knew. I loved being around his girlfriends who were, without exception, vibrant, bonny and as mad as him. Wonderful people to know.

So why, you are asking, is Shergar not racing Mother Theresa to sainthood? Well, in a nut shell, reliability. He was about as dependable as a politician's promise. Once he was on a job, he was generally OK as long as no-one opened a cold beer within earshot. Once you lost sight of him, however, then re-locating him was like finding your virginity again... he was in demand for cars, motorbikes, go-karts, women and parties; each and every one of which appealed to him a hell of a lot more than anything that floated. He had a tiny 'gorilla-bike' with a souped-up engine on which he commuted enormous distances to race meetings, parties, car-auctions and assignations at insane speeds, a tool-box on the back, his buttocks nine inches off the ground and his knees next to his ears. You could barely see the miniscule motorbike at all, and horrified Greek drivers flinched from the spectacle of a man passing them at high velocity looking like a squatting frog travelling on the bones of its arse. One never knew where he would be or when... he rarely did himself. As hard to find, in fact as... Shergar!

From the flotilla's point of view, there was one other slight flaw in Shergar's character too... he couldn't drive a boat to save his life. Thus the general bemusedness which accompanied Spiros's nomination of him as the master before God of *Molto Allegro*. I suppose there was some sense in it: true, he couldn't sail... but then, neither could the boat!

* * *

In the general mirth and incredulity which greeted this appointment, I happily noted some very positive Greek characteristics... they really can be lovely people. The first instinct of everyone was to shout 'Bravo!' and clap Shergar on the shoulder... and even though Greeks have an instinctive fondness for improvisation, this was a very generous reaction, when you consider the circumstances.

These were people whose livelihood was yachting, and there was an enormous amount of know-how around that table. O Geros and Megali alone must have had close to a hundred years' experience between them; Xanthos had been skippering since before he left school; Karrottos had started with his father at the age of ten, and although I didn't yet know anything about Yeorgaki he showed every indication of being a veteran.

Shergar, by comparison, hardly knew a main sail from a closing-down sale; he could not be anything but an embuggerance on the flotilla and, if he learned, he would only become a potential competitor. To boot, he was a foreigner. There aren't many places in the world that would have given him anything more than a luke-warm nod in the circumstances, but within seconds a jovial crew was beating him on the back and making jokes about *Molto Allegro,* about lady archaeologists, and, of course, starting to give him advice. And there is nothing, simply nothing, anywhere under the sun or moon, which Greeks enjoy more than giving advice.

Greeks give advice as copiously as the Amazon gives to the Atlantic, and as eagerly as gravity getting to work on an unsupported anvil. There is a confidence and generosity about the entire nation that manifests itself in rhetorical counsel on absolutely any subject, in any forum, and under any circumstance. Put a Greek in front of a firing-squad, and he'll die reminding you to take the safety-catch off. I had come to think of the host nation, in this respect, as terror-didactyls, and now Shergar rolled his eyes and grinned as the concentrated and conflicting essence of decades of Aegean sailing experience broke and eddied around him like Napoleon's cavalry around Wellington's squares.

* * *

I suppose that everyone considered Shergar's appointment as the *non-sequiteur* of the evening, but Spiros had one last little surprise for us... specifically for me, and The Pretty Panzer.

The Pretty Panzer was a very charmingly rounded young east German lady, of opulent form and a cherubic, mischievously lovely face whom I might perhaps best describe as 'abundantly beautiful.' Chubby and dimpled, she glowed with apple-cheeked colour. As tall as the average man and as demure as Foghorn Leghorn, she was a blue-eyed, flaxen Saxon, square in the shoulder, generous in the hips, voluptuous in the belly, buxom, plump, a synergy of curves and flawless flesh that simply exploded with robust health and vigour. She shone with youth and enthusiasm, and the enthusiasm which glowed most radiantly was the one for a western European passport and a father for her children. These were still Iron Curtain days, and The Pretty Panzer, predominantly interested in putting all that socialist workers paradise nonsense firmly behind her, was unashamedly using her every advantage and wile in search of a husband of impeccable national and financial stock.

She was utterly guileless about her intentions and set out her stall with no inhibitions whatsoever... she wore clothes which had probably fitted her when she was twelve and sunbathed naked at the least excuse, she danced like a dervish, dined like a combine harvester, and wooed like a tsunami. She kept herself surprisingly fit for such a Rubinesque form, running daily in a skin-tight stretch outfit.

The Greeks were besotted with her, and she trailed a string of Honda Fifties as she destruction-tested her Lycra every morning, but she held fast to her goal of a mate of impeccable financial integrity; not many of whom were to be found lying around unmarried on the island. Shergar swore it as gospel-truth that she kept an engagement ring in her bag in case she should meet Mr Right while out of doors.

This latter information Shergar had offered to me with an enormous grin, as the arrival of a British ship's officer on the island represented a veritable sturgeon in the very small pond of the Poros males whom The Pretty Panzer considered to be eligible bachelors. She had thus been exceedingly obliging to me, from the moment that Shergar had introduced her in a blatant effort to get her off his own front porch.

"He's the sort of chap you want, PeePee. Really rich... he's even got a credit card!*"

'PeePee', as she was content to be known, took my initial rebuff as a mere negotiating ploy and stayed as close as she could. She got very chummy with

---

* An asset which was at once exceptional, prestigious and almost completely useless. Greeks treated plastic money like an exotic animal with big teeth; they were quite fascinated, but they weren't going to pop into the cage for a cuddle. The closest they got to such a trusting, not to say taxable, means of payment was to put Visa and Mastercard stickers on their shop doors. Any tourist attempting to construe this as an invitation would be told the machine was broken, and politely shown the way to the bank.

Kyria Fotini, so that she was often around the house, and constantly asked me for English lessons "becauze I vood zoooooo much like to lif in Inglant, alvays it vos my tream to see ze Bockingkham House."

Next, she found out that I like to cook.

"Oh, pliss to teach me zis cooking... I vant to make sooch vonderful sings for my hosbant. A voman should be able to please her hosbant in *every* vay, *nichtwar?*"

The draft caused by her eyelids made the candles gutter on the other side of the road.

When sober, PeePee was an unrelenting suitor; when drunk... an activity in which she engaged with the noisy, salivating abandon of a pig in an apple-store... she was a matrimonial carnivore, a maternal time-bomb, and at absolutely any time she could have eaten and drunk John Paul Getty out of house and home. She really was a very nice person... good hearted and full of joy, but she had an agenda, and her aura was so forceful that you could enjoy it just as well in the next street.

Even in the condition of celibacy enforced by the Poros winter season I made very sure that I was never alone with PeePee, and was careful not to get inebriated in her company. And these were now resolutions which were going to be a sight harder to keep, for Spiros announced that she would be accompanying the flotilla as hostess, and would be sailing with me in *Iraklis*. My knees turned to jelly at the prospect.

These, then, were the *Dramatis Personae* and *Dramatis Naviae* which made up the Grave-Robber Flotilla that set sail from Poros in March 1985.

CHAPTER THREE

DOWN TO THE SEA AGAIN

The making of a captain... complacence... heads you lose... down to the sea... the marring of a captain... Iraklis *finds a chief mate...* Hydra... *waiters, another digression... the misrepresentation of* Shergar... *dinner under the plane-tree... a musical soirée... I am content.*

The first consideration was to teach Shergar to park a boat, and with only one afternoon to accomplish that feat I set about it in the most basic and brutal way. He already knew the boat technically, because Spiros had a management agreement with the English owners, and Shergar had been given a few weeks work to dry-dock and paint her, give the engine a complete service and sort out the 'to do' list which charter boats accumulate; and sailing was not critical, because the boat couldn't. I just needed to teach him how not to crash it in harbours.

Firstly, I separated him from the rest of the team... it was bad enough that he was getting my lousy advice without it being contradicted by other lousy advice. Then we leapt aboard *Molto Allegro* and headed round to the North Quay where, over the course of the afternoon, I battered a few nautical basics into Shergar's eminently terrestrial grey matter.

Going forward and backward he soon picked up... *Molto* had a steering wheel, and this was not too strange to him; he loved carving the still water in a turn and since steering a boat astern requires it to have a bit of speed, that appealed to his racy nature too. In very short order, our new Columbus was confidently turning and reversing in the open, obstacle-free water in front of the ageing destroyer at the naval base.

Next I tried to enforce upon him the most unnatural art of moving very, very slowly... the staple safeguard of the inexperienced boater, but which Shergar was genetically incapable of conceptualising. It was as if he had been mauled by an accelerator in infancy, so that he now had a visceral aversion to throttles of any sort and, wherever he saw one, he simply had to push it as far away from him as possible. Otherwise what was the point of the confounded thing? Decelerating was something Shergar only did with flashing lights in his rear-view mirror, and even then only when there was no narrow side-road close ahead, so the compromise we reached on the issue of slow speed was of United Nations-scale uselessness. Giving that up as a bad job, I progressed to parking.

The Mediterranean moor (by which I mean the recognised way of parking a boat between Gibraltar and Suez, and not the sultry chap you wouldn't want your daughter to marry) requires the anchor to be let go some way from the quay. The boat is then reversed towards the land, paying out chain as she goes; ideally she will then be stopped just as she reaches the quay and some sprightly crew-member or a helpful passerby ties the stern end to whatever can be found ashore... bollards, trees, discarded boat engines, taverna pergolas, fishermen... and finally the anchor chain is tensioned to leave the yacht securely held between anchor and shore, comfortably clear of the dock. All very simple with an empty quay on a calm day, but empty quays are rare in Greece and they coincide with calm days about as often as pigs are given clearance for take-off at Heathrow. To cope with the usual crowded waterfront in a cross-wind requires a degree of coordination which is not often instilled in a complete greenhorn in a single afternoon; so I showed Shergar the basics and then taught him 'the fall-back plan'... an inelegant but effective remedy which involves anchoring clear of the quay, rowing ashore with a long rope in a dinghy, and then pulling one's argosy in with the winches. Shergar, having not the least sensitivity with regard to his nautical prowess, was perfectly content with this.

By sunset, we were smugly pleased with our progress, but aching from the experience... Shergar and I shared a sense of humour and a taste for the ridiculous which made us a dangerous pair. Once we started extracting the absurd in any situation or idea, we simply fed off each other until we both ended up a giggling pile of dysfunctional body-parts in the nearest corner. A whole afternoon together had battered our thoracic musculature (such as it was) like a bout with a heavyweight boxer.

We completed the training of Shergar by retiring to George's Cafe, where I swiftly précised the entirety of nautical lore and law into two digestible pieces of advice: The International Regulations for the Prevention of Collisions at Sea* were abbreviated to 'keep right,' and as far as sailing was concerned I was just a little more comprehensive.

"Keep an eye on me. If I put a sail up, you put the same sail up the same amount. No less, and *definitely* no more. If I let it out, let yours out. If I pull mine in, you do the same. To trim sails, get the boat on course. Then let the sails out until they flap, and then pull them in until it just stops."

He looked at me quizzically.

"You'll do fine!" I assured him, and we both dissolved into a fit of the giggles.

Spiros turned up at this point, bringing with him a pantingly keen Pretty Panzer who was even more radiantly happy than usual at her inclusion in the Poros yachting scene, and openly carnivorous at the prospect of sailing with me. Alerted by a pout which would have alarmed a grouper, I ducked out of an attempted embrace and 'accidentally' obstructed her advance with a chair whilst I looked for an excuse to escape. Spiros! I buttonholed him, and drew him to one side, as though to have a private word. And I couldn't think of a private word to have, so I said the first thing that came into my head... which, in fact, had been in my head all afternoon.

"Spiro," I whispered conspiratorially, "I've been thinking. Shergar doesn't know anything about sailing. He's bound to cock something up somewhere along the line. Wouldn't it be better to put some of the kids on his boat? They'll be partying... they won't care how he drives. But the lecturers won't be fooled, and they're the chaps who *organise* the whole trip."

A look of concerned astonishment came over his face, the sort of look General Custer might have given as he said, "*How* many?"

"What? No, no, I can't do that... no-one else wants to sail with the *lecturers!*" Spiros looked at me as if I was a complete idiot, and the penny finally noticed the signpost saying 'down'. Of course not! The skippers all wanted to be near

---

* A noble and complex work consisting of 5 parts containing 38 rules plus 4 appendices

the girls… Spiros couldn't find anyone to look after a pack of staid, dusty old lecturers without making it worthwhile some other way. I don't doubt that he had serious misgivings about Shergar captaining the expedition leaders, but not so serious that he was actually prepared to *pay* someone to do it. Shergar's time was already being paid for by the *Molto*'s owners in far away England. Spiros was just going to rely on his silver tongue to mitigate any fallout.

* * *

Dawn in Poros. Rising in the last moments of night, I made coffee and took it onto the veranda overlooking the Poros channel to watch the eastern sky turn its coat from union blue to confederate grey. Then the begonia glow of dawn ignited the high ridge above Belesi and the blaze of light gradually flowed down the hillside, filling the east end of the strait. Muted voices and the occasional clink of cup on saucer drifted up from the waterfront below me; the dockside stirred. There was a tinny clash as an aluminium gangway was moved, a few motorbikes rasped and then, with a rumble and a popping of exhausts, the *Delfini Express* backed off the quay and headed for Piraeus. The growl of her engines faded until the calm of the morning was again broken only by the sawing and coughing of the mules which collect the garbage daily in the narrow lanes at the top of the town.

I washed my cup, showered, threw the last items into my toilet bag, and closed my grip. Kyria Fotini was already sweeping the *avli*[*] as I descended, and she bade me a very fond *kalises anemes,* or 'fair winds', as I let myself out of the gate. As I walked down through the town, grip over my shoulder and sunglasses taming the already-brilliant light at the end of the harbour, I felt enormous self-satisfaction. Several people greeted me on my way, already recognisable faces although not, as yet, names. The winding little paths, with their impeccable whitewash, were by now familiar and my step was sure. The brilliance of the morning sky, the dazzling chalky walls, the riot of colour which cascaded from every window-box and flower-pot all delighted me. What possible need had I of worn-out tankers and ungrateful employers if I could make a living like this?

---

[*] Courtyard.

Emerging confidently from the labyrinth at the side of Petros' cafe I took an ouzo and a small *mezé* of cheese and olives, simply because it was so definitely *the* thing to do in this seafaring town; as I sipped the ouzo, and took a profound private pleasure in stripping the olive-pits as efficiently as any man to the Mediterranean born, I exchanged grave nods with Petros' other seagoing clientele, which in one respect or another was pretty much all of them. The grip at my feet formed a bond previously absent; for now I too was a Mediterranean sailor, on his way down to the sea. Smugly savouring this new sense of comradeship, I exchanged a few knowing words about the weather with my peers, and casually let it be known that I was taking out 'the big boat.'

"Ah, neh?*The BIG boat!" they all acknowledged, and nodded significantly to their neighbours. One or two of them raised their glasses to me.

Having indulged myself with my Band of Brothers, I ambled down the dock, pausing to confer my gracious benediction on the fishermen's catches as they sold them direct from their boats, and to exchange greetings with other waterfront characters. Finally my regal progress ended outside a restaurant where *Iraklis* was moored alongside, her high hull presenting a large step up from the quay. I slung my bag over her railing, purloined a restaurant chair to stand on- another source of contentment, as one needed to be an intimate of the waterfront to know that this was quite acceptable behaviour provided that you patronised the restaurant from time to time… and swung myself up into my kingdom.

As I sat at the wheel and gazed complacently around, the first hydrofoil from Porto Heli grumbled into the channel. The boat bucked gently and plucked at her moorings… she seemed as eager as me to cast off the idleness of winter and feel the first of the summer miles washing past her keel. I had a sense of purpose, of nobility, of place, of independence, of aspirations high above the grimy imperatives of the life of the common man. In fact, I think pride and narcissism had inflated my chest to almost the size of my stomach when Spiros passed by with a cheery, "Good morning! Oh… I forgot… the forward toilet is blocked… but it's OK, you've got an hour or so to clear it before they arrive…"

---

* Yes.

The skipper who cheerfully greeted his boisterous charges at the ferry pier about ninety minutes later was one with slightly fewer misconceptions of the romance of commercial yachting, a little less self-esteem, and a strong whiff of antiseptic soap about him.

* * *

They were a bouncy lot, my archaeolonauts. We herded them all into George's Cafe where Spiros made a charmingly charismatic welcome speech… during which I noticed that he suddenly developed a rather engaging Greek accent whilst he set out his stall as the genial and genuine Hellenic host… and introduced the boats and the skippers. There then followed a cheerfully anarchic mêlée as the kids sorted themselves out according to the crew-mates, yacht and captain they liked the look of.

I shortly found myself patiently shepherding a platoon of dancing, chattering magpies past the souvenir shops towards the boat, where I simply said "This is my bed. The rest are first come, first served…" and was then rather pleasantly trampled by a good-natured phalanx of predominantly female body-parts. When I had enjoyed this to a point barely on the respectable side of perversion I left them to sort themselves out, and returned to the cockpit… a cockpit now inhabited by a very hyper Pretty Panzer, who was suddenly rather more conspicuous than she had been during my travails with the toilet. I figured that I now at least knew how far she *wasn't* prepared to go to get her man.

Eventually I mustered them all into Petros' cafe, and tried to make sense of the names and nationalities. I found I had two couples and eight young ladies, originating from places as mutually remote as Iceland and Okinawa. English was more or less the *lingua franca*, although an Italian boy and his Czech girlfriend didn't seem to have any language in common with anyone, including each other. The boys both looked a little soft, with a strong hint of mum's cooking still about them, but the girls were pretty much how I had imagined young archaeologists would be…a healthy, practical looking lot for the most part; somewhat earnest, inclined to be analytical, and highly inquisitive.

I was a (fairly) young, single and single-minded man, and so the equality-conscious reader will perhaps forgive the fact that, through the diminishing effects of the years, I have retained rather more detail about the girls than the boys. To the latter I was perfectly indifferent, but as regards the former I was highly delighted with my haul. Before me appeared a very pleasing selection of international womanhood; fit, intelligent and homely looking lasses with outdoor complexions not always found in students. There was one outstanding beauty amongst them; the Icelandic girl, who had some of the most delicate facial features I had ever seen; high cheeks, a sharp little nose and elfin lips, set off with silver-blond shoulder-length hair and the ice-grey eyes of a wolf. Her figure was equally mesmeric, and her character was delightfully open and warm. It was fortunate indeed that she had one flaw which brought her down to a level at which a mere mortal could interact with her…her name sounded like a wolverine eating porridge. My instant and no doubt lamentably sexist first thought when I met her was that she must be truly committed to archaeology,* because there ought to have been any number of modelling agencies willing to shovel dollars through her window with a fork-lift.

As we got introduced, and I concentrated desperately on trying to create *aides-memoires* to help me remember everyone's name, I heard Shergar addressing his team at a nearby table.

"No, honest!" He grinned, "I haven't a clue. I'm just going to follow Julian."

I winced, but his four earnest passengers chuckled contentedly; and then, as Shergar disappeared out of earshot to get more beer, I heard the confident rumble of a trans-Atlantic accent say "British understatement!" and her confederates tapped their noses and nodded knowingly.

* * *

We left the dock at about one o'clock. I had some notion of giving everyone something to do and making it a bit of a lesson, but no-one seemed very much interested in my ideas. The boys had both withdrawn into private cabins with

---

* Later- too late to do me any credit, I fear- it did occur to me that her commitment must have been even greater than I imagined. The life of an Icelandic archaeologist presumably requires considerable tenacity when you consider the hardness of their ground. There are also perceptible difficulties in having a quick look under a glacier, and if you go peering into holes you are likely to get a face-full of hot water or lava. All credit to them, say I.

their partners, and the rest of the girls were preoccupied with staking their claim to lockers, with unpacking and, to my amazement and delight, with changing into bikinis. It was a sunny day, to be sure, but the air was not really warm and if you stood in a shadow you soon felt it. I was wearing an open body-warmer over my shorts and cotton shirt, and most Greeks still had their overcoats and felt trousers on; but the northern element of my crew, which was most of them, were nothing daunted and the Icelandress, or whatever the correct term for them is, declared that she felt positively summery.

I trotted a few yards down the dock to help Shergar off the quay. This was no great challenge for him, as *Molto* was berthed with her stern to the dock. I let the ropes go, and he just headed straight out into the channel... and turned the wrong way, towards Methana. The rest of the flotilla was going to Hydra, and so when Shergar glanced back at me I gave my thumb a covert jerk the other way. He nodded imperceptibly, and a moment later I heard his voice booming over the water;

"We'll just go up this way a bit first, so that you can get a good look at the clock tower. Then I'll come back and follow Julian, because I haven't a clue where we're going!"

A ripple of contented laughter bubbled out of his crew. I shook my head at the insanity of it, giggled helplessly and hurried back to *Iraklis*.

We would have got away clean, had it not been for PeePee who, in her lunatic enthusiasm, cast off the lines of the boat ahead as well as ours. This resulted in me doing some rather rapid commuting up and down the deck to make sure she got them secured properly again. By this time, though, almost all of my crew were stretched out on deck in the sun. My migrations took on the nature of a hurdles race through a busy mortuary.

Having re-secured the other boat, PeePee made a wholehearted but elephantine leap for *Iraklis* and missed by about a metre. I ended up with my arms around her shoulder blades, hanging on for grim death as she thrashed about in a galvanic attempt to get a leg as high as the toe-rail... bikinied, fleshy and coated in sun-tan oil, it was like trying to hang onto a Teflon-coated hippo in an earthquake. My passengers lived scrupulously up to their name, observing with keen interest and doing nothing whatever to help as the now unsecured *Iraklis* drifted slowly astern towards Captain Yeorgios' fishing boat.

Fortunately, assistance was at hand. Blatchley's first law of nautical recreation is, 'the competence of the manoeuvre is in inverse proportion to the number of people watching it.' Half the waterfront folk of Poros, in particular the ones I had accidentally managed to tell that I was sailing 'the big boat' today, were in the vicinity to watch me leave, and the sudden abundance of bikinis had done nothing to diminish the audience either; a substantial throng was therefore available and very willingly grabbed hold of railings and shrouds to hold the boat and reduce her impact on Captain Yeorgios' newly-painted stem. Then a couple of grinning fishermen gave PeePee's ample posterior portion a shrewd hoick and she flew over the rail with a squeak of protest... propelled, I suspect, as much by indignation as force.

Regaining the wheel, I manoeuvred *Iraklis* out of the confined berth... it was a nice little bit of driving, if I do say so myself, but of course when you do something right, no-one notices. My reputation had already been established by preceding events, and a non-event was not going to change it.... especially since most of the crowd which had observed my inelegant departure were already on their way to the cafe to have a good chuckle about it, and the remainder were still bellowing advice. Ruefully, I turned into the channel, and just as my stern gland began to unclench the world suddenly became full of Shergar, roaring back out of nowhere with a huge grin on his face and an enormous bow wave under *Molto's* stem. I slammed my engine astern so hard that I almost broke the throttle-lever; black smoke erupted from under the counter as *Iraklis'* mighty eighty horse-power engine souffléed the harbour, and she stopped almost dead. Shergar crossed my bow with a cheery wave and a comfortable half-inch to spare. Had the bewitchingly vulpine eyes of Bjørk Someonesdottir not appeared in front of mine at that moment, he might have learned a thing or two about his IQ and parentage.

Sweating at the scalp and whistling to create an impression of imperturbability, I headed east down the strait, and consoled myself that, although I had performed ignominiously in front of about half of the people of Poros whom I most wished to impress, I could at least be grateful that O Geros and Megali were already out of the channel and had not witnessed our departure. As the senior local sailors, theirs was the censure I feared the most.

* * *

Hydra, pronounced '*ee*-thra', is a mere twelve nautical miles from Poros; a distance which a yacht can generally cover in just over two hours with a fair wind, or under engine if the day is calm. The wind that greeted us as we passed Bourtzi, a charming little fortified islet in the eastern approach to Poros, was a light north-easterly… enough to move us at three, or possibly four, knots at best. I decided to sail, however, because of Spiros' strictures about fuel consumption and also because I had this odd perception in the unexplored space between my ears that folks who had hired a sailing boat might actually want to sail.* So I swallowed a cup of hot tar and got nautical.

It was fairly evident from the inertia during our departure from Poros that most of the crew were at best ambivalent about boats, and they had so far shown no inclination for physical activity. I decided to make sailing an optional activity.

"Anyone who is interested in sailing, come and join me in the cockpit."

I wasn't trampled in the rush. The inevitable Pretty Panzer, fully recovered from her indignities and keen as ever, galumphed aft from the mast, and I had one other taker; a square-featured, stocky, curly-haired brunette with a cheeky grin who rose vertically out of the main hatch like a Polaris missile leaving it's silo.

"Oh, rathER!" She enthused in public-school English, and vaulted over the coaming into the cockpit with all the decorum and daintiness of an SAS trooper dropping in at the Iranian embassy.

"Ready, willing and able, what, Skip!"

She stood beaming and keen, blue eyes sparkling, button-nosed, apple-cheeked and shapely, attractive in the curvy, substantial sort of way that does not get into the fashion magazines, playing an imaginary piano with her fingers in anticipation of something to do. I groaned inwardly. A hearty Hooray-Henry type… the sort of girl farmed out to the Pony Club from the age of six, who can bare knuckle-box an inflamed stallion at puberty and crush a carthorse into submission with her thighs before she can vote. I had an immediate mental picture of a highly impractical creature of immense strength and enthusiasm but little sagacity tearing the clews out of *Iraklis*' weary old sails.

"OK, great. Er… it's Chloe, isn't it?"

"Clemmie, ectually. Short for 'Clytemnestra'… never forgive my ruddy Pater for that, what?" she bubbled.

---

* This was a premise which continued to misguide me throughout my professional yachting career.

Clytemnestra. It would be! Absolutely NO jokes, Julian!

"Right Clemmie… er… ever done any sailing before?"

'Please, Gods, let her say no!' I prayed… the last thing I needed was a Solent yellow-wellie who was going to say, "That's not the way we did it on the Hamble!" to everything… because I am a self-taught sailor, and I have not the foggiest idea how anything is done on the Hamble. Well, outside the Rising Sun, that is.

"Well, just a little bit, don'cher know?"

Grieving inwardly that, out of all the demure and elegant specimens of young womanhood on board, it was only these two gung-ho Amazons who apparently had the slightest interest in anything I might be able to teach them, I fixed a cheery smile on my phiz and led them through the steps of hoisting the main sail.

Tip-toeing as discretely as possible through the tangle of body-parts which strewed the deck, I gave a clear, step-by-step commentary… halyard up… not too tight, no vertical wrinkles at the luff. Reef-lines and topping-lift eased. Outhaul tension checked. Kicker lightly tensioned. All this was attentively followed by PeePee and Clemmie, and might as well have been a speech by the President of the European Commission* as far as anyone else was concerned.

Returning to the cockpit, I trimmed the track and main sheet with similar sagacious observations, and then turned slightly off the wind so that *Iraklis* heeled gently to starboard as the light south-easterly breeze filled the mainsail. It seemed I could just about lay a course to Tselevinia, perhaps having to make one tack, but that would do me just fine. I stopped the engine and, instructing Clemmie to let go the furling line and PeePee to heave in the sheet, started to roll out the genoa.

PeePee, in her eagerness, made a complete pig's ear of it. First she wound the sheet round the winch-barrel the wrong way three separate times… a situation exacerbated by a combination of her tendency to forget her English under stress, and my unaccountable failure to remember, in the heat of the moment, that the German for 'clockwise' is *Im Uhrzeigersinn*.

When she did finally get it right, PeePee tried to make up for lost time and face by unleashing her full upper-body strength combined with an

_____

* Anyone know the incumbent's name? Nationality? Sex? I rest my case.

almighty pump of her formidable thighs in a titanic heave… the experience of her previous effort with the rope wound backwards obviously left her expecting a similar resistance on the sheet, but the now correctly loaded winch spun easily and the genoa was rippling gently in the breeze without wind in it. There was no weight on the rope at all. PeePee took off across the cockpit like a long-jumper in reverse, just as *Iraklis* rolled to port on a wave. Under the twin influences of her fearsome quadriceps and the yacht's momentum she crossed the cockpit quicker than I can tell, shredding the air with flailing appendages. Her enormous impetus carried her clean over the bench, and she landed doubled-up, in an undignified half-reclined posture on the deck beside the cockpit, with her elbows over the middle lifeline, her knees next to her ears, and her sweet but highly puzzled face peering uncertainly out of a chasm of cleavage.

Before I could get around the wheel to correct things, the purposeful figure of Clemmie stepped into the breach. With barely a glance to either side, she stripped the line off the winch again. I started to tell her that it was perfectly OK as it was, and then shut up as I saw that it had developed a riding-turn, which Clemmie cleared as deftly as she had identified it. Then, with three cobra-strikes of her right wrist, she flicked the sheet thrice around the winch and, giving it an expert pull, set it screaming as it recovered the slack. At the instant that the load came on, Clemmie leaned easily back on the rope and tensioned it with perfect timing; then, in a move so fluid that it disgraced waterfalls, she scooped a winch-handle out of its pocket and slapped it into the winch. With a series of powerful but elegantly choreographed strokes of her arm, she then brought the genoa smoothly in until it formed a lovely curve a perfect four inches from the spreader.

Clemmie subjected the weary old sail to a critical look and, muttering to no-one in particular, "Track back a bit," she nimbly adjusted the tension of the foot of the sail. Then she stepped back, whipped the winch-handle back into its pocket with the panache of a Hollywood gunslinger holstering his smoking Colt, coiled the free end of the sheet onto the side-deck, loaded the windward winch ready for tacking, and gazed around with a look of complacent competence.

Iraklis was heeling easily and bubbling away on the port tack towards Tselevinia, PeePee was still in her recumbent posture looking as if she was only waiting for someone to say 'push' before giving birth, and I had finally managed to close my mouth.

"And the 'little bit of sailing' was where, exactly, Clemmie?" I enquired

She grinned wolfishly.

"Oh, between Sydney and Hobart. At Cowes. And a few times around Fastnet and back."

A minute before I had had her neatly docketed as a useless, effete rich-bitch, and was wishing that *Iraklis* had a chief mate; now I was wondering whether she had the right captain. What on earth is the point in having stereotypes if people won't conform to them?

* * *

The Grave-Robber's course lay southwards about three hours lazy sailing to the bijou port of Hydra, with a pause for lunch and a swim in a bay where every fold of the sandy seabed showed clearly through three fathoms of sparkling crystal. The water was still pretty cold, but that didn't deter our young clientele.

Hydra is a wonderful first destination for a charter, being a delightful port at the end of a short but interesting sail through wonderful scenery. There are narrow passages to negotiate and large ships to encounter. There is a castle and some monasteries to look at, and towering mountains, misty islands and shimmering horizons to romance over, and there are a couple of well-frequented but never the less charming swimming-bays to lurk-and-lunch in. Possibly most important of all, there is A Corner To Be Turned.

This latter is a very significant point, because a mere five-and-a-half miles south-east of Poros one rounds Tselevinia, closing out the verdant, forested, pine-scented slopes of the Saronic Gulf and opening into the arid, terracotta magnificence of the craggy Eastern Argolic. Between the precipices of Hydra and the vertiginous south face of Dokos are scattered the barren rocks and spires of numerous islets, all tinted various earthenware shades, and these stud a sea which radiates an almost electric blue glow wherever the sun has not turned it to coruscating spangles of white-gold. The contrast is marked, and fosters a sense that the voyage is going somewhere, that enormous progress has already been made, that this is merely the first in a succession of sensory delights.

The town of Hydra plays its part in this drama to perfection. A direct approach from Tselevinia to the harbour brings one first to a fortified outcrop which bristles with cannon under the vivid red, white and blue of the Hydra flag. Whilst the attention is on this feature, and the windmill-strewn cliffs above it, the town seemingly sucks in its belly to lurk the better out of sight, metaphorically holding a silencing finger to its lips. Then, as the yacht rounds the corner, it leaps out with a loud 'BOO!' The crew, moments before quite entranced by the towering rocks and the fortifications, are now completely overwhelmed by the abrupt manifestation of an entire fairy-story town.

Grey stone, sand-stone, whitewash, mandarin roof-tiles, ornate campanile, bright flags and softly faded awnings of all hues sweep up into the sky; beneath soaring, craggy peaks, the hillsides are carpeted with stylish little townhouses, studded here and there with imposing mansions and white monasteries. Cannon seem to poke out of every wall. The houses are closely packed around the three steep sides of the port, so that to me they resemble the audience in an ancient theatre, rainbow-hued and leaning earnestly forward to enjoy the performance below them… and a performance there often is, for the port of Hydra is small and busy. The skipper needs confidence here, and a spot of luck doesn't come amiss either.

I managed to get in reasonably early, and baggsied a place on the North Quay, which I would have managed to get into easily if only the crew had not tried to help. Clemmie handled the anchor very nicely; the problem was the rest of them. PeePee was being over-earnest with the ropes, half of the others were getting in everyone's way whilst taking photographs, and the remainder suddenly decided to take an interest in things nautical. In their eagerness to grab hold of other boats, these latter provided me with about two dozen appendages to worry about as they reached out with hands, legs, etcetera. The fact that most of them were rather pleasantly-shaped and very scantily-clad appendages didn't help my concentration much either.*

On our anarchic way to the quay we had an entirely unnecessary contretemps with another charter-boat. This was due to me shouting myself

---

* I will never, to my dying day, understand why people pay good money for fenders and then prefer to use delicate and difficult-to-replace body-parts to try to make sure the poor dear fender doesn't get squeezed. For woolly thinking, it wins best-of-breed in the merino class.

hoarse at people to put boat-hooks down and keep their extremities inside the railings when I should have been steering; but the boat we hit was well-fendered and crewed by some very charming, competent Dutch people who fended us off and held *Iraklis* whilst I tried to get her tied up to the wall. This wasn't going too well when Pan materialised at the opportune moment to take our ropes.

Pan, the waterman of Hydra and already an acquaintance of mine, fitted into the extrovert Hydra waterfront panorama perfectly... which is to say, he was about as inconspicuous as a hippo in a hamster-cage. With hair half way down his back and a spade-beard covering his chest to the third shirt button, a sartorial taste which brings to mind a suitcase after an air-disaster, a bass voice that can command bulls and a personality so cheerfully forceful that it can be enjoyed from the mainland, Pan is not a man who 'arrives' or 'appears.' Rather, he manifests himself, as he did now. One of his conversational Bashan bellows, combined with his startling appearance and magnetic presence, controlled the girls in a way that my five minutes of ranting had not come close to achieving. Having restored order, he nimbly secured our stern-lines and settled the passerelle on the quay with a deftness which hinted of sorcery. Then I abandoned *Iraklis*, leaving Clemmie in charge, and set off with Pan to get *Molto Allegro* tied up.

Throughout the trip, Shergar had, by dint of his masterful engine, kept his anchor a faithful thirty metres from my rear-cleavage. To this point he had done very well indeed, for a beginner, but to ask him to park (or even turn around) in Hydra was taking it too far. I hastily whispered the situation into Pan's ear... or rather, into the thicket of hair which I presumed concealed his ear... and moments later we were afloat in Pan's wonderfully shapely little red work-boat. Shergar simply dropped his anchor when I told him, and then we took his stern-line ashore, Pan standing in the stern and leaning forward on his oars in the style of a gondolier. In no time at all *Molto* was tied up about three boats along from *Iraklis,* and with none of the commotion which had attended my berthing.

The sun was about to dip out of the bowl of the harbour, so I made a quick arrangement with Pan to fill up my water early in the morning, and told my crew that they could shower as much as they liked, but only until the water stopped coming out of the taps. Then I accepted the offer of a sundowner with the tolerant Dutch crew before heading to the cafe for the evening rendezvous.

Just as I got seated at the Corner Kafeneion, the taller of the two American lecturers who were sailing with Shergar breasted determinedly through the nearby mule-rank, scanned the terrace, and surged through the chairs to my table. The very definition of purposefulness in khaki utilities, with a wide-brimmed hat and a jaw broader than his forehead, he looked as if he had a full-length drawing of Indiana Jones in his dressing room, and studied it daily.

"Jew mhaind if ah set wuth yew uh whaaal," he said, and when I had translated this from Profound Alabaman into contemporary English I inserted a question-mark at the end of it and smiled my assent.

"Most welcome!"

It was a waste of breath. He was already collapsing his six foot frame into the chair next to mine.

"Whutcha drenk'n?"

I said a cold beer would not be unwelcome, and he set about calling a waiter.

"Wader! Wader!" He semaphored wildly, and bobbed up and down like a prairie dog, head swivelling after anything dressed in black and white. Sadly, most of the waiters then in view belonged to the adjacent cafes, so he got no satisfaction; but in any case this is not the way to attract a Greek waiter, as anyone with experience of the country will tell you. They are not summoned, they must be stalked, with technique and guile; and, as in the pursuit of all wary and elusive creatures, the hunter must know his quarry. Oh, dear, I'm off again...

* * *

Greek waiters are very often highly skilled at their profession, especially in up-market cafes. The best of them rarely use a notepad, no matter how large the order, and the menu is never referred to for the price. Our man knows his bill of fare intimately, can explain any item in a useful selection of languages and often makes excellent suggestions when the client misapprehends, or if his indecision is wasting valuable time. He is entertainingly adept at manoeuvring enormous trays through the dynamic bustle of a crowded terrace and often presents his wares with a pleasing display of showmanship, which may include the one-handed opening of beers, the juggling of bottles or glasses, or simply a smooth flourish as he pours drinks.

From his professional handling of glasses, bottles, ashtrays and the like, one gets the impression that he went to a waiter school (he probably did; most towns have them in the local technical college) and he is proud of his profession. But he is a Greek before he is a waiter, and he is even more proud of *that*. He is no-one's inferior… he is smart, polite, welcoming, and will be energetic in setting up your table to suit your party, but he is always your equal, and that air of deference expected in good cafes in other lands is not to be found. The Greek waiter will come when his time allows, he will give priority to his regular customers, he will take the time he needs to do his job without apology,* and that includes a few moments to make conversation with his valued clients. You can't deflect him when he is engaged in something else, so flapping your hand in his face as he passes is useless, and you can't shout or whistle at him across the tables, because he is not your dog. And when he doesn't want to see something, he could ignore a crocodile… even if it was in the bath with him!

This ability of Greek waiters to fail to notice clients when they chose is one of the remarkable phenomena of the country, as iconic as Doric columns on a headland above a sun-drenched cobalt sea. His eyes may appear to be riveted to your very breast, but no amount of semaphore or calisthenics will evince the least flicker of an eye-lid. He can make what appears to be the most thorough scan of his tables, during which his pupils track directly across your face, and not respond to any level of attention-seeking activity short of a clown on a trampoline.

His hearing is equally selective… as The Bard has it, 'Thou but offend'st thy lungs to speak so loud'. And he can be just as unobtainable even when receiving payment… several times in my early days in Greece I muttered ferociously 'OK, I'll get up and leave… then he'll soon give me some attention, the swine!' He never did. All I ever got for my pains was an

---

* I had a Greek language course which pointed out that when ordering, the waiter will often respond by saying 'A méssos, Kyrié', which means 'Immediately, Sir.' "Although," the voice on the tape then continued rather wearily, "…sometimes, in Greece, it does take a little longer!"

increasingly guilty feeling as I walked away, and after twenty fruitless yards a humiliating walk back to my seat.* On one occasion I ran off to deal with a problem on the boat and ended up having to leave the port. I went back to pay about a week later, which the waiter appeared to consider entirely satisfactory. He knew exactly what I owed, gave me a grave nod and counted out my change without any comment.

Foreigners attempt to be polite to overcome this blindness…when entreaties in their own tongue cannot prevail, they learn Greek. Unfortunately, the native English-speaker tends to translate directly from 'excuse me' to the Greek *sygnomi*. This means the same, but a Greek will use it only when apologising… which, it must be remarked, is not a common national pastime. Greeks simply aren't that self-effacing; and they don't expect you to be, either. Many foreigners who have spent some time in Greece have come to believe that *sygnomi* really means 'ignore me'.

The word you should use is *parakaló*…'please'. But use it just the once… the waiter will have registered it, and repeating it will only harm your cause. He'll be with you as soon as his personal schedule allows. Even better, give a discrete signal, such a single raised finger, as he performs his reaction-less scan. Don't expect a response, but if you are then cool about it he will probably materialise behind your shoulder before too long; and if he doesn't, then even throwing plates won't change things.

Mostly it is best just to be as relaxed as everyone else in the kafeneion, but if you really, desperately need to pay and be gone just count up the bill, leave it on the table with a small tip, and give the waiter a wave as you leave. He'll generally just give you a wave back.

On the day in question, Billy-Bob's[†] aerobics had doubtless put us at the bottom of the list and our expectancy of being served would probably have been sometime in the early hours of the next day had Pan not made one of his abrupt materialisations. He, of course, commanded instant attention; but Billy-Bob seemed to think it was his performance which had done the trick and appeared a little mollified.

---

* Don't try this if you really are planning to leave without paying… I've seen a good few people try it, and it doesn't work. This just proves that they do know what is going on!

[†] Can't actually remember his name, but if it wasn't Billy-Something then it should have been.

As we chatted for a few minutes, looking, I suppose, like Indiana Jones having a drink with Father Christmas and his apprentice, I regarded Billy-Bob somewhat guardedly... people who drink fresh orange juice at six in the evening are not a species I can claim to have extensive experience of, but he seemed pretty intense and I assumed he had something (probably Shergar) on his mind. I wasn't wrong.

Pan, spotting a massive gin palace approaching the outer mole, left with his customary abruptness. Barely had his neon shorts left his chair than Billy-Bob set down his glass firmly, gave me the eyeball and laid his fore-arm purposefully on the table.

"Nauw, lookee here; this guy Shergar... has he ever been on a boat in his goddam laaaife?"

I adopted an expression of extreme bewilderment.

"Shergar? Why?"

"He's ayuctin' laike he ain't never seen a boat. Ah meyun, he's a naice guy, but he don't seem to know whar he's goin' or how t'git thar! Seyez he needs to stay near yeu so that he knows whut t'do!"

I allowed my expression to clear and change into a grin.

"Ah, I see. He's up to that old game again, is he?"

"An' jes whut gay-um wud thayut be?"

"Oh, he's a bit embarrassed about telling you who he is... a bit of British understatement."

"So, he knows whut he's about?"

I leaned conspiratorially across the table.

"Shergar," I said quietly, "is an Olympian. A gold medalist."

It wasn't exactly a lie... there is a go-kart track at Olympia, and Shergar had several medals for winning races there.

"He's rather shy about it, though," I added, "and he has a very dry sense of humour."

Billy-Bob sat back and laughed.

"Jee-yuz! The guy's behavin' laike he don't know sheeyut! So he's OK?"

"Take it from me," I said. "*Molto Allegro* is in very good hands."

Looked at in a constructive way this was almost true... Shergar had wonderful hands. It was just unfortunate that they were the hands of a mechanic and racing-driver, not a sailor.

* * *

The whole flotilla enjoyed a rambunctious 'welcome' meal that evening. It was eaten under a massive plane-tree in a square so perfectly whitewashed and so quaintly furnished that it looked like a decoration on an iced cake. A yellow light oozed from the strings of lamps overhead, creating a bowl of golden-warm conviviality ringed by the purple-blue shadows of the dimly-lit, narrow lanes. In this refulgent haven our young charges regaled themselves on *moussaka*, *dholmadhakia**, *keftedakia*[†] and Greek salads whilst *kanatas* of cool rosé wine went the rounds, and cheerful black and white waiters swirled and smiled. The gardens of the Hydriots were concealed behind high walls, but the floral scents which filled the air were eloquent testimony to their luxuriance. To complete the ambience there was, seated under the tree, what looked like a moustache with legs wearing a Greek fisherman's cap and twanging popular Greek airs on a bouzouki... *Frangosyriani,* followed by *Dirlada, Who Pays The Ferryman, Zorba's Dance* and *Never On A Sunday;* then back to the beginning. The kids loved it.

When all the food was eaten and the *kanatas* ceased to arrive, Xanthos and Yeorgaki deftly guided the youngsters towards a disco high up over the edge of the town, sufficiently far removed that we couldn't hear the screams, and the rest of the skippers retired to the Pirate Bar in the port to relax for an hour or two. Then we went back to our boats to be available in case anyone came back and did anything silly.

As I waited, I admired Spiros's organisational skills; the food and drink had been emphatically traditional, and the setting had been a choice of genius. It had been undoubtedly touristy... it was only a wonder Anthony Quinn himself hadn't danced *Syrtaki* through the middle of it... but none the worse for that. Yet despite being a distinct success, the meal had been a budget event... salad, meat-balls, vine-leaves, moussaka and some wine; no beer, grilled meat or fish... tasty, traditionally Greek, and it wouldn't have cost much. In addition, I don't doubt that the gratitude of the disco-owner further defrayed Spiros's expenses. He had me working for him for half-rate, PeePee was doing the job

---

*   Vine-leaves stuffed with rice and herbs
[†]   Meatballs

just for experience, Shergar was being paid by someone else and some of the skippers had probably paid Spiros for the privilege of attending… and I hadn't seen a client frown all evening. The man really was a genius!

There were a few shenanigans on the other boats when the future of archaeology began to traipse back from the disco, and I did help fish two promising academic careers out of the water further down the quay, but my gang came back decorously enough; boisterous, but not stotius. They got settled into the cockpit, then Clemmie produced, from gawd-knows-where, a violin and began playing wonderful, racy, sparkling gypsy-sounding folk music. In between, I became involved in some strenuous folk-singing, and the bubble of conviviality echoed around the darkening little arena of the port.

As the town closed down for the night, I kept a wary eye on the dock and the other boats for any sign of complaint about the noise, but all that happened was a number of people came down to the sea-wall and took a seat to enjoy the violin, and the boats around nodded serenely without objection. Shergar and Pan joined us at a late hour, and streaks of crimson were beginning to slice the sky beyond the battlements as we finally heave-ho-and-a-rumbelowed our way down the companionway steps.

* * *

Next morning I awoke relatively early, courtesy of an enterprising Hydra cat which decided to try his luck in the galley and mistook me as a footpath from the hatch to the promising remains of a sandwich on the work-top. Even the fuss of Moggy's eviction did not rouse anyone else, however, and all was still in the boat.

It looked like one of those cinema scenes from the inside of a submarine, when the exhausted crew are sleeping off a jolly good depth-charging… clothes and half-unpacked bags lay on tables and the floor, artefacts littered every surface. Legs and arms lolled out of cots, and the 'clop-clop' of water against the hull was overlaid by a deep, steady susurrus of relaxed breathing.

I was going to make myself some coffee, but even without looking closely it was apparent that the general standard of nightwear wasn't high, and what there was of it was not all where it should have been. The cabin looked like someone had gassed a nudist colony. It seemed a bit voyeuristic to hang around, and so, muttering to myself, "It is a far better thing I do than I have ever done," I trotted ashore for a coffee in Tassos' cafe.

I sat in that cafe in a state of quiet contentment. It was mid-morning already, and the quayside was teeming. Mules brayed, boats jostled, people swarmed. Wafts of coffee, bacon and eggs, baking bread, mule and donkey by-products and boat-exhaust ebbed and flowed over a constant scent of pine. In this vehicle-free* environment the chatter and clatter of conversation and eating utensils is like plain-chant sung to the metronomic clopping of mule-hooves. Scantily-clad tourists and elegant socialites mingled with the locals in their heavier working-wear, the former boasting early sun-burn, and the latter gravely contemplating the world over a selection of magnificent moustaches... for Hydra was moustachioed on an almost Cretan scale, with styles ranging from the Gallic Spiked through the Revolutionary Extravaganza to the 'This-Cat-Is-Delicious' schools of facial hair. The butcher looked like one of those early scuba-divers, with two enormous tubes coming over his shoulders to meet under his nose.[†]

As I sat over my yoghurt and melon I took in the kaleidoscopic, pungent, vibrant, all-function workout for the senses that is Hydra and had the greatest sense of satisfaction with the almost involuntary turn my life had taken. This, I thought, I could put up with for a while.

---

* Almost... the only motorised transport on Hydra is the garbage-truck. It is the only place I know where the refuse-collectors kerb-crawl. Since only the most attractive ladies are usually honoured with their attentions, Hydra is surely unique in considering it a social cachet to be seen being taken out with the trash.

[†] ...and still does!

CHAPTER FOUR

STRUTTING AN HOUR ON THE STAGE

A skipper's lot... crewed behaviour... competing for Miss Iceland... musical beds... PeePee jumps ship... the Nob and the Oik... table dancing redefined... the many ways of beating one's chest... needs must... Iraklis expires... post-coastal depression... gale-force altruism... more of Blatchley's nautical philosophy... an extant sextant... the captain and his mate.

Thus the flotilla proceeded for four or five days. We visited Spetses and Ermioni, had a barbeque on the lovely, uninhabited island of Dokos and spent a night anchored off a beach taverna somewhere east of Thermissia. Shergar was managing very well, all things considered, but every night Billy-Bob and the American lady on the faculty crew took time to assure me that he was still acting as if he didn't know one end of a boat from another, and to tell me the latest 'Shergarism'.

Apart from the lazy, late morning starts, the pace of life continued to be somewhat hectic... the general pattern which developed involved a short, quiet sail in the late morning, with hangovers being slept off on deck; some sort of activity (swimming, water sports, water-fights, etcetera) in the afternoon; an evening meal and then a party into the early hours. For the skippers, it could get a bit wearing... late at night there were all sorts of problems to be sorted out; documents and hand-bags gone astray; misunderstandings about bills; people to be pulled out of harbours, mule-bites to be salved; unwanted suitors to dislodge. Also, of course, the skippers had to constantly replenish the water and make the boats ready, so they couldn't sleep late the next morning as the clients did. Any regrets were expressed cheerfully and ruefully, however. No-one dreamed of complaining.

The general atmosphere was very genial and good-humoured. The girls were not, of course, the anthropophagic wantons which chauvinistic alpha male fantasy, fevered by a long, womanless winter with nothing to do but tell lad's tales and consume caffeine, had contrived to imagine; but they were nevertheless very charming and it was fun to help them. As for the boys... well, I'm not sure anyone noticed them much unless they got into trouble, so they were perhaps a little less esteemed...

I quickly learned to enjoy my solitude in the early hours before the crew awoke. I would take a very leisurely coffee and a stroll; watch the world a while, and then set about my chores very, very quietly in order to be left with my thoughts a while longer. This was something which became very much easier after the second night, in Spetses, where we had a boozy cockpit-party late at night. The corollary of this was that a dishevelled and transparently euphoric PeePee emerged the next morning from Karrotos' boat, hand-in-hand with a blonde Canadian lad. I was delighted to assure Spiros that Clemmie and I could manage *Iraklis,* and PeePee was seen no more on board 'the big boat.'

This was by no means the only liaison which was made on the Grave-Robber. There was a fair amount of late-night smooching... referred to by one of the American girls as 'mashing', which I thought a splendidly colourful and accurate description... and quite a few people changed boats during the course of the trip. At night there was great variation too... the boat one sailed on was not necessarily the boat one slept on. People migrated like nomads with defective compasses, and laid themselves down to sleep wherever affection, fatigue, alcohol or sheer convenience deposited them. On two occasions we left people behind, skippers thinking they were on other boats, and they had to catch up by ferry, and there was one Welsh lad who, I think, slept on a different boat every night. I found him snoring contentedly on the beach the morning after the barbeque.

There was enormous competition amongst the other skippers for the attention of my Icelandic goddess... which she returned with graceful acknowledgement of the compliment, and not the slightest hint of interest. This, of course, merely made the Mediterranean blood boil all the more effervescently for her.*Yeorgaki, Karrotos and Xanthos were locked in a good-humoured contest for her favour, and by my reckoning the cheery, rotund

---

* Greek men do not have a problem with rejection, because they simply don't recognise it. It isn't really on their radar.

Yeorgaki was a narrow head in front of the other two and still getting absolutely nowhere. I highly approved of this jealous devotion, as it made it unnecessary for me to have to worry about her being bothered by men in the towns we visited. Her suitors guarded her from each other and from outsiders with equal devotion, and she proceeded through the streets like an American president surrounded by the Secret Service.

I trust I do not give the impression that our archaeologists were a depraved lot: we all wished that had been so, but it was not. They were just healthy young people with a truck-load of vigour, in mixed company and a vibrant, stimulating foreign country, feeding off each other's energy. There was an end-of-term sort of atmosphere, and it was party-time. Some might think the studious, committed nature of archaeological study and frenzied revelry unlikely bedfellows, and perhaps they become so with time... the lecturers who accompanied the tours were sensible, abstemious sorts by and large... but there appeared to be no sense of incompatibility amongst the student body. Even the more mature scholars were likely to end up jumping into harbours in the early hours; and, on consideration, perhaps there was an element of catharsis in their carousing... an archaeologist, after all, is someone who will spend a week in silent, single-minded concentration gently brushing dirt out of a gladiator's coccyx in an attempt to separate his *pilum* from his prostate; there must surely be a reaction to such a degree of absorption.

* * *

On board *Iraklis* things were becoming quite well organised by the morning of the third day. Clemmie had assumed the role of chief mate as smoothly as she did everything else, and I had no qualms about letting her berth and unberth the boat... she was completely competent. Then, to my great surprise, our Nordic beauty abruptly began to pay attention and progressed quickly to Fender-Tender First Class.

The Italian boy... time, time, the thief of all things, what was his name? Giovanni seems to strike a chord... turned out to simply adore helming. The only occasion when he willingly left the wheel was when Jana, his Czech consort, disappeared into their cabin... then he was gone like a missile leaving its silo, regardless of whether anyone else was there to take the wheel or not.

On more than one occasion I heard a door slam, then felt the boat coming up into the wind, and hopped up on deck to find a *Marie Celeste* situation in the cockpit... and presumably another Czech getting bounced.

A Scots lass called May, who was a climber, knew a few knots and took a bit of an interest... mostly in shinning up the mast. She could go up it like a monkey fetching coconuts, and spent a good while happily sitting on the crosstrees until Spiros took her to one side and quietly explained how long it takes to get to hospital from a boat. She also became one of my 'trusties,' capable on the wheel at sea and on deck in harbour.

Other than that, my crew were occasionally inspired to get involved but generally just made the boat untidy. At sea they took little interest, and it would have been fine by me if they had been the same in port as well, but they did feel it incumbent upon them to do something when we were berthing, which was really when I most wanted them to sit down and keep their extremities inside the boat. Then, on the third day, I had a stroke of genius.

One of the party had a yellow portable stereo with a bulging circular speaker at each end, an implement I regarded as the death-knell of civilisation because I am a musical caveman who tends to the opinion that music ceased to be written the day Teddy Elgar turned up his toes. The term 'boom-box' was in current usage for such an 'asset' at the time, but because of its suggestive shape we called it the 'boob-box.'

Since they had so much energy when we came in to port I suggested that our status as Largest Vessel should be emphasised, and revealed that I had a cassette recording of the works of Offenbach about my person... and you know what *he* wrote. Thereafter, every time we came in to port, all the spare girls donned whatever they had in the way of a short skirt, lined up along the boom and, with Offenbach's most recognisable work crashing out of the boob-box, they performed the Can-Can with enormous gusto. This amused everyone, entertained hordes of cheering Greeks, and kept the girls well out of harm's way. It also had the fringe benefit that they paid for significantly less of what they drank when ashore.

Being the principle sailors on *Iraklis*, Clemmie and I were more often with each other than with other people. She always stayed to help me with the watering, engine checks and general care of the boat whilst the rest were in town or at the beach, and we often wandered off and had a drink together, or ended up enjoying the cockpit in peace and quiet whilst the mob were marauding in the discos.

Clemmie's far-back upper-class accent and dated slang grew on me, and we teased each other unmercifully about our breeding, or lack of it. Offenbach had outed me as a classical music hound and, although she was primarily a folk- and ethnic-music aficionado, Clemmie had been brought up playing the classics. During the evening on the island of Dokos we wandered away from the barbeque and she played me a stunning improvisation on Bruch's Scottish Fantasy as we watched the sun set over Ermioni.

We weren't an item. She was still rather too much of a hearty to appeal to me romantically, and I had no delusions of being irresistible to her; so there was no romantic tension. We worked and conversed easily together, I admired her as a sailor and a musician, enjoyed her company and very much appreciated her help. We laughed a lot.

* * *

The penultimate night was quite amazing. We anchored off a beach some way east of Thermissia, with a single taverna on an otherwise deserted beach. Spiros had pre-arranged the meal, which was followed by a spectacular display of unbridled Greek waiter machismo.

The show started with some Greek dancing. Notwithstanding the rural setting, the restaurant boasted five waiters all impeccably attired in black-and-whites. They now supplemented their costume with scarlet sashes, and heel-slapped, high-stepped and genuflected their way through a couple of dances to much applause.

Then they started to get competitive. First they danced individually, with bottles on their heads, turned somersaults, and generally tried to outdo each other. Whilst awaiting their go, they also began to drink quite freely with their customers. Next, one of them made a standing jump onto a table,* alarming the occupants so much that two girls overbalanced backwards off their chairs. This led to a competition as to who could make the most consecutive such jumps, and I think one chap managed six or seven.

---

* Try it… it isn't easy! And these guys were taking off from soft gravel.

After this, the rest of the waiters demanded an opportunity to showcase their own particular talents, and it rapidly got silly. One of them squatted, gathered up a girl in the crook of each arm, and lifted them both off the ground.

The next tried to repeat the feat with an additional girl sitting on his shoulders… and succumbed to gravity spectacularly, ending up compressed under a wriggling assortment of female anatomical components (which may, of course, have been his intention all along). The surface was loose stone chippings, so no-one was really hurt.

Then other waiters started to load themselves up with girls from the table-tops and stagger under the greatest possible load to another table about five or six metres away, some with quite successful results, others with hilariously abortive ones. Some of the male archaeologists tried their hands… or, rather, their entire skeleto-muscular systems… at it too. And finally, of course, one of the waiters had to try it on the rickety pier extending over the water, and that ended inevitably in a rapid succession of three loud splashes. Laughter, squeals and bouzouki music flowed into the calm night air.

It would of course be an intolerable breach of storytelling convention had such an evening not had a finale, and the reader is easily forgiven if he suspects that, to give my story the classical form, I gild the lily to create the predictable denouement; but to doubt the existence of a definitive climax is to misunderstand the flamboyant nature of Greece and Greeks. There is *always* going to be a finale… that is the quintessentially theatrical nature of the place. It really happened.

The most thick-set of the waiters, a moustachioed enthusiast of about fifty years, who looked like the villain in an Arabian Nights tale, bellowed for attention and then tore off his shirt… quite literally, cloth sundered and buttons pinged into the audience… to reveal a body somewhere between stalwart and stout. His chest and shoulder blades were thickly forested with greying hair. He stalked around the circle of onlookers as though looking for someone to eat, and selected a slim American girl as his partner for the next event. She went willingly enough, giggling and rolling her eyes at the waiter's hairy body, and he took her waist in two hands and swung her up easily to stand on a table. She looked a little nervous, but bowed left and right, gamely playing her part. And then she looked a bit puzzled as the waiter produced a blue plastic bottle and commenced squirting fluid up and down three of the legs of the table.

By the time the waiter had finished, she was beginning to show a little more agitation, but if she was going to bail-out she delayed too long. The waiter squatted down at one corner of the table, placing his chest against the leg and holding the side of the top in both hands. Then he took the corner of the table-top in his teeth. And stood up.

The whole restaurant gasped. The powerful little chap made it in one smooth, clean lift, holding the weight of the girl and table with his bared fangs and keeping them level by the pressure of the leg against his chest. The girl staggered and squeaked, but he had the table-top quite horizontal and unbelievably steady, so she hung in there, teetering a little with her arms spread to balance her. Then the waiter spread his arms out wide, and an acolyte started *Zorba's Dance* on the stereo. He began to move slowly, smoothly. The girl pleaded, half seriously, to be let down; but she didn't jump. And then the assistant performed the second part of his supporting role... he flicked his lighter quickly one-two-three against the table legs, and they burst into flame.

From the blue-ish hue of the conflagration it was obviously only methylated spirit, but you can imagine the reaction of the girl. After an instant of incredulity, she felt the warmth on her ankles and, emitting a shriek that would have put a band-saw to shame, she launched herself sideways into the audience, collapsing half of the front row. The table spun the opposite way, one blazing leg coming into contact with the waiter. He righted the table serenely and danced on, eyes wide, and now a trickle of flame was extending over the table-top towards him. By the time he dropped the table there was a definite smell of singed hair, a suspicion of smoke around his Adam's apple, and any mere mortal would have beaten his chest like a gorilla after happy-hour; but our Hercules paraded around his applauding audience like a victorious prize-fighter, arms high, until he came to his erstwhile partner as she adjusted her clothing and eyed him with wild-eyed consternation. Then he gathering her into his powerful, hairy arms and, drawing her into his chest, gave her an enormous hug. C'mon, baby, put out my fire.

The girl took it extraordinarily well. She even laughed about it. Eventually.

The waiters weren't the only macho ones. The skippers weren't exactly deficient in testosterone either, and were always in competition. We raced whenever there was enough wind, naturally, but that was very indecisive, as the boats were not evenly matched, so the competition took other forms... fanciest dive off a high rock, deepest dive, biggest fish caught, biggest octopus, longest time underwater. The Greeks were in their element, of course... they all had spear-guns, which they used at every opportunity, and knowing the water temperature they also had wet-suits. They spent hours fishing, and when not in the water they prowled the rocks and harbour-quays with their *kamakis,* the long, wooden-handled octopus spears. They took the girls out in the dinghies in the evening and bounced their octopus-hooks across the seabed. Daily they brought in their harvest to feed the barbeques... Karottos in particular was a fine spear-fisherman who could stay under water about three minutes, and generally won the deep-diving contests.

All this was stuff I couldn't possibly compete at, so I threw down the gauntlet in my own field, and just tried to down-right out-sailor them all. I made sure that I tied the fastest, flashiest knots, and I sailed every possible inch of the way. With Clemmie's help I got my sails up and down as quickly and smoothly as could be... it was counted a deep disgrace if *Iraklis* didn't have her mainsail up before she left the harbour... and I sailed in and out of anchorages without the engine. I pontificated on navigation and seamanship and, despite the fact that we were never more than a couple of miles from land, I desperately regretted the fact that my sextant was lying idle in Kyria Fotini's best bedroom. I shamelessly expounded maritime lore... history, mythology, nautical etymology of common words and phrases... and analysed great naval battles and shipwrecks.

Even I soon realised that I had overdone it... the kids would go away happy and I would never see them again; but if I wanted to stay here I had to co-exist with Karottos, and Yeorgaki, with Xanthos and Megali and O Geros. It belatedly occurred to me that if I ever had to face a major test of my prowess, I was going to find it somewhat difficult to live up to the image of a maritime oracle which I had made for myself.

And so we came to the last day. Leaving Spiros on the beach near Thermissia, arguing about compensation for damaged tables, we set out to round Tselevinia and return to Poros. A race had been planned, but there wasn't enough wind to bother a butterfly, so we motored. The plan was to get most of the mileage done whilst the worst hangovers were still being slept off, and then stop at Aliki beach outside Poros for lunch and a swim before going in.

Iraklis led the fleet out of the bay, and should have led all the way with her speed, but Shergar, full of confidence after several trouble-free days and in thrall to his innate belief that unused horse-power was an affront to nature, gunned his mighty engine and steadily forged past me. I gave him an indulgent wave as he passed, happy to see my fledgling taking flight, and got on with talking about astro-navigation with an earnestly interested Clemmie.

Clemmie was keen to learn astro-nav, and her questions were insightful and serious. To stay a step ahead of my student I had to concentrate quite hard at recalling my college days, and although I had a mental register on where Shergar was, it was quite a while before I realised where he was going.

Poros is separated from Hydra by a long, thin, high spur of the Peloponnese which extends eastward and ends in two islets called the Tselevinia Islands. One has to make a dog-leg of more than ninety degrees around the end of this peninsula, changing course between north-west and south-west, or vice-versa, depending which way one is going. There is a channel between the Outer and Inner Islands which looks deep and easily navigable, and this is in fact the case; it is an easy passage which almost everyone uses, even hydrofoils and ferries, as it saves at least a mile going out around Akra Skyli on the outside. But between the inner island and the shore there is also a channel which looks as if it may be navigable... and nothing much bigger than a duck should try it! It is rocky, shallow and, although a few small fishing boats with years of local knowledge go through in calm weather, it should never be attempted by anything with a keel.

The thing with these two passages is that they are not aligned. Whichever direction you approach from, one is masked so that you see only one channel; and if you come from the south-west, then it's the bad one. Shergar, knowing nothing about charts but remembering that on the way south he had gone through a channel, had added up two and two, arrived at the answer of eight-point-nine recurring, and was blithely heading *Molto Allegro* and her crew of erudite archaeological savants straight towards a passage full of rocks at full speed.

I shot down to the chart room and picked up the VHF radio mike.

"*Molto Allegro, Molto Allegro*, this is *Iraklis*, over."

Nothing. I tried again. I fiddled with the squelch knob, using the static to test the speaker volume. Maybe he was not on the working channel. I switched to channel sixteen, the calling and distress channel.

"*Molto Allegro, Molto Allegro*, this is *Iraklis* on channel sixteen, over."

Getting desperate now.

"Shergar! Shergar! This is Julian, over."

'*You're wasting your time here, big fella,*' whispered a treacly smug voice somewhere inside my head, '*Time to get out there and show some of that nautical omniscience you have been spouting about!*'

I estimated that I was about half a mile behind Shergar, and had perhaps twenty minutes to get his attention. It is pretty hard to make up half a mile in a stern chase in twenty minutes under any circumstances, and Shergar was a petrol-head with an engine that would have been adequate for the *Lusitania*. As I rammed the throttle forward, and *Iraklis* spouted filthy smoke from under her counter, I knew that I wasn't going to make it.

I was cooking up some scheme for encouraging all the crew to shout at once when I abstractly realised that the exhaust from the engine was irritating my throat, and we were probably motoring at close to seven and a half knots. Some long moments later it dawned on me that we had wind from astern, and glancing back I saw a dappling on the water with occasional white flecks… there was something of a gust coming up from behind us. Hope flared. I called Clemmie.

"Can you fly a kite?"

"Oh, rathER! Have we got one?"

I nodded. "Get forward!" I said, and then, "Giovanni, take the wheel… yes… you… Si! Prendo il… the… bloody wheel! *Conductore!* Timoneer, you, savvy? Steer! Take the wheel!"

I galumphed forward and dragged the spinnaker out of its cave. There were perhaps four other girls on deck, May and Miss Iceland fortunately amongst them, and I soon had them all working, passing the sheet-lines and letting the main sail out to catch the new wind.

Clemmie and I feverishly dumped the sail out on the deck and swiftly ran our hands along the luff and leach to check that it wasn't twisted. No time to re-pack it and launch it from the bag… we'd just have to send it up from the deck as it was. It lay there, an enormous, prolapsed heap of thin red, white and blue nylon which spasmed occasionally in the rising breeze; not a hint yet of the great, powerful, arrogant belly of barely-controllable power which it represented.

"I say, Skip, what's all the ruddy bally-hoo?" asked Clemmie privately, and I needed her on top form so I told her. Her eyes lit up.

"Roger-dodge. Mum's the word, what! Bit of a lark!" she grinned, and I thought, I like this girl. A lot. Despite the P. G. Wodehouse vocab.

I had an enormous struggle to release the spinnaker-pole; it had lain unused so long that the outer piston was almost seized with salt, but I levered and battered it with my knife, and got it free. The pole downhauls looked as if they had seen better days… a spinnaker puts enormous lifting strain on a pole, and the downhauls control this. Anyone who has seen a down-haul break under a well-loaded spinnaker will also have seen an enormous balloon of enraged nylon shoot vertically up above the top of the mast and either become hopelessly entangled, or heave the boat right over on her side. Or both. So I quickly improvised some reinforcement out of a sturdy mooring-line, and hoped for the best.

I headed back for the wheel, and Clemmie took the halyard. I set the pole-guy and had May and Giovanni stand by the sheet. And up she went.

For a moment all was quiet; I steered down a bit to allow Clemmie to get the spinnaker up in the lee, or dead-wind area, behind the main sail, which was straining gently out to port now. The luff of the spinnaker snapped petulantly once or twice, and Clemmie came aft again with the crouching gallop of an experienced foredeck hand, which is a very good trick if you can do it. Then, with Clemmie on the sheet, I had May bring the pole square using the guy and brought the wheel around to fill the sail.

It flickered twice, and then blossomed in an instant, filling with an angry 'boom' that rattled the rigging and heeled the boat ten degrees in an instant. The luff began a slow, sullen flogging as Clemmie and Giovanni winched in frantically on the sheet to tame it and then, as the flogging stopped, the sail began to develop its potential. The bow dipped and *Iraklis* settled. You could feel her accelerate. I pulled back the engine-throttle and put her in neutral… she was already sailing faster than she could ever motor, and the wind was rising still.

Clemmie knew her stuff with a kite. She never even looked at me, but did the sheets-man's job to perfection, trimming the sheet and issuing instructions to May on the guy. The spinnaker swelled out, a great, proud distended belly of straining red, white and blue, its enormous power transmitted to the boat through the straining mast head, the thrumming sheets and the creaking pole. *Iraklis* was flying now, nine knots coming up on the log and her wide, creamy wake hissed like tearing linen as it curved past her flanks.

I could feel some weight coming onto the wheel as the great sail tried to bring the boat up to windward. Heads started to appear in the companionway, complaints at the disturbance and angle-of-heel giving way to a delighted chatter as they saw the great, noble bulging kaleidoscope above their heads.

I probably still wasn't going to make it in time to stop Shergar, but at least now I was sure someone would point out the spinnaker and make him look round. I hoped so, because otherwise I was going to have to sail into the bay after him… and wind does funny things in Greek bays. Being in a Greek bay with a spinnaker up is like walking through a tiger-park with a pork chop tied around your neck and bleating like a lamb.

At last I saw it, the flash of flesh-colour above Shergar's T-shirt-du-jour as he turned to look back, and I raised my hand high and stabbed emphatically off to the right. He got it second go, and I saw him turn back to his crew, point for a while at the passage he was almost into,[*] and then lazily swing the wheel. *Molto Allegro* curved smoothly out of the bay, and just as smoothly my blood pressure fell away. An unimaginable lightness of heart and a great feeling of peace fell upon me. All I had to do now was get this rampaging great boat out of the bay it was entering without alarming any of my crew… who, with the exception of Clemmie, were still under the blissful impression that I was in control.

"Everyone sit down!" I called, my guts twisting as they took their time finding comfortable places. They finally managed it, after about a year or so. And then I slacked the pole forward, and brought *Iraklis* around slowly.

A spinnaker becomes more difficult to control as the angle of the wind comes more on the side of the boat, and it also becomes more powerful, because the relative wind-speed increases as it comes forward. Clemmie was still doing very well on the sheet, there was no flogging, but the heel of the

---

* Probably telling his crew, "You don't want to go through there!!!"

boat increased by another ten degrees and the speed rose over ten knots. I had a good bit of weight on the helm now, she was trying to bring her head up into the wind where the spinnaker would flog and damage something. If you get this completely wrong you may even broach, losing all control as the boat goes over on her side and then, if the spinnaker sheet is not released pronto, you could be in dismasting country. Clemmie was doing exactly the right thing; looking straight into my eyes, calmly ready in case I told her to dump the sheet. *Iraklis* was almost on the edge, but not quite. I still had about a turn on the wheel before I lost steering control. We screeched out of that bay like Herbert von Karajan leaving a rap concert, almost eleven knots showing on the log and the crew shrieking with nervous exhilaration.

We got the wind behind us again and Clemmie and I got things more under control. I sent *Iraklis* screaming past *Molto Allegro* a mere twenty feet to her windward side, exchanging insults with Shergar whilst the pupils abused their lecturers. Vegetables were, of course, thrown, and fire returned... Billy-Bob scored a direct hit on Miss Iceland with a tomato, and May put a yoghurt right into a Swedish lady's cleavage... but so great was our speed that we were soon out of range.

I didn't try to go through the 'right' channel, not with the kite up... we carried on outside the island, and there found the wind decreased a little and went a bit more southerly, so we very gingerly gybed the spinnaker and main, and set off for Poros at a spanking eight knots with the wind over our port quarter. Of the rest of the fleet, O Geros followed. Never to be outdone he quickly set his own spinnaker, but couldn't close the gap. The rest dwindled far behind, apart from the motoring Shergar, who, I noticed, followed us around the outside... he had apparently had his fill of channels for one day.

* * *

The wind started to come ahead of us again about three miles out of Poros, and we dropped the spinnaker. Plodding lazily on with the main only, Clemmie and I tidied it up and put it away... I wondered how long it was since it had seen the sun; how long it would be again. And then I went back to start the engine. It ground, and it whirred, coughed and stayed resolutely inactive. We set the genoa and Clemmie sailed slowly north-west on the dying breeze as I tried to look confident and descended into the engine compartment. And let me tell you, what I don't know about engines… well, it would fill a very large, useful book about engines.

I poked around, uttering mendaciously confident platitudes to my concerned passengers whilst looking hopefully for something very simple and obvious which was within my capabilities… such as a large switch set at 'OFF'; and then I suddenly remembered that, in the exhilaration of setting the spinnaker, I had put the engine in neutral but I hadn't stopped it. It must have stopped itself. Fuel starvation? The tank was still at least a quarter full. Finally I realised that, with the engine running whilst the boat was heeled hard over, we might have got an air-bubble in the fuel system. At least that was something I could deal with.

After five minutes of pumping and grinding the starter, then slacking and tightening the injector-feeds, the engine suddenly roared into life. I walked on deck feeling a million dollars, wiping oil from my hands, trying not to look smug in front of my admiring crew, and casually put the engine in gear.

An appalling grinding noise, like a noisy ogre being sick into a cement-mixer full of rocks, clattered out of the companion way, and with a massive shudder the engine stopped dead again. Oh, deary me. Well, that is the essence of what I said. My actual vocabulary was probably just a fraction more authentically nautical.

My mechanical guru, the elusive Shergar, had already passed me and was thundering into Aliki bay, a useless half mile ahead again and with his VHF radio still tuned to Planet Zog. Without him I didn't have a clue where to start with this problem, so figuring that whatever happened now couldn't do any more damage than had already been done, I optimistically put the engine in neutral and restarted it.

It started with no problem, and ran perfectly. I thought for a minute. Gearbox problem, then. Well, there's two in there… if one won't work try the other.

As Mr Spock would have said, "It's logic Jim; but not as we know it." But it worked. *Iraklis* went smoothly into gear astern, and began to gather sternway. We quickly dropped the main, and with Clemmie and I each side of the wheel to hold it straight *Iraklis* completed the Grave-Robber in unique style, blithely reversing half a mile into the Bourtzi channel and so to anchor off Aliki beach. Here Shergar attended, certified the gearbox as dead on arrival, and so we enjoyed a lazy lunch by way of a wake for it before towing *Iraklis* effortlessly back to Poros. *Molto Allegro's* great, purring beast of an engine barely raised a sweat.

* * *

There was a very merry last night. I took all my crew to Petros's cafe for sundowners and then we met up with the rest of the gang for another meal of cheap but tasty traditional Greek dishes, some of which mysteriously became airborne. Spiros played master-of-indignities with raucous abandon, dishing out silly little prizes for the dumbest deeds of the trip. I got one for being pillock enough to sail into a bay under spinnaker. (Spiros had originally been a bit cross about that, until I explained why I had done it; but then he beamed and said, "*Bravo, Palikari-mou!*" 'Palikari' translates as 'good lad', and is something of an accolade. It is the sort of thing one calls a trusted friend, and is used in folklore to describe the younger revolutionaries who fought well against the Turks, so I enjoyed that).

The party went late into the night. Some of the kids went to the Kavos and Korali discos up on the rocks at the end of the dock, others stayed in the cafes or retired to the boats. I made a random last minute effort to chat-up the Swedish lecturer with the yoghurt-flavoured bosom, and after I had been very charmingly told to go and boil my head the American lady lecturer drew me to one side. For a moment I thought my luck was in, but she only wanted to talk about Shergar.

"Y'know," she said (in a crisp American accent which was at the other end of the evolutionary scale entirely from Billy-Bob's sub-Mason-Dixon porridge), "He never let up, right to the end. Last dang thing he said was 'I don't think I'll ever be any good at this sailing business.' He was an absolute hoot!"

The wine was in, the wit was out, and I couldn't resist it.

"Well, he's a very truthful chap!" I said. Her brow creased.

"Whad'ya mean?"

"He's a racing car driver, not a sailor," I said. "He's our mechanic. He really doesn't know anything about boats at all. We were short-handed."

She looked at me uncertainly for a minute, and then let out a whoop of laughter.

"Ah, you Brits and your sense of humour! You're worse than he is!" And off she went, apparently perfectly convinced that she had been in safe hands all week.

We saw about sixty hangovers off at the ferry quay the next morning. The rattling old *pantouffle* farted and puffed its way back off the dock and plodded doggedly out of the bay. The skippers all sagged slightly. We bad each other weary farewells, and went our separate ways.

Shergar and I traipsed sluggishly back to the South Quay, where we collapsed on Petro's terrace and consumed a pyramid of bacon sandwiches. He brought us both a beer on the house as well. We sat quietly, both quite drained by five frantic days. My body was pleading for sleep, and my get-up-and-go had not just got-up-and-gone, it had changed its name and emigrated without leaving a forwarding address. But a quiet day would soon sort that out, I knew, and then I would want to be out on charter once more... I had loved the experience, and it depressed me that there was no immediate prospect of doing it all over again. I didn't think Spiros would have many other charters, even for a '*palikari'*, until after Easter at least. In all probability it would be the height of summer before he needed me. I could expect some deliveries, but it could be months before I skippered a charter-boat again, and the thought deflated me.

I glumly cleaned up *Iraklis* and walked away from her, leaving the poor thing broken and forlorn at the quayside, waiting for someone to come and fix her gearbox. I settled down at Petro's with a *kanata* of retsina, and as Mine Host did not have much business he sat with me for a while. He gave me his world-standard sardonic smile.

"How was your big boat? You got towed in, huh?"

I nodded, and said, a little defensively, "Gearbox. No idea what went wrong... I could only go astern." He nodded.

"S'always problems, that boat. Gets towed more than a caravan."

I thought about this a moment.

"It's had engine problems before?"

"That boat? Always! Engine, gearbox, electrics... s'a pieca shit. Las' year the oil leaked inna the bilge an' got pumped in the harbour... the cap'n spent two days in jail. The owner don' spend no money. They gotta name for it… stead of *Iraklis,* they calls it 'Horror-klis'. Nobody in Poros gonna drive that thing."

So now I knew why no-one else was qualified to drive 'The Big Boat'. They weren't stupid enough!

* * *

Three days later there was a powerful blow and strong rain overnight, to which I was awakened in the early hours by unsecured shutters crashing against the windows. Blasts of enraged wind buffeted my house high on the hill, sending chilling jets of air squirting into the room at every ill-fitting window-frame. Salvoes of heavy rain flayed the roof-tiles, and the flash and grumble of thunder stalked the mountains around the bay. The noise in my un-insulated apartment resembled that in a speeding underground train.

Sensible people would have burrowed deeper into the duvet and luxuriated in being dry and snug on such a night, but I love dramatic weather and take a macabre interest in its effects. Hastily donning my waterproofs, I hurried down to the quay to see what was going on and help out if anyone needed a hand. After years of dealing with my own maritime mishaps, I find it utterly delightful to assist other people by way of a change, and a higher altruistic plane is always achieved when I perform in full waterproofs; thus I was in a state of beatific smugness (a good trick if one can manage it) for the next hour or two as I assisted fishermen and yachtsmen to sort out various predicaments in the driving rain and gusty wind.

On the North Quay there was a real shemozzle for a while, a motor boat having dragged her anchor and fallen across two charter yachts. It took until after daybreak to get that sorted. Then several grateful boats offered me coffee in their cockpits… coffee which the wild weather dictated had to be laced with something to keep out the cold… and we chatted away the early hours contentedly. It was some time after the first ferry from Piraeus had chugged in before I got ashore again, reflecting as I did so on the astounding number of wonderful and varied folk I would never have met if someone hadn't made a cock-up in a boat. I've seen common endeavour for the preservation of fibreglass unite people across any social barrier you care to name… national, cultural, social, class, economic, even soccer… and I cogitated upon this phenomenon as I pushed my way along the North Quay through the still-boisterous air.

Sailing is a definitively international pursuit; and it is socially varied too. The racing scene, with its jet-set image, luxury sponsors and hallmark events like the America's Cup, has a strong whiff of elitism about it, but there are far more do-it-yourself types out on the water than plutocrats, and even the rich chaps with their carbon-fibre speed-machines need lots of proletarian grunt to wind their winches. The result is that the sailing world throws together people from all backgrounds. In a yacht-club, or even some marinas, you may find stratified society; but on the harbour-wall you meet the world.

Yet, as much variety as there is in the waterfront world, you do need a catalyst to make the final bond. Like does tend to cling to like. Racing men don't have much in common with passage-makers, family cruisers or live-aboards; people sailing their own boats keep a very leery eye on charterers; all the rag-flappers combined are united against motor-boaters, and the divide between any type of leisure-boater and professional fishermen or ferrymen is generally of Berlin Wall quality. But the one place all these disparate users of the waters cannot avoid interaction is in harbour cock-ups, and the upshot of this is that you can meet an amazingly catholic selection of people in the sailing game, but mostly only in times of crisis!

One is attracted to people who acquit themselves well in adversity, whether in terms of skill, imperturbability or simple good nature. Having passed through the fire in company, and seen one another in misfortune, one recognises qualities in people one would otherwise probably never have even looked at. It is the 'Band of Brothers' syndrome: 'For he that shreds his boat with me today shall be my brother; be he ne'er so vile, this day shall gentle his condition!'

As I pondered this it struck me abruptly how many of my friends I had first met when the wind was piping and the fibreglass flying, friendships often begun at odds but fashioned into bonds by mutual suffering. It occurred to me that, in such circumstances, I had even exchanged civilities with jet-skiers; and upon that very shocking thought, I believe, I formulated my Second Law of Nautical Recreation… 'One meets a better class of person in collisions'.

* * *

The sense of virtuous accomplishment which I accumulated from both the morning's events and the formulation of a new nautical axiom left me feeling as perky as Pinky's brother, and I also found myself exceedingly keen on the idea of breakfast. I set off for George's Cafe beneath a scudding sky of low, grizzled cloud, the tail-end of the gale ripping through my hair and beard.

As I reached the ferry quay I met Shergar coming the opposite way on his little gorilla-bike with, behind him on what there was of the pillion, Miss Iceland! She gave me a great, cheesy grin and a wave as I stared open-mouthed.

"Oi, Captain!" bellowed Shergar, with an unmistakable smirk, "You'd better get up home. There's something going on up at your house!"

I waved acknowledgement and trotted up the steps. It is quite a way up, for a seafaring gentleman like me who enjoys his table; and the direct route from the Heroes Square is pretty steep. By the time I arrived at the house, marginally concerned about what I might find there, I was drawing breath like a blacksmith's bellows and feeling distinctly over-heated under my waterproofs. I was, thus, not quite the calm, collected chap I might have wished to be as I entered the *avli* and found Clemmie sitting on my steps, doing Cheshire Cat impressions.

"Wha… how… Clemmie, dear girl! How the devil are you?" I panted.

"Top hole, Skip. In the pink. How about you?"

I gestured to my sweating face.

"Even more… in the pink… as you… see…" I puffed. "What are you doing here? Err… delighted of course… pleased to… see you…"

"How very flatteringly you put that! Well recovered… we'll make a pretentious bourgeois upstart out of you yet! Wellllllllllllllll…" She looked at me appraisingly, "I have about ten days before I have to go to Turkey, for the Ephesus visit, don'cher know, sooooo… I came back to see if you were telling the truth."

"I doubt it!" I said. "I'm sure I would have remembered. About anything in particular? Or are you after The Truth… is there a God? Why are we here, what's it all about, all that stuff? I charge extra for that."

She stood up, pursed her lips as if mulling something over, and rather suggestively scratched the door of my room.

78

"Have you *ryally* got a sextant in he-yar?"

I nodded.

"We're not talking about one of those plastic things, are we? You have a real, live sextant? Brass, glass, enamel? Sort of thing Ahab and Horatio Wotsit would recognise?"

"Made by Cooke of Kingston-upon-Hull, serial number 5904. With an eight-by-thirty monocular sight for stars. I can even work Venus in daylight on a clear day."

"Ah. Tempting. Very tempting. Because, you see, I ryally would like to learn astro-nav."

"Ah ha! Well, I've got everything you need, including Nories tables, a star-finder and this year's nautical almanac. And a short-wave radio, for the time signals."

Clemmie sighed theatrically.

"Oh, you silver-tounged devil, you. What's a girl to do? One tries to be virtuous, one tries to be good, but it's a wicked world, full of things we want..."

"I'll have to get a chart and some parallel rules... they've got them in the chandlery..."

"Oh! There you go again, talking dirty!" She grinned. "Is it a deal then? You'll teach me?"

I tugged my forelock and bowed my head.

"Most 'appy to be of 'umble service to yer Ladyship!" I servile-ed in my best Faaarmer Joiles accent.

"Jolly Dee. But there's just one thing..." She grinned impishly and looked me straight in the eye. "Regretfully, one has to stoop to grubby commercialism when dealing with the lower classes... and you really are a fearful oik, you know. Pater always insisted on paying the menials... God knows why, but there you are; but he also said a lady shouldn't carry cash. Can I pay with Sexual Excess?"

I opened the door to the room and waved her in with a flourish.

"That," I said, "will do nicely!"

CHAPTER FIVE

PERIPETIA

An unjustifiable but heartfelt digression on Greek light, visibility and ancient mariners...Ayios Yeorgios, and musings on the utility of rocks... High Noon in the Plum Pudding Club... Choras... Serifos by night... Sifnos by day... the consequences of dolphins... Irakleia... boiling old goats, the desirability of... anemos-ity and indecency... sweet sorrow.

About half way between the Peloponnese coast at Poros and the chain of islands which mark the western edge of the Cyclades* is a high, rocky island called Ayios Yeorgios, or Saint George. Scarcity of fresh water and the lack of safe access means that it is uninhabited, apart from a large flock of very hairy, horny goats; another of hairy, horny sheep; and... briefly, on very calm days... a hairy (and let us charitably infer no more) goatherd; yet despite the lack of facilities or society, Ayios Yeorgios is a most valuable chunk of rock. I feel a digression coming on.

* * *

The air in Greece is famed for its clarity. The Artist's Light, they call it; and indeed there are days when one can see a hundred miles if one can get high enough... I have seen Mykonos from the heights behind Galatas, which is almost ninety miles. But those days occur mostly in the winter, or in the later

---

* The accepted English spelling 'Cyclades' is generally incorrectly pronounced by English-speakers in one of two ways; the first suggests unwell gentlewomen, the second an immunity deficiency caught from a bike. The correct Greek pronunciation is 'kick-LAH-thess'.

autumn and early spring. When the weather gets warmer, the visibility drops dramatically as a gentle haze invades the atmosphere.

This is in no way like fog, mist or pollution… well, not once you get out of Athens, anyway. The sky still radiates pure blue, the few clouds are perfectly defined. Nothing hinders the cataract of radiant heat crashing onto the dry rocks from a blast-furnace sun overhead. When close in with the land, the large buzzards can clearly be seen wheeling lazily high on the crags over the harbours. It is close to the horizon that the air becomes less distinct… not unpleasantly so; it is a rather warming diffusion of light which enhances the colours and softens the features. In summer, this haze turns the Aegean into a magnificent impressionists' canvas, giving the islands and mountains an ethereal quality. You might think of it as excellent value for Monet.

Yet however this haze enhances the scenic qualities, however it delights the artist and the visitor, it can be a bit of a pest for sailors. The only time you can clearly see where you are going is the winter, when the weather can be very rough and pretty chilly. As the conditions become calmer and more congenial for sailing, the horizontal visibility drops away until, by the heat of early summer, a large island can sometimes only be seen at six or seven miles; even less on occasion.

All this barely matters today, since almost every boat has a satellite-navigator, but in 1985 very few yachts had them and even commercial ships had the old orbital satellite systems which sometimes left them without a fix for hours at a time. If you couldn't see the next island, you needed to proceed on dead-reckoning,* extending your course from the last-known position by estimating speed, drift and leeway whilst wondering vaguely where it was going to lead you.

Dead-reckoning is an imprecise science even for modern vessels, which have current atlases, tidal charts, reasonably reliable compasses and speed-logs; but no such luxuries assisted the Ancients, of course, as they forged the earliest maritime trade routes through these waters, or launched the odd

---

* If a doctor isn't too sure whether you are going to live or die, he doesn't, of course, say 'Your ticker's on its last legs, so I hope you didn't waste your money on a return ticket.' That would be highly unprofessional, and not at all the sort of thing that even a patient patient would pay his substantial stipend for. The doctor will take refuge behind something like 'anomalous myocardial dysfunction' and in extremis may go so far as to predicate 'an uncertain prognosis'. Navigators are no less careful of their professional image. If they use the term 'dead reckoning' it means 'we guessed'.

thousand-ship excursion necessary for retrieving ladies of questionable virtue from the Trojan side of the tracks.

The Ancient Greek navigators had nothing but their eyeballs, and the direction of the sun to guide them… they hadn't even developed maps. It was strictly daylight navigation only when they crossed any open water, with one eye firmly fixed on the nearest shelter at all times. In fact, the difficulties these chaps faced are now enshrined in one of our most cherished axioms, "the face that launched a thousand ships." It did indeed launch them… ancient navigators were so wary of the sea that they pulled their ships ashore when they weren't using them; and, since they didn't have very good anchors either, that included most nights when they went to sleep.

Contrary to the popular belief in The North that the Mediterranean is a benign lake, it is in fact a capricious, giddy-headed schizophrenic; and to people who were still slightly behind the eight-ball with regard to physics and thermodynamics the Aegean's moods were so inexplicably fickle that a quirky, bored and irascible God stirring up the sea with a big fork was probably the most logical idea the Ancient Greeks *could* have come up with.*

So the Ancient's dilemma, still familiar to yachtsmen until quite recently, was a dichotomy. The good weather and long days for daylight navigation occur in summer, when the visibility is often rather poor. And this, coming finally to the kernel of this latest outrageous digression, is why Ayios Yeorgios is esteemed far more than its barren inaccessibility would suggest.

The island is a great sentinel in the middle of the forty-something miles of otherwise empty sea between the Argo-Saronic islands and the Cyclades, a way-point at which the half-blind navigator can either renew his confidence in himself and his calculations or, alternatively, put his affairs in order. By the time the Peloponnese side fades from view, Ayios Yeorgios is just appearing. By the time it fades astern, there will usually be only a short time before the Cyclades come into view. With a lighthouse at each end to guide the night-time voyager, Ayios Yeorgios stands, like a great traffic policeman on eternal overtime, pointing the way from the marinas of Athens to the islands for yachtsman and dividing commercial ships left into Piraeus or right to the north Aegean, Dardanelles and Black Sea.

Clemmie and I, contentedly navigating with the sextant, had no essential

---

* No dafter than the concept of a single monopolies commission, at any rate

need of Agios Yeorgios, and so I apologise for the above digression and can only mitigate my sin by asserting that the island did serve as a check on our celestial fixes, which helped to give my pupil early confidence, and that therefore, like countless sailors before us, we smiled our acknowledgements as *Mucky Duck* sailed slowly past its triangular southern peak.

* * *

Mucky Duck was a modern forty-foot Gib-Sea sloop which I had acquired by Machiavellian means. In need of a boat for a week or so, and feeling that I also needed to re-assert myself after having been duped into taking *Iraklis* on the Grave-Robber, I had done a deal with Spiros.

I was already designated to take *Mucky Duck* from Alimos to the port of Pythagorion in Samos, a large island hard against the Turkish coast, to start a charter just before Orthodox Easter. Samos is right next to Kusadasi, which is the Turkish port adjacent to the ancient city of Ephesus; and that was where Clemmie had to be in about ten days' time. So, knowing that Spiros wasn't going to pay me much for the Grave-Robber, and wasn't going to do even that until it suited him, I cornered him in a Piraeus waterfront shebeen called the Plum Pudding Club and made him a proposal.

My suggestion was that, in lieu of half of the wages owing to me from the Grave-Robber, I should set off with *Mucky Duck* early, and take my time about the journey. The owner of the boat was in Western Australia (whose state emblem, the black swan, inspired 'Mucky Duck', which is evidently what passes for wit in those parts) so he wouldn't know where the boat was. I didn't say a word about Clemmie, but rather let Spiros think that I would be improving my chartering curriculum vitae by reconnoitring ports and bays, the better to delight *his* clients. I would then prepare the boat for charter and stay to hand it over to the clients in Pythagorian at no extra charge.

Spiros bargained back at me, of course… this is simply Greek. You always haggle, no matter what. It is expected; it is ingrained. For a Greek, accepting a deal without an argument is like breathing in and forgetting to exhale… it is an entirely automatic reaction. Hagglers are not resented, but rather admired… astute foreigners soon learn that they may be very well liked, but they will never be truly respected if they don't bargain effectively.

"But Julian!" he expostulated, "I only owe you for four days... you are asking me for a free nine day charter for two days' pay!"

"You owe me for *five* days, and you weren't going to pay me anyway; so the rest is interest."

"Good Gods, how much interest are you charging?"

"As much as it takes! Come on, Spiro... it saves you money, and doesn't cost you anything. And I'll be able to do a better job with your next clients. I'll also do some tidying up on the boat... rope work, that sort of thing, so the owner is getting a deal too."

"Well, do the delivery for free too, then. Then I don't have to deduct the delivery from the owner's charter income."

I didn't think an owner almost ten thousand miles away was ever going to know very much about how or when his boat got to Samos, and I had my doubts whether his rebate was robust enough to survive so daunting a journey; so I grinned my disagreement.

"Tell you what; I'll take the delivery fee, based on two days sailing and two travelling, but I won't charge for cleaning the boat and handing her over. You fill her up with fuel, and give me enough to put fifty litres in her after the trip... I'll cover any extra, plus water, and I'll leave her full at hand-over of course. And you pay my ferry fare back."

"Thirty litres of fuel. You wouldn't need more for a straight delivery. And the owner wants electric shower-pumps putting in, and the fresh water pump needs changing... you do that on the way, for free. And I will pay you for the fuel and delivery when you get back to Poros."

"I think I had already guessed that!" I grinned.

We shook on it, and my soul soared.

"Oh, by the way," I added casually, "It's best to have some crew for a long trip... when you fix the papers could you please put this name on the crew list?"

I gave him Clemmie's name and passport number scribbled on a ferry ticket. His eyes rolled up and he invoked the wrath of the Gods* on me as he realised he had possessed the advantage in the argument all along. But a deal is a deal; he wryly did as he had agreed, muttering darkly that he was sure I

---

* A polite way of putting it. Greek vituperation is generally a complex and long-playing series of contradictory insults heavily inclined to allegations of ambigous sexuality, auto-erotic proclivities, hagio-sexual blasphemies and... well, sex and saints generally.

had some Greek blood in me somewhere, and I contentedly sailed *Mucky Duck* down to Poros that evening to pick up Clemmie and my gear. The next morning at four o'clock we were heading out of Poros leaving a deliberately vague idea of our itinerary behind... just in case Spiros had any bright ideas, like taking some paying passengers, or doing a charter on the way.

The wages of sin, in this particular case, were well worth the effort. *Mucky Duck* was a good sailing boat of the modern type, two or three years old and in fine condition. She was a Gib-Sea 402, a very reasonable compromise between the older, classical style of boat and the new high-volume types which were taking over the market. She had the wide-beam hull which was now ubiquitous for new charter- boats and a big, broad, comfortable cockpit. Down below there were two double cabins aft, a large vee-berth cabin forward, and a big saloon. We found her a good performer under sail. Because she belonged to an Australian she had an enormous fridge, a cruising chute for going downwind and a 'Bimini'... a canvas sun cover over the helmsman's position, which was a very rare feature in Greece at that time. If we had hired her, she would probably have cost a thousand pounds per week in high season.

As *Mucky Duck* nodded lazily past Ayios Yeorgios, Clemmie and I basked mother-naked in the midday heat, delighted with our fortunes and just about as contented as the human condition is disposed to be.

* * *

The cool of the evening saw us entering Livadhi harbour on the island of Serifos. It had been an almost perfect day... the wind for most of the daylight hours had been a steady, warmish southerly force three, which had kept us moving at about four and a half knots on a close-reach. There had been some light, high skeins of cloud through which the sun had shone without much dilution, so that the middle hours of the day had been agreeably toasty. Lunch had been a poem... I had managed to get a couple of crayfish from a friendly Poros fisherman, and Petros had filled two of the five-litre, handled bottles the Greeks call '*damzans*'* with his crisp, fruity rosé wine for the trip.

---

*   A corruption of 'demi-john'.

The sea had not been too skittish, allowing me to teach Clemmie the rather strange swaying motion which is necessary when using a sextant. This is a lateral rocking motion which causes the sun to move in a curve across the horizon, allowing the observer to take the measurement at the lowest point of the arc; teaching how to do this is most easily done by grabbing the trainee's shoulders and physically imparting the motion, so instructing a naked member of the opposite sex can rarely be anything other than enormous fun... such fun, indeed, that it would probably have led to some extra-curricular activities if *Mucky Duck* had only had an auto-pilot, but sadly that was one refinement she lacked. We got second prize, however; by late afternoon, a delighted Clemmie had managed three fairly accurate position-lines all on her own.

Serifos is a roughly round island, rocky and high, with whorls of ancient terracing looping around the intricately folded hillsides. The main port of Livadhi is on the south-east corner, a deep bay in the shape of a reversed letter 'R' cutting over a mile into the island, with a ferry quay forming the central indent and a great sweep of beach around its head. Once upon a time minerals were mined here, and there are several ruined loading gantries around the shores; but now there is only tourism, and the week before Easter the port was still mostly closed and shuttered. We moored *Mucky Duck* at the yacht-quay and, after a quick look at the dusty, closed-up restaurants and shops around the bay, we took the bus to the chora.

There is a 'chora'* on almost every central Aegean island, the main and usually highest village. It may have another name as well, sometimes that of the island itself, but the thing that makes it the 'chora' is height, protection and predominance over other settlements on the isle. Here, often in hopelessly inaccessible places, you will find the *Dimarxeio*, or town hall; the main (and probably only) bank; the post-office; and generally the school. Of the island's official entities only the police and port police will be down by the ferry quay, where most of their business is and where there is room to park their Toyobishi Dumpsters.

Aegean Island Greeks of old lived largely from the sea, for these are not fertile islands, like those of the Argo-Saronic. The Cyclades, with the notable

---

* Pronounced 'Hora', with a guttural 'H' and the stress on the first syllable. It literally means 'village'. The ubiquitous Greek salad is actually a 'choriatiki' or 'village' salad.

exception of Naxos, are craggy and windswept, magnificent in their starkness, with few uncultivated trees and little pasture. Some vines, olives and crops are grown on terraces or in sheltered areas near the sea, but island people developed mainly as fishermen, traders, merchants, and seamen. It made sense to live by the shore, where the work was and where the lower land was more sheltered and easily farmed. It made no sense at all to live on top of a mountain, far from the workplaces of the community and exposed to the frequent strong winds; but there the choras are… perched high on beetling crags, accessed by serpentine roads painstakingly quarried out of solid rock, a testament to immense labour. For centuries the people of the islands have descended to work, and every evening they have climbed back up the mountain again; there to cook, eat, recreate and sleep high above the world, where the winter chill is keen and the wind screeches more than two hundred days a year. The reason for this retreat from the sheltered lowlands and the sea, of course, was piracy. And I'm off on a tangent again.

* * *

The Eastern Mediterranean of Medieval and Renaissance times was not a good place in which to live by the seaside. Seafaring marauders, all with a keen understanding of ships and the sea, could be found in almost every waterside community; often they traded or buccaneered alternately, as opportunity allowed. Piracy had been a threat to the Venetians, who had used their maritime might to control it somewhat; but the Ottomans pushed the Venetians back, and the Ottoman Empire never really understood sea-power. Commercialism and seafaring were pursuits below the dignity of an Ottoman, whose only real function in life was supposed to be waging war or high politics, so the Sultans left all the pecuniary stuff to their subject Arab and Christian populations. So long as a reasonable amount of tax came in they were free to get on with. And get on with it they did.

The entire north African shore was Ottoman in name only for most of the time… sometimes the Sublime Porte, the Ottoman government, would throw its toys out of the harem and brutally execute a bolshie Bey who had gone a bit too far; but generally they were too busy trying to extend the Empire into Europe, fighting the Knights of Saint John or sneaking into the seraglio, and the local Pasha would be left to his own devices. The Egyptians and Algerians were particularly active sea-raiders... names such as Barbarossa became feared, and the Barbary pirates were a force into the early nineteenth century... and Corsicans, Sardinians and Sicilians all played a part. The Greeks themselves were also notable pirates when opportunity arose,[*] and whilst one island might not prey on its immediate neighbours there certainly were fratricidal raids against distant Greek populations. Settlements were not only robbed, there was also a ready market for slaves on the Barbary Coast.

The Ottomans didn't really care about this... their trade was mostly conducted by their subjects, so they suffered little direct loss. And in their outlying provinces the ruling Pashas were behind a lot of the piracy in any case, so what came around went around. It was only individuals who suffered, and there was no relief to be had... even if the Ottomans had wanted to stop it, their control of the Pashas was rarely more than nominal, and their inefficient naval forces were far too ungainly and inept to prevail against the skilled, ferocious corsairs in their fast-sailing galleys and xebecs.

The only protection from this rapine for an islander was therefore to live high up, with narrow streets to aid defence, where you could see who was approaching and, if necessary, run the other way. It wasn't, in fact, often necessary to run; ill-disciplined corsair crews were not much inclined to climb massive hills and assault alerted, desperate people in narrow alleyways. The mere existence of the chora was usually sufficient deterrent.

Thus centuries of necessity made the chora the place where the islanders lived; and now in the modern age when local piracy is a no longer even a memory and the beaches are the source of most of the islands wealth, ancient custom still takes the population back up the hill to the chora at night.

* * *

In Serifos we climbed up and up through the narrow lanes, between buildings of biblical simplicity. Somewhat less than half of the houses seemed to be occupied... front doors were open in many, and stable-type half-doors were

---

* i.e. when they saw a boat smaller than their own.

common. Despite a chill in the air old folks sat outside on the spindly, rush-seated Greek chairs, talking quietly. Not one of them failed to welcome us as we went by, and almost all used the greeting *xáirete.**

It seemed impertinent to gaze unbidden into these open doorways, but returning the courtly greetings gave us the excuse to snatch fleeting impressions of the interiors of the iconic cube-dwellings. Some doors had linen or beaded screens providing some measure of privacy, but most were not curtained.

The interiors were simplistic to the point of being Spartan... a trendy architect would call them 'minimalist' or some such neological guff. We glimpsed flag-stone floors, with occasionally a rug but no carpets, and plain, plastered walls; unadorned chairs and tables, sometimes varnished but often painted in bright primary colours; some wood-burning stoves, and a few simple electric hot-plates or gas-rings. There seemed to be many old-fashioned enamel oven-dishes. Beds were made up in living rooms in several houses, and the walls were sparsely hung with icons, photographs, simple plate racks, and lace. Lace seemed to be the only frippery in these austere homes fashioned almost into the rock.

Apart from the cooking arrangements, the only definitively twentieth century appliances I saw were light bulbs, rather dated transistor radios and the occasional refrigerator. There was the impression of pristine cleanliness and the pride of the inhabitants was evident in the carefully maintained whitewash within and without, in the bright colours and in the sheen of the floors.

Dinner in the square by the town hall was pleasant, and we had a drink or two in a bar near the bus-stop before we realised that we had misread the time-table... we were reading the times for the Easter weekend. The bus had already finished for the night, and when I asked if there was a taxi the

---

* I love this salutation... when people are in a hurry, or being merely polite, they more often say good morning, good evening, or whatever; and these are the forms more usually heard in towns; but in rural areas one still meets xáirete, which conveys rather more than mere acknowledgement. Deriving from 'Xaire', meaning 'hail' it is pronounced 'hxair-ettay', and the stress on the first syllable can be prolonged for anything up to half an hour or so, when nothing else is pressing. It really gives the sense that the most important thing in the world is saying hello to you, and that all day is available for the task.

bartender said yes, certainly… in June. So we set out walking under a half moon.

It is probably five or six kilometres to the port, maybe more the way the road winds, but we didn't really care. We chatted and chuckled, held hands at times, and enjoyed the panoramic view of the bay and distant lights on the adjacent island of Sinfos. We would probably have burst into song once we left the houses behind, but suddenly lights flared behind us and a great air-horn nearly blasted us off the road. The bus screeched to a halt, and a grinning face beckoned us in.

Apparently the driver had been having a drink after work, and someone had told him we were walking down, so he had come especially to get us… unspeakably nice of him, but he was in a hurry to get back to his friends and the way he went down that road quickly had me wondering how many drinks he had in fact managed to consume before hearing of our plight. I gripped the rail in front of me until I almost bent it. The driver heaved the wheel back and forth with great, dramatic arcs of muscular forearms as he bellowed his undying commitment to Olympiakos and Leeds United over his shoulder. Clemmie started out holding me, but soon decided I wasn't firm enough and shifted her grip to the rail; I meanwhile braced my foot against the seat on the opposite side to prevent us both being flung into the aisle on right-handers.

The bus dumped us by the quay. The driver did his duty to the community by accepting our fares, which wouldn't even have paid for the rubber he had lost off the tyres in his waterfall descent. Then he solemnly handed out two tickets and the change, declined to accept a tip, and roared back up the hill. We stood on the quay watching the lights weaving up into the night, the crescendo and clash of uphill gear changes still audible faintly in the still air and the blare of the horn reaching us a few seconds after the bus turned each corner.

We ended the night with a final glass at the single taverna open on the beach, very satisfied with life and thinking how wonderful the bay of Livadhi must be on a hot summers evening, with music spilling out of the numerous tavernas and the tables on the sand under the flame-trees.

* * *

Next morning found us motoring south-east. We had wanted to see the island of Naxos, which is unique in the Cyclades for its forestation and fertility. Clemmie, whose expensive education had inevitably included a hogshead or two of mythology, had gleefully informed me of the policy of Phaedra and her Maenads with regard to men on that island*, but I am sure that it was really the weather report from the port police which dissuaded me from visiting. Some strong southerlies were forecast in about two days' time, and the pilot book was not enthusiastic about the safety of the harbour, so I decided to drop in to Sifnos and then duck underneath Paros and Naxos to take a look at Irakleia, which faced north and looked like a great place to hide from a southerly. Then we could head north-east for Samos via Dhonoussa if the southerly was not too strong, or hide for a while if it blew a belter.

We tied up in sleepy Kamares, the main port of Sifnos, for a few hours and took lunch in the village of Artemonas, which is a short, stiff walk above the chora, Appolonia. From the terrace of our restaurant a stunning tableaux of islands lay before us... Dhespotico, Anti-Paros, Paros and Naxos stacked neatly one behind another; below them Irakleia and Skhinoussa; and far away to the south the fuzzy humps of Folegandros, Sikinos and Ios. The thought that all this lay at our whim and pleasure was almost too much to bear; and we experienced a bitter-sweet conflict of emotions, the joy of such freedom and choice countered by a deep regret that our time was so limited.

We loved Artemonas, with its whitewashed purity and panoramic views in every direction. It sits on the crest of the island, open in places to the east as described and also to the west, with views to Serifos and Milos. We would happily have lingered but, like children at Christmas, we simply had to open the next present before playing with the first. In barely three hours we were back aboard *Mucky Duck,* setting our cruising chute to a soft northerly.

As soon as the water began to chuckle under our bow, a lazy school of dolphins appeared and flickered effortlessly under the forefoot. Great, grey creatures, over two metres long and as clear as could be in the pellucid water, they rolled sideways and returned our enchanted gaze with that slight hook to their mouths that dolphins have, and which so resembles the loving but

---

* Possibly the first people to suggest that the way to a man's heart could be through his stomach. Or his kidneys. They seem to have enjoyed taking the scenic route.

slightly smug smile of a parent who has got the better of a wily child. Every rippling muscle, every mark, every scar on their bodies and every notch on their fins, even the pupils of their eyes could be made out in the crystalline, cobalt sea. When they left, we dropped the sails on deck and left *Mucky Duck* to her own devices for a while… no-one of any sentiment at all could possibly have done anything else.

We passed that evening anchored in beautiful Dhespotico. I bought a large, fresh *fagri*, a red bream type of fish, from a fisherman, and whilst I grilled the delicious, firm, flaky white flesh over a fire on the beach Clemmie played her wild, romantic folk tunes and the sun sank behind Sifnos. No amount of money could possibly have given us more than we already had… except time.

* * *

The next day dawned under a sulky sky, a grizzled canopy which exuded discontent like a child which has five sprouts to eat before it can have its ice cream. We set off eastwards using the engine and wearing rather more clothing. The cloud put paid to astro-navigation, so we did a bit of chart-work to mitigate the tedium of motoring under the miserable clag; but after an hour or so the promised south wind began to set in and we got some sails up.

By the time we reached Irakleia, we felt more as if we had landed in a different continent by aeroplane rather than travelled a short distance by boat. The grey, blustery showers, the increasingly miasmic visibility and the deserted appearance of Irakleia seemed a hemisphere away from the radiance, clarity and amiability of Sifnos twenty-four hours before.

The harbour at Irakleia is roughly square, with a sandy beach across the southern side and short quay partly closing the northern one. Yachts usually make fast on the inside of the quay, facing south towards the beach; but with a southerly of unknown strength forecast I decided to use the north side, effectively tying up on the outside of the harbour. There was, for a change, method in my madness.

I was already aware of the funny things that wind does when it hits an Aegean island. It goes up the windward side all well-behaved, as if butter wouldn't melt in its mouth, but what it gets up to at the top I simply don't know… perhaps it is tired and cross after the climb, or maybe it holds a trade union meeting, or something. Possibly it absorbs from its contact with the land the characteristics of the Greeks themselves, and it is merely reckless enthusiasm which compels it to behave like a harum-scarum kid on a skateboard. Whatever the reason, it comes down the other side in a series of powerful squalls which the Greeks call *spilliades;* tumultuous gusts that howl like a banshee and batter the bejaysus out of anything in their way.* Knowing this, I snugged *Mucky Duck* down on the outer northern side of the quay next to the ferry-ramp, where the wind would hold us off the jetty and the weight of these *spilliades* would be taken on our stern-lines.

The crew of the only other yacht in the harbour, early charterers with an Italian flag at the crosstrees and conventionally moored inside the mole, watched these proceedings with veiled incredulity. They were a stylish group, two couples of probably forty or so. The men were senatorial, distinguished, edged with silver types, and the women were svelte, long-limbed and elegant. Their grooming was universally superior. They were utterly unreserved and friendly, but entirely monoglotal.

In loud, slow Italian, and with many gestures, they earnestly tried to explain to me that the harbour had an inside and an outside, and for people of style there could be but one choice. In English For The Unimproved Foreigner, laced with a few attempts at something which I thought might be Italian but obviously wasn't, I tried to tell them that they would shortly be on the windward side of the quay praying for their anchor to hold; but we could find no common tongue. I tried my schoolboy French, my war movie German and my Central American dock-rat Spanish, whilst Clemmie tried in Latin (what else?); but by no means could we make them understand that a) they weren't in a good place, and more importantly b) that I wasn't a loony. We parted from each other smiling broadly, making no sudden gestures, both parties keeping their hands visible and making all possible soothing, amicable gestures to appease the dangerous nutters on the opposite side of the quay.

---

* I call these katabatic gusts 'Poseidon's Bullets'; and the yachtsman who is new to the Med, and particularly the Aegean, is well advised to watch out for them. In Northern Europe we are somewhat conditioned to running into the lee of the land for a bit of shelter, but in the Aegean this can be a very bad idea indeed. It is best to keep at least two miles away from the lee-side of any high island when there is any strength in the wind, and if you have to come in close then reef down, be ready to release your sheets, and keep your eyes on the water to windward.

Irakleia was a very quiet little island... apparently, less than a hundred people lived there during the winter. The port boasted a wonderfully soft, sandy beach under shady trees, a small shop and two tavernas, both of which offered, at this very early part of the season, not very much at all. There was considerable consternation at our arrival. Fridges were thrown open to display no more than potatoes, olives, cheese and the odd tomato.

My nascent Greek was not up to the voluble explanations which accompanied this out-turning of the cupboards and so, by means of eldritch screams up and down the beach, a teenager was summoned to interpret. We were offered fresh fish, and the much-vaunted local goat... but would we please order now, as someone had to go to the chora to get it?

We allowed ourselves to be talked into ordering *yido-makaronada*, goat-meat with spaghetti... heaven knows why; we must have been in an enquiring frame of mind... and then settled down with a bottle of Naxian wine whilst a clattering old pick-up truck was sent for our supper.

It seemed hours before it was ready, but we were quite happy sitting under a great tree in a courtyard, chatting and practising our Greek with the kids. The adults kept coming to apologise for the wait, and the children enthusiastically told us how worth waiting for it was... people came from Naxos, from Santorini, from Athens even, for Mum's *yido-makaronada*.

I suppose we had sort of expected the meat to be in a sauce, but the name turned out to be scrupulously correct, and what we got was a soup-bowl full of goat and spaghetti, with just a hint of clear juice at the bottom of the bowl. It seemed the meat had simply been boiled, and there wasn't much likelihood that it was kid, or anything young and succulent, either; the flesh had a sinewy, coarse-grained appearance that suggested a draught-animal beyond economical repair. From irregular chunks of the greyish meat protruded splintered ends of substantial bone, and dotted here and there were lumps of yellowy fat. It looked like something you might find stuck on the front of your car after speeding through a sanctuary for elderly warthogs.

The smiling, obliging proprietors assembled in an expectant line to watch us enjoy this culinary pearl, and only the compulsion not to give offence to what looked like four generations of the proud family gave us the courage to try it. And do you know, a pearl it was!

The spaghetti, we later found, had been prepared in the water used for boiling the goat, and had a delicately gamey flavour very nicely spiced with rosemary. The meat itself was tasty, juicy and as soft as butter. Second helpings were offered and accepted. Boiled superannuated goat with spaghetti... try it sometime!

* * *

Overnight the wind picked up just as forecast, and we awoke to the tinkling of the halyards inside the mast, a low humming in the rigging, and the occasional sharp heeling of *Mucky Duck* as a gust struck her spars. Smugly secure with our stern to the weather, we snuggled under the duvet and enjoyed being safe in port in a blow... it is a wonderful feeling for a sailor, to be cosily contemplating a leisurely breakfast and an idle day in the taverna when a different decision might have meant being out in the dawn, moving to a safe place, lashing things down and generally combating the elements.

I ruefully lamented the fact that, in accordance with my first law of nautical recreation, nobody was around to appreciate my omniscience. Clemmie told me to quit moaning and make the coffee. We then engaged in a wonderful little wrestling and tickling match to determine who was going to quit the pink, rosy ambience of the duvet and put the kettle on, during the course of which we discovered to our surprise that we didn't really want coffee all that much anyway, and continued the wrestling and tickling for the sheer fun of it. And then, at frankly a most inopportune moment, there was a horrendous grating close by. An instant later *Mucky Duck* took a great lurch to one side, and I came perilously close to suffering what is hopefully a very rare form of whiplash.

I shall spare the sensitive reader a graphic description of the next few moments; suffice it to say that I deserted Clemmie in the most boorish manner by virtually traversing her north face and base-jumping off her head. Tumbling naked and disoriented into the cabin, I then spent the next few moments like the dog in the dilemma of being equidistant from two bones. With fear for the boat in my heart, nautical contingencies in my head and every other organ of my body still in the service of Eros, I performed a headless-chicken impression of Oscar winning standard between the hatch way and a desperate search for clothes. It wasn't made any better by a babble of panicky voices outside and another few lurches at critical moments.

I picked things up, changed my mind, put them down, lost them. At one point I got my substantial thigh stuck tight in a pair of Clemmie's knickers… nothing kinky, I merely mistook them for underpants… and at another I found myself staring indecisively at a left foot sandal and a right foot rubber boot. Eventually I found a pair of swimming shorts, heaved them on with great difficulty… they appeared to cling to my legs like rubber… and following a prodigious struggle with the main hatchway I erupted into the cockpit through a shotgun blast of storm-driven raindrops.

The Italian boat was pressed up against *Mucky Duck's* port side, with her bows towards the quay and canted sharply so that her stern was across our stem. A regular succession of violent gusts of wind pressed her bow to starboard, and she should have just blown away and gone clear; however, her anchor was hooked over our stern-line so that her front end was firmly attached. Something similar had evidently occurred at her back end too, as that was also held tightly against us. The side of the Italian boat was hard against *Mucky Duck's* un-fendered port bow, and four howling, frantic people in matching day glow foul weather gear were desperately trying to hold the two boats apart whilst forcing fenders down between them. This was an utterly dispiriting business for them, as there was no way under the sun that they were going to manage to compress the fenders sufficiently to force them between the upper edges of the two decks; and they were up to the usual nonsense of pushing as hard as they could on life lines and stanchions.

I bellowed at them to stop that before they broke something and, doing my best to ignore the assault of the ferocious elements on my naked torso, I ran forward with a fender taken from the other side. This I dropped to sea level, let it float between the boats and then hauled it upwards so that it wedged itself between the hulls from underneath. A couple of mighty heaves jammed it so tightly into the narrowing gap from below that the hulls were held a few inches apart. I dragged another one in there from the other end, and told everyone to take a breather. This the Italians evidently misunderstood, as they immediately commenced a massive argument.

Clemmie appeared next to me at this point and took in the situation with keen interest, looking as fetching as ever with a twinkle in her bright eyes, a quirky smile and her curly, dark hair positively Medusan in the anarchy of the gale. Her bare, shapely legs protruded below her waterproof jacket, terminating ludicrously in a pair of cut-off green farmer's wellies.

We watched avidly as the two women on the other boat got stuck into their men folk like reapers into a wheat field. I got the impression that this was merely the first instalment of a fulsome and remorseless remonstration for broken fingernails and spoiled hairdos; and there was none of the screeched, semi-articulate loss for words which these affairs often engender, either. Both ladies appeared to be powerfully coherent, their scorn-laden phrases clearly enunciated and forcefully projected without deviation, hesitation or repetition so far as we could tell. The men defended themselves with passion. Jaws were thrust forward, arms flew about without quite making contact... it was all rather like a third-rate kung-fu film.

At any other time I would have poured a drink and sat down to enjoy the show; however, at gale strength and laced with light rain even the mild south wind was cold enough to begin to bite, and I reluctantly interrupted.

I made a couple of half-hearted efforts to interrupt them, but passions were flying fairly high and nothing remotely polite made any headway. And then I remembered a bit of dock-Italian I had heard stevedores using during a difficult cargo operation in Trieste some years before. I decided to give that a try.

"*Basta, Stronzo!*" I cried, with all my not inconsiderable vocal power. It was probably registered by seismic monitoring stations around the area... but all it accomplished was to enrage the Italian men,[*] who now turned on me. Until, that is, the blonder of the two Italian ladies bested my effort with a penetrating "*Tacere, vecchia pentola a pressione!*[†]"

This had the effect I had totally failed to achieve, and she turned from her startled and speechless men folk, saying to me sweetly, "'*Scuzi, Signor!*"

I was in charge. Wonderful. Now what was I going to do? I took a look at the situation.

Driven away from the windward side of the quay by the ferocious gusts off the island, the Italians had presumably tried to move around to the lee side

---

[*] Hardly surprisingly, with hindsight, since I am now informed that it means 'Zip it, Shithead!'

[†] 'Shut up, you old pressure cooker'... Oh! I would have given a major appendage to have come out with that one myself!

next to us, and I supposed that they had decided to lay a stern anchor and moor bows to the weather… a sensible thought, but one which gave a dreadful premonition that the entanglement at their stern might well involve their anchor-rope, my anchor chain, and/or a propeller. Dimly aware that something was still very wrong with my shorts, I made my way forward and peered over the bow… the Italian's rudder was over my anchor chain, and in the clear but agitated water I thought I could see a loop of their anchor line around my chain and back into their propeller.

We quickly got some lines ashore from the Italian's bow, and then one of the men donned his snorkelling gear and cut the anchor-rope free from their propeller. This done, the other boat drifted away from *Mucky Duck* and lay to the wind. We knotted the two ends of the anchor-rope together again, pulled hard to make sure that their anchor was holding, and presently had them conventionally moored. Peace was declared, universal good will broke out, Clemmie brought me a fleece jacket, and one of the Italian ladies handed round small glasses of grappa.

Whilst the other lady prepared magnificently aromatic Italian coffee for us all, I trotted ashore to deal with their anchor, which was still over our stern-line; and as I did so I realised what was wrong with my shorts… in my haste to get on deck, I had put them on back-to-front. I ignored the matter temporarily and concentrated on the other boat's anchor, which I supposed they had left hanging from the roller whilst moving around from the inside of the harbour. It had hooked over our rope when they approached the quay. I didn't want to slack our moorings in this wind, and I couldn't be bothered rigging another line, so I slipped a rope around the head of the anchor with a boat hook, asked the Italians to slack the chain a little, and lifted the anchor onto the quay.

I was quite enjoying the attention of everyone as I performed this manly feat, and I posed a moment as Clemmie took a photograph. She still has it, I believe… it captures my open-mouthed expression at the very moment when the abused shorts finally gave up the ghost, and preserves me for all posterity, virtually naked from the waist down apart from a boot on my right foot and a sandal on my left. The keenest of observers, with patience and concentration, may just be able to make out The Pride of the Blatchleys making a very successful job of hiding from the inclement elements, and Clemmie's lace-frothed knickers still gartering my extravagant thigh.

We left Irakleia early the next morning with a cool but exhilarating north-westerly force five over our shoulder and raced eastwards under Skinoussa towards Amorgos, fortifying ourselves against the temperature and flying spray with occasional drams of fiery, invigorating Italian grappa. We also bore with us some Limoncello liqueur, both bottles insistently bestowed by the Italians after a boisterous evening of mutual incomprehension and mirth in the taverna. Lacking the means to discuss anything other than everyone's profound satisfaction at having witnessed my inaugural efforts at indecent exposure we had just laughed, drank incomprehensible toasts, brutally murdered some opera, and then basked in bonhomie whilst Clemmie's violin filled the house to capacity. By the end of the evening they seemed to have bussed most of the islanders in from the chora and we finally parted in the wee hours, feeling like honorary Irakleians and Freemen of the city of Firenze too boot.

I thought, as we fizzed across a rolling, grey sea and Clemmie stole a few more minutes sleep in the pilot-berth, how very easy it would have been to get angry about the Italian's mismanaged manoeuvring; and what a pleasurable experience we would have missed if we had done so. A confirmation for my Second Law of Nautical Recreation… one meets a better class of people in collisions.

* * *

Evening. A cafe table on a picture-postcard harbour front, and a view across a narrow strip of water towards a rocky, rising landscape. Clemmie and I sat strangely upright in our easy chairs, unusually quiet as we toyed with our evening G-and-Ts. For the first time since we had met there was a constraint between us. Both of us were painfully aware that the repartee had dried up, and the silence had none of the companionable tranquillity which normally marked any hiatus in our conversation. Neither of us dared mention it.

It was a pensive silence, full of reminiscence and introspection, pregnant with unspoken thoughts; for the harbour front on which we sat was Pythagorion, on the south-east side of Samos. The land rising a short distance across the straits was in Turkey, the start of a new continent, and the last thing we had done before ordering our drinks was to book a taxi driver for five o'clock in the morning to take Clemmie to the ferry port in Vathi. I was staying in Greece to hand over *Mucky Duck*, and Clemmie was leaving me, Greece and Europe to continue her archaeological studies.

Even my insensitive temperament recognised that the moment bristled with opportunities to say something *really* crass. Our relationship had been born out of camaraderie, not romance; our intimacy had developed as a simple extension of friendship, begotten out of badinage and carried on in the same teasing vein with the unspoken and mutual expectation of a brief, sub-emotional tryst. No involvement, no commitments, just healthy physical fun which provided the crowning condiment in a delicious banquet of companionable experiences. We were jocular about our relationship, mocked each other about our respective social origins, and jested that living together was a mere matter of logistical convenience. It was always a finite thing. We spoke easily about it.

We weren't speaking about it now, however. The imminence of our separation made me suddenly starkly aware that I was going to miss this girl, possibly more than I'd ever missed anyone, and it seemed to me that Clemmie had realised this and didn't want any last minute emotional nonsense. She had in front of her a career which would require her to travel freely; she was younger than me and a hell of a lot better looking. She couldn't follow her own vocation and me, and she wasn't interested in giving up her own worthy ambitions to become an asset to help me enjoy my life; not even if she did share any of the feelings I was now belatedly discovering.

Mutually preoccupied, both of us searched cluelessly for a neutral subject of conversation. Periodically there were farcical outbursts where we both tried to speak at once, deferred to each other and fell silent again with nothing said. When we did speak, we uttered inane blether, neutral, uncontroversial and pointless. Mostly we pretended to be absorbed in the scenery, and just let the awkward silence have its way.

As we watched the dusk fall and lights begin to twinkle on the Turkish coast, all I could think of was what a perfect time this would be for a soliloquy. I'm rather fond of The Bard and, lacking anything original to say, I searched my memory for an appropriate quote; something witty or comic to defuse the tension. But The Bard was treacherous that night, and all that came to mind, over and over, was a gentleman of Verona intoning, "What joy is joy, if Sylvia be not by?"

Clemmie declined another G-and-T, so we moved to a restaurant and poked some food around our plates for a while; then we went to bed early and lay there in the dark for what seemed like ages, both quite aware that the other was wide awake.

Eventually we must have slept, because the alarm woke us in the early hours. Clemmie dressed quickly. I got up and, too stupid even to make her a farewell cup of coffee, stood clueless and useless as she threw the last few items in her backpack. The purr of a car engine announced that the confounded taxi driver was true to his hour. Clemmie gave me a sisterly hug and a kiss on the cheek. It was absolutely the last chance to say something, and Blatchley will never, at the last, remain silent; so I cleared my throat and, with a nervously hoarse tenor which belied my bantering words, I said, "Well, enjoy your grave-robbing. I don't suppose I can persuade you to stay and do my ironing and child bearing?"

She froze for an instant, and then turned to me and took me gently by the ear lobes.

"Sorry, Skip," she said softly, "No can do. You are awfully sweet, but I couldn't dilute the bloodline... my family hasn't had an oik in the gene-pool for centuries!"

"Quite right too!" I said, with what flippancy I could muster, "Your elitism does you credit! Well, you have a good time, Clemmie. Dig up a pot for me, would you?"

"You'd only break it, you ox! I'll look for a sword, or a bloody great big axe... that's more your style!" Then she hugged me, and kissed me very gently on the lips.

As she climbed out of the hatch, I realised that she had left tears on my cheek.

CHAPTER SIX

THE LITTORAL TRUTH

Dynamic inertia and the rigours of cafe society... what not to do when in Greece for Easter... beware of Greeks bearing gifts... an inviting prospect... a visit to the butcher... the sage counsel of Kyrie Manolis... advice on the spitting of pigs... a helpful hint for persons planning armoured invasions of France... a late surge... porkrastination... entroparty... the littoral truth... the monolithic muleteer.

One of the enduring pleasures of living in Poros is doing absolutely anything at all.

If that seems like a fatuous statement, then go there and try it yourself. It doesn't matter a jot what you do... you might fancy a hair-cut, or a cup of coffee; you might want a light-bulb, some alka-seltzers, or a bottle of gas for your cooker; you might need to take money from the bank, a letter to the post, or an unsatisfactory partner to the ferry. You always end up having fun. Even if you go out to buy flowers for your mum's funeral, you'll probably have a smashing time. The reason for this is the waterfront.

Almost everything you want to buy or need to do in Poros is located on the waterfront, known as the *paralia*. It is a wide street, with nothing but flowerbeds and lampposts on the open quay side. This open aspect ensures that each and every one of the cafes, restaurants, hotels and shops which line the other side of the road enjoy stunning views over the waters of the bay to the surrounding hills. The architecture of the *paralia* is a charming mixture of classical and traditional buildings, quite grand in some places, quaint in others and everywhere picturesque. Immediately behind the first row of buildings the land rises steeply to become the massive chunk of rock upon which the houses of the town are built. There is very limited motor access to the high part of the town, and few people bother to walk up and over when they can walk around on the flat, so all life circulates around the *paralia*.

Whatever you do, you end up passing along this waterfront, which means that you will see everyone and everyone will see you. Even if you have only been there two days, you will be greeted by every waiter and merchant who has served you; and as your acquaintance grows you will be hailed with metronomic regularity. As your familiarity increases you will be stopped at regular intervals for a leisurely greeting, a snippet or twenty of gossip, and then gradually you start to receive invitations… to stop and talk, to take coffee, or to join a party at a kafeneion.

As you become even better known you will be offered sweets or cakes by people celebrating their saint's name-day. People will stop you with news from your home country, or to ask your opinion of news in Greece; you will be advised of apartments for rent, new businesses, impending weather changes. You may be offered things for sale, ranging from fresh fish through hunting puppies to real estate. I have returned from a walk along the front with invitations to barbeques, parties, weddings, christenings, funerals, football matches… and very, very often I have not returned at all. As for sport… show the merest hint of an interest in soccer or basketball, and your progress around the *paralia* probably wouldn't match that of an arthritic snail traversing a glue-spill.

If you are at all sociable, this is a very pleasant atmosphere in which to live. You don't need to plan a day at all… just invent some nebulous reason for leaving your house or boat and venture forth. The chances of you not being diverted… into conversations, cafes, trips to the beach, lunch appointments… simply do not exist.

For holiday purposes, this state of affairs could hardly be improved upon, of course, but if you are living in the town it can make it a little difficult to achieve objectives. Every time you set out with any sort of goal or deadline, you end up hours late, unsure of what you had originally intended, and so full of caffeine that you keep trying to climb the lampposts.

You may, for instance, go out purposefully early in the morning with every intention of getting some money from the bank and buying some screws to fix the wonky shelf above your bed; you return home pleasantly inebriated at about midnight having been inveigled into four cafes, wandered over to

Galatas for an ouzo, gone to the beach, started lunch with four friends at three p.m. and finished it at eight-thirty with eleven, and spent the rest of the evening back in the cafe watching the world go by and setting it to rights. You then roll into bed, muzzily wondering who paid for it all, as you never got within two hundred yards of the bank, and wake up cuddling the shelf which fell on your head in the night. So you get dressed and go out for some screws…

Living in Poros is very pleasant, but as your acquaintance grows… and not only with the locals, for many of the visitors return very regularly… it gets harder and harder to get anything done. People for whom this is a tribulation don't come back; people who enjoy it stay. This, of course, continually purifies the laid-back demographic of the island, the bloodstock being constantly refined and sieved of purposeful elements. Charlie Darwin could have saved himself all those iguanas and got the job done in a fraction of the time it took him to get to the Galapagos if he had only studied the natural selection extant in Poros cafe society… if, that is, he had ever managed to sober up long enough to have a quick think about it!

* * *

From my earliest days in Poros I recognised the siren song of the waterfront, but I never comprehended its true puissance until the Great Inaugural Pig-Roast. It happened like this…

I handed over *Mucky Duck* in Samos on Easter Sunday and booked myself a night-time ferry ticket back to Piraeus. This was a great mistake… Easter is the largest event in the Greek calendar both spiritually and socially, and you need to hunker down somewhere and enjoy it.

I had a general awareness of this, but I didn't think much of it at first; partly because my own attitude to Easter was conditioned by the much more muted British celebrations, and partly because the 'Big Week' before Greek Easter is one of mourning and deep religious observance… bells toll, melancholy scriptures are read through the church loud-speakers and sombre, candle-bearing processions wind silently beneath half-masted flags: Many people keep the Lenten fast, some businesses close altogether, and no music is played… to the uninitiated, it doesn't seem much like the precursor to a fun festival.

As a result of this atmosphere, combined, no doubt, with a sizable portion of self-pity at Clemmie's departure, I made no effort to participate in the feast but spent Easter Sunday morning working on *Mucky Duck*. I handed her over to the clients at midday, and then spent the afternoon wandering around Vathi, the main harbour of Samos, waiting for the ferry and trying not to think of Clemmie, who was still just across the straits in Ephesus and tantalisingly close. I found no restaurants or bars open, as everyone was at private parties, and the air was everywhere scented with roasting lamb, roasting goat, and rosemary. I starved and slavered whilst listening to the merry clink and chatter of ubiquitous celebration.

Quite by chance, in the early evening, I was observed by some revellers and dragged in to a garden for a very pleasant hour. I would happily have stayed longer, but it was already late in the day; the party was succumbing to entropy, the ferry was leaving, and all the brief interlude did was to remind me that Greeks are hospitable and that I was a total pillock for managing to be the only person in the country who had contrived to spend Easter alone. On the empty overnight ferry I dozed in a reclining seat where, plotting to even the score, I determined to host a feast of my own as soon as I got back to Poros. I passed the waking hours of the voyage carefully compiling an eclectic guest list.

In the garden at my room by the clock tower were a large barbeque and a traditional stone oven, of which I had the use on request; and although Poros has any number of idyllic locations for al fresco recreation, I decided to hold my party at the house. It was a delightful setting. The space was just right for a group of perhaps twenty people; a rock-and-earth surface rising unevenly from a slate courtyard which offered numerous convenient places to sit, and was about half-covered by a shady pergola made of brightly painted steel pipe. The pergola, garden railings and the house walls were festooned with climbing plants in spring bloom.* There was also a budding vine over the courtyard; and throughout the garden, wherever there was overhead support, hung dozens of dried gourds painted kaleidoscopic colours in disparate designs. The backdrop to this riot of colour was the view across the straits to Galatas on the one side and along the bay of Poros to the Sleeping Lady on the other. The water of the bay lay almost sapphire under the high afternoon sun,

---

* Don't ask me what they were. I spent my biology lessons doodling sailing-ships, and couldn't tell a primrose from the Great Barrier Reef. If you showed me an oak tree, I'd have a fifty percent chance of guessing which end goes in the ground.

the hills a patchwork of fawn and olive, the sky a milky blue studded with puffs of pristine cloud. This high on the crest of the town a cooling breeze generally blew in the afternoon which, together with the help of the shady pergola, tempered the fierce sunshine of spring afternoons. The scents of flowers and pine came and went as the wind eddied around.

As attractive as the garden was, there was another reason for holding my event there, instead of at a beach or on an island... my landlady's family had been so generous that I strongly felt it was time for me to reciprocate. Barely a day went by when I wasn't offered a coffee or an *ouzo-mezé* in their courtyard, or given a portion of the day's dessert, and the British instinct is to give in return. I had, however, managed to master the urge so far... for I had learned that Greeks do not esteem a kindness being promptly returned.

True Greek hospitality... and there is still plenty of it around... is freely given, without the expectation of repayment, so to reciprocate is to negate their generosity. For a Briton, raised in the tradition of standing his round, it can be uncomfortable to receive without reciprocation; but I soon found that people became rather stiff if I returned kindnesses promptly. Fortunately for me, Petros witnessed an early *faux-pas* on my part and explained it to me.

When Greeks do you a favour, either something asked of them or something which they have taken upon themselves because it will benefit you, it is registered and there is a score-card kept. A reciprocal gesture is expected, and appreciated when performed. But when someone does you a kindness unconnected with benefit... such as buying you a drink, giving you a piece of Mum's delicious *kataïfi** or a pot of this year's olives... then it is meant as a gift from the goodness of their hearts. To return it is impolite, as it gives the impression that the giver expected something in return, which devalues the gesture. One must learn to accept graciously, and this can be an uncomfortable thing for a Northern European, as the generosity can sometimes be quite significant. Very large rounds of drinks may suddenly materialise 'from Kyrios Yiorgios', and on occasion one may even find that one's entire meal bill has been paid by someone who hardly knows you, but who has had a good day and just wants to share his happy condition.

Once I understood this, I compromised between Greek and British custom by accepting any generosity as graciously as I could, then waiting a

---

* Basically a Shredded Wheat soaked in local honey and dusted with almonds... delicious!

decent time before reciprocating liberally, but in as different a manner as possible. It was in line with this policy, mindful of the many small kindnesses I had received from my landlady, that I decided to feast at my apartment. It would provide a charming, comfortable and well-equipped venue at which it would be entirely natural to include Kyria Fotini and her family... it was their garden, after all... and thus I planned to kill two birds with one hangover.

* * *

The day I got back from Samos I began issuing invitations, regardless of the fact that I hadn't yet planned the event; and as I have already described, even when one has organised conscientiously, the Poros waterfront is a formidable adversary. Engaging it unprepared is simply to cast any hope of self-determination into the teeth of a gale. The first spanner it threw in the works was the utter destruction of my carefully compiled invitation list.

From a perfunctory survey of the garden and courtyard I had a vague notion of how many people it could accommodate in comfort. I also considered how many bodies it would be acceptable to invite into what was, after all, someone else's house. To Kyria Fotini I suggested that I might ask twelve people, and her family in addition, which might mean a total of twenty if she happened to be on speaking terms with her siblings on the day in question. She gave this judicious consideration and an eventual grave nod, which I took to mean that this, but not much more, was acceptable. So I selected twelve names from my list, a considered mix of locals and foreigners calculated to provide good conversation, added three or four names as first reserves, and set off into the waterfront to find my victims. This, of course, was somewhat before the advent of mobile telephones, which came surprisingly late in Greece.

Finding them took no time at all; they were, naturally, on the *paralia,* but the problem was, of course, that they weren't all sitting together. They were sitting with other people, and I am not the sort of chap who can walk into a group of five people and invite just two of them to a party. And since they spent most of the day on the waterfront, it wasn't much use trying to catch them alone elsewhere.

First of all, I joined groups where my intended guests were sitting and stayed until people went to the lavatory, when I finished my drink hurriedly and followed them to accost them alone; but people seemed to have bladders like buckets that day, and by the time I had managed to have a *tête-a-tête* with even half of my targets I was hours late, on the outside of about two pints of wine, and probably beginning to acquire a reputation as a stalker with exceedingly indiscriminate tastes.

About half way through the morning I managed to isolate Charlie this way, and as I delivered my invitation just outside the toilet the rather insubstantial door was almost torn from its frame to reveal PeePee, hurriedly re-tensioning her nether garment and squealing delightedly, "Oh! A Partee! Zat vood be *vunderfool*. Vot shoot I pring?" Okay, then, thirteen.

Next I found Monique sitting on her own in the Blue Ouzerie, so I sent an ouzo down to see how the wine was getting on inside me whilst I invited her. She accepted, and so did Willy and Ilsa whom I had not noticed at a nearby table. Well, thirteen is unlucky anyway.

I slogged on to Petros' cafe and there, over a free nip of *tsipouro,*[*] I invited my mentor; then I spotted Joe Burke in a corner... I hadn't realised his boat was back in town, but I couldn't not invite him. He gleefully accepted... and introduced his niece who was sailing with him.

At the Mouragio restaurant I was pressed to try a glass of retsina whilst Dimitris thanked me very effusively for the invitation and said that his mother also loved a party; then I was inveigled into the adjoining Lagoudera with another glass on the house, which could not be refused as I had been seen to accept next door. Passing George's Cafe, I invited Gina and Andrea, two girls who worked in one of the bars. They hadn't been on my initial list, but they looked so gorgeous sitting in the sun that no heterosexual male... not even a sober, respectable one... could possibly have omitted them. In any case I thought I was safe... they were nocturnal animals who generally slept on a beach in the afternoon before working until dawn. I was wrong. The police had closed their bar for a week for making too much noise, so they were not only free but also unemployed and hungry. They were more than happy to accept a free meal, and kindly promised to bring two other girls who had just arrived looking for summer work and would be agreeable to looking attractive in return for a few calories.

---

[*] A sort of local grappa, made from the lees of the wine pressings.

The reader will, by this point, have got the picture. By the time the sun crossed the meridian, I had firmly invited about twenty-five people, suspected I had been overheard by many more, and my breakfast was dissolving gaseously in about a gallon of exceedingly miscellaneous intoxicants.

Then I weaved off looking for a butcher.

Up to this point, I hadn't really made friends with a butcher in Poros. Eating out in Greece was so ridiculously inexpensive that there was no temptation for a bachelor of even modest means to cook. I didn't want to be alone, to do washing up, or to carry a load of stuff up a steep hill, so my fridge contained only some cheese, olives and salami in case I got the midnight munchies… I don't believe I even knew how the cooker at the house worked. Even on boats I only cooked if there wasn't a taverna in sight when my belly started looking for a union official. I didn't really know where to buy anything, apart from cheese pies, ice and cold drinks. I was choosing my butcher entirely blind… never a smart thing to do.

The meat market in Poros is a sort of arcade between the waterfront and a narrow alleyway behind, and in this alley was a very fine restaurant called Pandelis. Several nautical ne'er-do-wells were taking an early glass of *tsipouro* and I was inveigled to join them and add a tincture or two of this fire-water to my as yet lunchless tripes.

I eventually swayed into the meat market as they began to close up for *mesimeri*… the afternoon break, or *siesta*. One of the singular and enchanting features of this market is the rather ingenious use of a ceiling-fan to keep flies off the meat… a sloped display table is sited below the fan, to the blades of which are attached frayed rope's ends which almost reach the produce below. The fan runs at low speed, whisking the frayed ends just above the meat and effectively deterring the flies. In that simplicity of mind which tends to accompany a whole morning of drinking mixed wines and spirits, I swayed and communed with the fly whisk for a quiet, contemplative moment or two; and then I went completely mad.

In the glass refrigerated case was a pig's head, regarding me critically through half closed eyes, and it gave my befuddled thinking-muscle an idea. I had always wanted to spit-roast a pig, and it occurred to me that Kyria Fotini's barbeque was equipped with a business-like looking *souvla*, or spit; so, on the spur of the moment, I decided to give it a go… without, of course, the least idea how to go about the business, nor a moment's consideration of how silly I would look if I got it wrong in front of a crowd of people. Without any consideration of how this was to be achieved, I engaged with the butcher and stated my intention. And, on an island as gregarious as Poros, every action is a public one and there's no honourable way of going back from that point.

My butcher listened gravely to my expectations of twenty-five people, and advised that I needed a piglet of about twelve kilos. I had just enough wit still about me to check how long that would take to cook... three to four hours, I was told... and I put in my order. The pig would be ready for collection the next morning from seven thirty onwards.

Collecting the impoverished and hungry Gina and Andrea for company, I made a half-hearted effort to sober myself up with a steak lunch away from the infernal waterfront; but the owner of the butcher's taverna up in the town was grateful for a recent party of tourists I had sent his way and insisted on giving me a free kilo of retsina, so that didn't work. It did, though, help me persuade the girls to take care of preparing the salads for the following day.

Whilst waiting for the shops to re-open I tried a couple of strong coffees in a cafe, but if I did in fact sober up at last, it wasn't the caffeine that did the trick; it was the sudden realisation that half the waterfront was by now aware that I was roasting a pig in my garden the next day. An astounding number of people managed to find themselves in front of me, some openly hopeful, some (predominantly those I had met earlier in the day and not invited) mildly reproachful. By the time I had engaged Apostolis from the Kava* to deliver wine and beer, asked Petros to send up some ice, and bought a bin-bag full of paper plates and plastic cutlery, I was vaguely aware that I had weakly admitted another imprecise number of people to the guest list.

* * *

The day of Piggy's passion dawned bright and clear, and I legged it down to the butchers in optimistic mood, a spring in my heels and rosy with anticipation. True it was, I had a nagging concern about what Kyria Fotini

---

* The wine-store, a cavernous, dark hole in the south side of the waterfront whose ramshackle shelves supported enough intoxicants to tranquilise Luxembourg.

would say when a battalion of hunger pig-chompers swarmed into her garden, but there was no longer anything I could do about that; so apart from hoping mildly for an outbreak of a debilitating pork allergy, I ignored it. The butcher had been true to his word, and there was Piggy, in all his glory in the glass case. As I took delivery a moustachioed, bespectacled Groucho Marx look-alike, whom I recognised as the chef from one of the beach tavernas, was attempting to conceal a half-dismantled scooter under a heap of pork chops.

"About three to four hours to cook, you say?" I asked the butcher; but with the deal done and the cash in his pocket, his answer had none of the assurance of the previous day. He shrugged, then waved his hand at Groucho and said, "Kyrie Manolis cook pig. Many pig he cook. You ask him."

I raised my eyebrows towards the bristling moustache, which switched rapidly left and right a time or two. Then he fixed me with intense black eyes, and lifted one finger of his left hand and two fingers of his right.

"Two kilos, 1 hour," he said, "No less. Two kilos, one hour"

"Eh?"

As the implications of this hit me, Groucho marched round to the back of the cabinet, opened it, and hefted the piglet.

"*Dhódheka kilá*! Twelve!" he announced. "Six, seven hour."

"Seven hours!!!" I cried in anguish… I had invited everyone for drinks at midday and food at about two o'clock. I didn't even have the fire hot yet.

"Not less!" admonished the moustache. "Maybe more, not less. Anybody he say something another, no you listen nothing. Two kilos, 1 hour. *Káli órexi!*"

He straddled the only remaining visible part of his scooter and, trailing several dogs and a music-hall raspberry, he wobbled off along the waterfront. I screamed for Shergar, and moments later we were legging it up the hill to my house, piggy slung between us, looking like Burke and Hare doing a quickie.

Putting out fires in Greece is often exceedingly difficult, but starting them rarely presents a problem. A handful of last year's dry vine-twigs, a match and we were away. Any Greek garden will yield some kindling… there is always a bit of collapsed pergola, an old window-shutter, a failed attempt at a plate rack, or a moribund chair somewhere. The flames were soon thrusting keenly up through the charcoal, and Shergar and I set about spitting our pig. Simplest thing in the world, you would think. Big spike, insert in bottom, vigorous thrust, job done. Not so. It is a grim business, involving repeated efforts, indignities that Egyptian mummy embalmers would have quailed at, and, in extremis, resort to the non-too-delicate application of a hefty hammer. By the time the guest of honour was installed another forty-five precious minutes had fled into the cerulean sky.

It was by now almost ten o'clock, and a disaster confronted us. The garden was not prepared, the fire still not hot enough for cooking, we had as yet no ice, no salads, no cutlery or crockery, and no help. You can't face debacles of this magnitude sober, so we popped the first beer-cans, toasted ineptitude, and cracked up laughing.

Gina and Andrea arrived at about eleven to find Shergar and I, already in a very rosy frame of mind, poking and peering experimentally at the pig. We had it low down over the coals with some vague notion of making the skin crisp before cooking the meat at a higher level.* Being men, of course, we wouldn't have read how to do the job before attempting it, even if we had known where to find the instructions; and the girls were unable to help, as it appeared that they had been playing truant the day their domestic science class addressed the dos and don'ts of ramming an eight-foot spike up a pigs bum and bunging it on a bonfire. Nonetheless, appropriate things seemed to be happening... the first, fleeting savoury wafts began to taint the air, and the skin was starting to whiten and blister in a way that brought crackling to mind. Our innate optimism, assisted by some liquid accelerant, allowed us to believe that we had the job nicely under control. We adopted a policy of turning Piggy about sixty degrees every five minutes or so, and started arranging tables and chairs.

Apostolis arrived with the drinks, and we were trying to get them all into the kitchen fridge, when Joe Burke's brogue outside bellowed "Mary, Mother of Jesus! What're ye doing to that poor pig?"

I trotted outside to find a roaring inferno entirely engulfing our lunch. Shergar and I galloped up to the flames, seized an end of the spit each, plucked the beast out, then dropped it as the metal seared our hands. As we plunged our own roasted flesh into the yard-bucket, Gina and Joe gallantly put out the fires on the pig's skin with a towel. Then we all stood looking at the

---

* About the only thing Shergar and I ever did at a higher level.

smouldering, blackened remains whilst the barbeque, which so recently had been a respectable, well-behaved bed of hot, grey coals, raged like a rocket-engine.

We soon worked out what the problem was. The skin of the pig had been starting to weep some fat, which made the fire smoke and flare a little, although not enough to be a problem; but just before we had gone inside, we had turned the spit belly-down... anxious to appear as if I knew what I was doing, I recalled having made some completely fabricated but plausible remark about 'getting some heat into his hams'... and obviously the fats which had been created inside his belly cavity, captive when he was on his back, had run into the fire with a rush when he was turned; and there they had ignited.

A plan 'B' was obviously required. Experimenting feverishly, we sprinkled water on the fire just sufficiently to quench the flames and then raked the coals to each side of the barbeque, leaving a bare space immediately below the spit. The girls washed the worst of the soot off Piggy, as nonchalantly as if self-immolating porkers were ten-a-penny in their native Lancashire.* Then we put the sorry-looking pig back on his pyre, and stationed a fire-watchman with a water-bottle.

It was plain by now that we didn't have a hope in hell of serving lunch much before dinner time, so I sent Shergar down to town to buy some sausages to keep people going. We also didn't have enough room in the fridge for all the drinks, so Gina was sent to her bar to try to borrow an ice-box. Also, the girl's efforts at a salad... potato salad in one bowl, coleslaw in another... were quite charmingly presented, but probably only enough for a dozen people at most, so Andrea was despatched with Joe's niece Morna to buy veggies to make a big *horiatiki* salad. Joe and I remained to battle the flames, which still periodically flared when fat pooled under the spit and threatened to turn a culinary event into an *auto-da-fe*.

By one o'clock, despite the constant battle with the flames, the guest of honour was starting to brown nicely and a very appetizing smell was eddying around the garden. A second, small, portable barbeque had been started and sausages were beginning to sizzle.

---

* Possibly they are... the Pendle Witches come to mind, and a culture which can venerate black pudding and clog-dancing is surely capable of anything.

Cold beer and wine was now in abundance. Unable to find her boss, Gina had used her initiative and bought a plastic dustbin... plastic-ware in Greece was ludicrously cheap... and the bottom half was now our ice-box. We filled it with ice which Petros had sent up with the garbage mules, mules which were now contentedly consuming the neighbour's window-boxes and turning the street outside into a midden whilst the muleteer seated himself by the barbeque. Helping himself to a glass of ouzo, he contentedly set about telling us what we were doing wrong, and looked about as likely to move as the Western Front in 1917.

The lid of the dustbin also came in handy... propped upside-down on three bricks, it became a man-sized salad-bowl, full of the traditional *horiatiki* salad... olives, sweet little reddish onions, tomatoes, cucumbers and feta, all drenched with olive oil and vinegar. Kyria Fotini now made an appearance and inspected the salad critically. She sniffed in a non-committal manner and brought some capers to add to the mix, which instantly turned a competent salad into a speciality.

We were ready. The beer was cold, the first tranche of sausages were hot. The salad glistened, packets of picnic utensils gaped, and the gentle strains of *Dhirlada* and *Frangosyriani* oozed out of my old cassette-player. Over the rebellious fire the pig glistened, spat and steamed. Charlie arrived, florid from his climb, but no-one else apart from him. My wishes for a pork allergy appeared to have been granted; people stayed away in their thousands.

So, there we sat: Joe and Morna, Charlie, Shergar, Gina, Andrea, the garbage muleteer and I, making small talk and contemplating having to eat a twelve kilo pig and a dustbin lid-full of salad. As one o'clock faded and two o'clock loomed, I grimly distracted my thoughts by addressing myself to the problem of the flaring of the fire, and came up with a solution... I borrowed two narrow baking-tins from Kyria Fotini, and placed them below the spit. Now all the fat was collected in the tins, preventing the fire from flaring, and we could also use it to baste the beast. I was quickly finding out that the skin wasn't as crisp as I had expected, but it looked pretty scrumptious all the same. Not that anyone would ever know, I thought in a resigned way.

The muleteer watched my efforts with mild approval, and seemed to be turning over a matter of some weight in his mind. Eventually, he approached the spit and gestured to me to take the pig off the fire. He used a large clasp-knife to quarter some lemons and oranges, which he plucked without so much as a by-your-leave from trees in the neighbouring gardens, and then did the same with three onions left over from the salad. All of these he ladled into the stomach cavity of the pig. Then he twisted a piece of rusty wire out of the fencing, used it to deftly close up the belly, and gestured for us to put it back over the fire.

I instantly understood that this was a wonderful tip... the fruit, of course, would steam as the heat increased and the juices would be infused into the meat. The muleteer nodded gravely at my thanks, refilled his glass, and returned to his seat. It was quite evident that his secretary had cancelled his appointments for the rest of the afternoon.

Charlie too settled in very readily. He quenched the inner fires ignited by labouring up the hill with a couple of rapid-fire beers, and then settled down with a mug full of wine to tell us a story. I was ready enough to listen to anything at all, to distract me from the apparent snub which my absent guests were delivering, but as it happened it was a wonderful tale and remains one of my favourites.

* * *

Charlie sailed an old Westerly centre-cockpit boat called *Aquafrolic* and was a rotund, jolly, mischievous chap with twinkling blue eyes, a bald patch like a monk's tonsure, and a carbuncular nose that looked like one of those animal shapes made out of twisted balloons. I knew that he was retired, that he was a widower, and that he lived year-round on his boat, roaming the Eastern Mediterranean from Cyprus to Italy. Other than that, I really only knew that he was immensely likeable and a walking databank of entertaining stories which he told in a lazy, liquid, warming Devonshire burr.

I had always had a feeling that Charlie was an ex-serviceman... he had never said as much, but he had a Royal British Legion sticker on his boat, and on the rare occasions when I saw him actually doing something he was decisive and authoritative in a way which had 'N.C.O.' stamped all over it. It now turned out that I had been right, for he confided that, during World War Two, he had served in a tank regiment in the desert campaign. By the time of the D-Day invasion, Charlie had been a sergeant in charge of a Sherman tank.

Charlie's squadron, it appeared, had been selected to land in the very first wave of landings on D-Day. Their unenviable task was to follow mine-clearing tanks across the beach, flatten the wire for the infantry, and then get off the beach and attack the defenders from behind: But, as Charlie graphically described, no-one had the least expectation of getting as far as the road. They all expected to be knocked out on the beach, and the cynical opinion of the crews was that the planners knew that perfectly well, and really intended to use the disabled tanks as shelter for the foot soldiers.

"Soo, y'see," Charlie said, "…We never bo-othered much with reme-emberin' all the stuff we wuz surppozed to do *after* we got off that ole' beach. It worn't gon' t'appen. We just pra-acticed gettin' out o' that ole' tank as quick as possible, an' troid to thi-ink about other thi-ings."

One of the other things they thought about was driving through a house.

Apparently, all of the crews had rather a thing about driving through houses. It looked very good on the films, but in the desert they hadn't had the chance… houses tended to be scarce. Also, their tanks were earlier models, too light and underpowered. They might have got stuck, and, as Charlie somewhat superfluously pointed out, getting stuck half way out of a house with a ton of masonry on top of your gun in the middle of a battle was not a situation people relished being in. He added that a few of the lads had found a tent to flatten, but it wasn't the same.

In training for D-Day back in England, of course, driving through houses was frowned upon. A few of the more adventurous souls had flattened a hen-coop or an old sheep-pen, but the deep and enduring satisfaction of going right through Number Seven, Magnolia Gardens, emerging in a shower of bricks from the other side with curtains across the turret and Granny in her bath on the engine-cover, eluded them. No such restrictions were expected to apply in France, however, and the Sherman, a very much heavier and more powerful tank than their desert equipment, was clearly just what a chap needed for indulging in the ultimate gate-crashing. To divert their minds from what was likely to happen to them on the beaches, the crews talked long and hard about how to drive through a house, what would happen when they did, and took bets on who would be the first to do it.

Along came the great day and, to his utter amazement, Charlie's tank churned across a Normandy beach with no worse harm than a few annoyingly loud noises as things bounced off the outside. In tip-top form the tank crested the dune, skidded sideways from behind a mine-clearing tank and roared away up a tarmac road. Then, just as Charlie was desperately trying to find out where he was and recall where he was supposed to go, he found slap in front of his snarling steel steed a smallish house with a machine-gun blazing out of a window.

"Oi'm ha-avin' that!" roared Charlie and, slamming his hatch closed over his head, he directed his driver to drive straight through the building.

He described how the garden wall went down, the frantic patter of bullets on the outside of the tank, the exhilaration and adrenaline rush as the house came closer and closer until the roof could no longer be seen through the narrow viewing slits. As they crossed the garden, Charlie fired the main gun into the building and swung the turret backwards, to protect the barrel; then, at full throttle, they crashed into the brick wall.

Charlie paused at this point in his story, looked thoughtful for a minute, and took a deep, reflective draught of his wine. Then he looked directly at me.

"'Ave you ever driven though a 'ouse in a ta-ank?" He enquired brightly.

"Not recently," I admitted.

"We-ell, son, whe-en you do," he said, and shook his head with a look of weary martyrdom, "When you do, try an' pick one without a bloody cellar!"

* * *

The clock tower struck four and the clock itself said six-thirty, by which I knew that it was a quarter to three,* and at that instant, a chattering started and gradually grew louder. Moments later, it seemed to me, half the village arrived.

Expanding from the chicane of the gateway like the opening of a peacock's tail, they filled the garden with noise and colour in what seemed like a matter of seconds. From a solemn gathering of self-conscious people spreading themselves expansively in an attempt to make the garden look busy, the party was abruptly transformed into a roil of jostling, bubbling humanity questing for a place to sit or even stand. I greeted as many as I could, all the

---

* They had a lot of trouble with that clock. Periodically it could tell five different times at once.

time religiously avoiding the incredulous eyes of Kyria Fotini which I could feel lasering the crowd from the relative safety of an upstairs window.

It was amusing to watch how the crowd sorted themselves out. The Greek women took no prisoners, single-mindedly appropriating all the chairs and moving them into the shadiest areas of the garden. That done, they assured themselves of a supply of drinking water, subjected the salads to a judicious inspection, and resumed their avid daily examination of village affairs. The Greek men congregated around the fire, lit cigarettes, and proceeded to offer advice and criticism of my cooking.

The Europeans* made a fairly orderly circuit, formally greeting people with whom they must have just walked up the hill, and all of them took the earliest possible opportunity to make the acquaintance of Piggy, intrigued no doubt to find out what atrocities the much maligned English cuisine was in the process of committing. It seemed that, on balance, they *just* approved. Men pursed their lips and nodded sagely, women shrugged and tilted their heads in vague acknowledgement. Then they made for the bar, and of course found the Brits and Paddies already in residence.

I never at any time found out how many people were there, but I doubt if even the excessive number I had invited accounted for more than a third of them. Piggy wasn't looking quite so plentiful now, with this herd of amiable carnivores drooling over his obsequies, and when I saw the speed at which the sausages were vanishing I sent the girls back down the hill for some more grub. Even the dustbin lid was starting to show through the salad at an alarming rate.

The retsina was going down very well, too. I had early on found that the retsina from the adjacent island of Aegina was a wonderful, heavy, oily wine of gravity with a smooth, resin tang. Many retsinas, especially the bottled ones, were rather too tart, but the Aegina farmers had the true secret. They didn't grow the grapes, but they imported the must and completed it themselves, and the farmer's market on the Aegina waterfront was where they sold it. Charlie had been happy to bring down a few '*gallonia*' for the party, and I was relieved to note that the locals obviously approved.

---

*   By which I mean the French, Italians, Germans, Scandinavians, etc. No matter how pro-European they may be, the British and the Greeks are united in subconsciously considering 'Europe' to be somewhere else.

I circulated for a while, and to begin with I beat my breast and said my mea-culpa's for the lateness of the feast; but the answer I received was always the same... an unconcerned shrug, and 'Oh, everyone in the cafe knew you were a bit late. That's why we didn't come earlier.'

The roast was starting to concern me. By the time the crowd arrived, the pig had been cooking for over four hours; the animal had shrunk somewhat and was loosening up on the *souvla*. A succession of men were turning the handle slowly but constantly now, and with each rotation the backbone was starting to come away from the spit and then fall back again. It didn't take an expert to see that this could end in disaster, for if the back broke the best of the pig might fall into the fire. Almost every one of the Greek men present sought a private interview with me, at which they kindly drew my attention to this. As five hours passed and six approached, and as the bar stocks declined, advice turned to warnings; then to pleas.

"Time to take it off!" they advised, and "It's ready now"... "You'll dry it out"... "It'll fall to pieces!"

As steadfastly as I could, I ignored them. In my heart I thought the meat was done too, but the persuasive mantra of Kyrios Manolis had me in thrall: "Anybody he say something another, no you listen nothing. Two kilos, 1 hour. No less. Maybe more."

In my time, I have conned some of the world's largest ships in some of its busiest and narrowest waterways. I have been shot at a time or two. I have tackled fires at sea, and had occasion to tell a Prime Minister to sit down and shut up. I have, to cap it all, thrice faced those immutable, dispassionate, disdainful dispensers of judgement, the Department of Transport Examiners of Masters and Mates. The degree of tension I experienced on any of those occasions was as nothing compared to the anxiety I now felt, isolated in opinion from everyone else at the party still sober enough to make an informed judgement, and quite a few others besides. The opportunity to look exceedingly silly here gaped like a shark at a shipwreck.

For the last hour of cooking, the tension knotted my guts in the manner of a model aeroplane's rubber band and my heart leapt into my mouth every time the backbone of the pig moved. Fissures opened in the skin, and anyone could see how tender and loose the meat was becoming. I took over turning the spit myself, in an attempt to be sure that it was turned as gently as possible, but this was a terrible mistake, for every time the pig moved on the spit I could now physically feel it, and each gentle jolt wound my inner spring a notch tighter.

As I refused steadfastly to do anything, the pleas to take the pig off became demands, and then to something close to anger. Hands were raised to the heavens, Greek pejoratives took to the air like a rookery disturbed by a gunshot, eyes rolled. And then, as we passed the sixth hour, the mood changed entirely. Everyone gave up, and sank back in defeat. It was reminiscent of that moment in the submarine films when the boat passes crush depth, and the crew stop turning valves, fall silent, and accept their fate.

"I told him!" ran the litany now.

"It's ruined!"

"*Ti na kaanoume?*… what can we do?"

"Foreigners! They don't know."

"Well, I told him!"

"You did! I heard you! I told him too. *Yiannis* told him!"

"Ah, well, at least the sausages were good."

Hopelessly they refilled their glasses and lit cigarettes, glanced sadly back at the spit from time to time and generally assumed the air of mourners outside a church waiting for a funeral to begin.

Seven hours. By this time, Piggy was almost bent double and lolloping around on his spit in the manner of a burst tyre on a speeding lorry. Turning him on his back, I used a long, thin knife to probe into the ham. Every fibre in my being yearned for the juice to be clear, but there was still a trace of red. Stoically, I returned to cooking. Equally stoically, the audience extinguished any final embers of hope in their breasts and forced themselves to speak gaily of other things.

Seven and a half hours. The juice was clear. With extreme caution, Joe and I lifted the spit from the fire and placed it on the table. Holding my breath, I carefully carved a piece of shoulder, and sudden hope kindled in me. My heart began to glow as I felt how easily the knife went through the meat, saw the juice bubbling up below the surface.

I made a bit of a ceremony about presenting the first cut to Kyria Fotini, who certainly deserved no less recognition for putting up with the annexation of her garden by a barbarian horde. The party fell silent as she speared an unctuous gobbet with her fork. She closed her eyes as she popped it into her mouth. A moment later they sprang open again, and a look of wonder passed across her face.

"*Loukoumi!*" she cried, "*Loukoumi iné!*"

Was that good or bad?

Good, it seemed... the Greek women present surged forward, brandishing paper plates, and as fast as I put meat on the serving-plate it vanished. When a piece of skin hit the porcelain, it was frequently pinned immobile for an instant by two or three forks, and then rent asunder. By the time I had stripped and served all the easy meat, a good few people were already ambling innocently back to the table casting sidelong, hopeful and enquiring looks at the carcass. They cast in vain. Piggy was sped.

Loukoumi, it turns out, is the word for Turkish Delight,[*] and is a term used to describe something soft, sweet and juicy; I could hardly have wished a finer accolade. My heart soared to see the fruit of my labours so keenly devoured, but my back felt as if it had been broken with a sledge-hammer... I supposed this to have been the result of a day on my feet, combined with the posture I had used whilst carving, but muscular tension caused by stress was probably also a significant factor. I shamelessly stole Gina's chair as she went for another drink, and compounded this un-gentlemanly behaviour by instructing her to get me one too. Then I sat with a pint mug of icy retsina in my paw, tension draining out of my feet. I felt like the amateur who has just landed the airliner after both of the pilots had the Chicken Tartare for dinner.

As I sat there limply, people congratulated me on the way Piggy had turned out. Several of the Greeks said, "*Poli orea!* Ver' nice, Tzoulian!"

I got a little of my energy back and expostulated keenly, "*Sas ipa!* I told you... two kilos, one hour; maybe more, not less. And if I had listened to you, we would have taken it off two hours ago, and it would have been raw!"

Entirely unabashed, they looked at each other in an enquiring manner for a moment, several of them shrugging and others tossing their heads and making the little tutting noise as Greeks do in negation. Petros roared with laughter.

"Nobody here ever cooked a pig before!" he crowed.

---

[*] Sorry- what am I thinking of? Greek Delight, of course.

But then, when did a little thing like complete ignorance ever stop a Greek from giving advice?

* * *

The sun was declining, the temperature was dropping, and the pig was a memory. The remains, picked so clean that they looked as pristine as a skeleton in a medical school, had finally been tossed over the wall to a couple of street-dogs. The muleteer and Petro had appropriated the head and skilfully stripped that before questing after the brains with the assistance of a log-axe. I had eaten very little pork for myself, contriving to secure only a piece of leg by way of tasting whilst carving. There hadn't even been an un-gnawed bone to regale myself on after my labours at the carving-table… that would annoy me on the morrow, but for now I was basking with contentment at the success of the day.

A few people had drifted away to sleep it off, but many remained, and some more people even arrived. Two of them were policemen, who came to investigate reports of a disturbance during *mesimeri,* or siesta time; however, they had evidently completed their own afternoon nap before investigating. Arriving, therefore, after the end of the official siesta, they naturally found no crime in progress, so there was no legal or moral reason they could not stay for a drink.

Similarly, three firemen wandered in claiming that some concerned citizen had reported smoke. Since I recognised one of them as the owner of a house just down the lane, it didn't take much of an intellect to work out who the concerned citizen had been.

Another late arrival was Big Savvas, a colleague of our eternal and stalwart muleteer; tall, rangy, dark and moustachioed, he was possibly the most Greek-looking Greek I ever saw; and he was one of the best Greek dancers too.

Morna and Ilse were in the lane feeding the remains of the salad to the donkeys whilst their inexhaustible owner continued disposing of wine by the embers of the fire. Every now and then one of the Greeks… generally Big Savvas… would start dancing, and we would all clap in time. Chatter filled the evening. The police and fire service vied for the attention of the girls. I sat, so relaxed in my chair that I moulded myself to it like a chocolate on a radiator, and chatted quietly with Joe and Charlie. Sunset turned the west to cerise, then to ice-flecked indigo.

The ebb-tide started when the policemen took their leave. Their example was catching, and the party began to die. The garden emptied quite rapidly, people calling out to each other to pass their adieus or making new assignations to reconvene in the waterfront cafes. They swirled around the garden gate before disappearing, rather like the last of the bath-water gurgling down the plug-hole, and as they ebbed the magnitude of the morrow's clean-up hit solidly home.

Almost the last to leave were Joe, Morna and Charlie, who made their farewells, collided in the gateway, and then linked their arms for support. They weaved down the lane, kept upright by judicious contact with the walls, singing an Irish goodnight song.

Kyria Fotini and her husband went tipsily to bed, climbing unsteadily but uncomplainingly over the slumbering Shergar on their steps, with no evident ill-will at the carnage I had wrought in their garden. I headed for my bed, only to find that it had been appropriated by Gina and Andrea. I fashioned a makeshift couch from a blanket, a repaired sail and some waterproofs in the lower part of the room and lay down on that.

In the moment or two before slumber overran my senses, it dawned upon me that this hadn't been my party at all… I had been merely the hapless mouse running on the laboratory treadmill; the commanding force, from start to finish, had been the whimsical Poros waterfront. Like some Olympian God meddling in the affairs of man to pass an idle hour, it had completely ignored my own intentions and wishes to create a party entirely to its own satisfaction. It had dictated the guest list, the menu, and the schedule. By constantly informing the guests of my progress… or lack of it… it had prevented people arriving early. When I needed extra supplies, it had provided them. When I needed people, it had made it easy to find it. When it was time for people to leave, it lured them away again. All I had to do was add money. Indeed, when I reflected on the deft and thoughtful manner in which the waterfront had managed things, I concluded that I could hardly have done better myself.

Smiling at that last thought, I made myself as comfortable as possible on the impromptu bed and closed my eyes. The last thing I heard was the cough of a donkey, the clink of a bottle on a glass, and the gentle crooning of the muleteer as he watched the last of the embers.

CHAPTER SEVEN

PRE-DATE-ORY BEHAVIOUR

Love is almost all around... how to make a miss-ogynist... captain's mates... a dramatic performance... homosapphians... why a sailor must know his flags... the gentleman's guide to crossing the Aegean... involuntary espionage... subornation... the beauty of Kamares... a souvlaki seller's dream... all the nice girls love a sailor... a profound farewell

The lack of a partner had not greatly concerned me earlier in the year, when prospective amours were few and far between and the end-of-Winter feeling had lingered; but as we progressed into May I not only hankered for the solace of female company but also began to feel that my continuing state of celibacy did not reflect to my credit.

Every house acquired a floral wreath on May-day, and with this tangible symbol of spring Greece finally conceded the passing of winter. The sun flew higher and brighter every day, the hotels came to life, the beaches opened. Waiters laid down their paint-brushes and took up their trays, ferries began to swarm and music drifted on the air. The locals, who had finally discarded their winter anoraks but remained well covered-up in heavier clothes, began to cede predominance in the *kafeneions* to more scantily-clad tourists.

The water, still far too chilly to tempt a Greek, was already warm enough for the increasing numbers of Northern Europeans who began to shriek delightedly as they frolicked in the astringent, glass-bright shallows. The skies were intensely blue, the flowers rioted on every hand, the bees began to buzz, and there was a lot of smooth young skin on display. Greece in the sunshine simply oozed sexual promise... but all I got was an IOU.

This wasn't entirely my fault. I was doing mostly delivery sailing at the time, which meant that I did not stay in one place very long, and also I often sailed on my own. I was not inhabiting a target-rich environment. However, the fact must also be faced that I was pretty damn feckless when it came to interacting with girls. I blame the circumstances of my childhood for this.

Dad was a classical music aficionado and, at an early and impressionable age, he cunningly took me to a performance of the 1812 Overture which featured the cannon of the Royal Horse Artillery. I would, of course, have roared like Caliban if forced to sit through even five minutes of orchestral music for its own sake, but to see real cannons fired I would have endured The Ring Saga in its entirety. I waited impatiently whilst they got the silly, boring music out of the way before exulting in the smoke and noise of the guns at the finale, and enjoyed it so much that I begged to be bought the recording of the performance. By the end of the week, Dad wished he had never thought of the idea because I was incessantly humming 'Pada-pom-pom-paam-paam-paam-paam-PAAAAAMMM-pa-paam' and crashing saucepan lids together.

Thus a classical monster was begotten, and ever after I found myself unable to derive much satisfaction from popular music. Nothing short of half-an-hour of music registered, and I inhabited a world where Status Quo was a snobbish Roman, and Meatloaf was a school dinner.

Shortly after this my school compounded the musical misdirection I had suffered by organising an outing to Stratford-upon-Avon, there to see a wonderful performance of Julius Caesar. This left me muttering 'It must be by his death!' when my peers were quoting Monty Python's Parrot Sketch. Then my strangely selective memory took a hand by auto-focussing on poetry... or perhaps I should say doggerel. Almost unconsciously, and for no good reason that I can determine, I started to learn great and pointless epics such as *Tam O'Shanter*, *The Ballad of East and West* and *The Man From Snowy River*. Protracted recitations of these occasionally afflict my associates to this very day.

What little room my thinking-muscle had left was very largely sequestered by the two most unconventional and charismatic teachers I encountered at my various schools; the unforgettably-named Mr R. I. Phillips (RIP), who taught history as if he had been at Agincourt himself, and only yesterday morning at that, and an intellectual English master called John Fielding who lurked behind a facade of bewilderment and failing faculties, from which ambush he lambasted the pompous and de-mystified literature. There wasn't much room left in my attic for more contemporary matters.

The final spectacular cock-up occurred when Dad changed his job and we moved to a Lakeland village where the local secondary school was boys-only. That revered and draughty old slaughterhouse drew half of its pupils ready-muscled from the surrounding hill-farms, and the other half seemed to be the sons of army P.T. instructors. I was so physically inferior to these feral manimals that I could not make the grade in any team sports, and I ended up a solitary protagonist in the esoteric fields of sailing and clay-pigeon shooting.

Needless to say, sex education at such an establishment consisted of advice to take cold showers and reading the swiftly-removed and often contradictory information available in the toilet cubicles. The only thing I thought I knew about sex was that it was as tiring as a ten-mile run, which wasn't much of an encouragement for an indifferent athlete like me.

The result of these events was to send me through childhood and puberty isolated from popular culture, sporting in solitary splendour, musing on Richard III, quoting Shakespeare, whistling The Pastoral Symphony, and singing Schiller's Ode to Joy in German. As for girls… they were like reptiles, in that I had seen them, in carefully controlled conditions, and I understood that they occurred naturally, were necessary, and that some were quite beautiful; but I had little idea how to approach one in safety. They were mysterious creatures whose language I could not speak, and I was so deeply ignorant of their physiology that my sole awareness was a vague impression that, once a month, they had to go to places called 'sanitary towers'.

It was in this condition of painful ignorance and ineptitude that I went to sea, thus entering a chauvinistic male world where every day of the week was lived like Saturday evening at the rugby club. The Blatchley who landed in Greece in 1985 was worthy of at least an honourable mention at any barbarian ravishing competition, but when it came to seduction a sloth probably had more chance of getting laid in the ostrich enclosure than I had on a Greek beach.

I have earlier remarked on the innately competitive nature of the waterfront world, and this put me under some pressure to nurture my *paralia* 'persona', which was an image created out of perceptions of my proficiency in two distinct disciplines; my sailing ability, and my social performance. As far as sailing went I was hitting all targets, maintaining boats, doing a lot of miles, sailing in some hard weather at times, and generally being Captain Courageous. Socially, however, my CV was incomplete. Compulsively gregarious, I kept myself noisily in evidence but my lack of a consort was eventually going to be remarked upon.

Most of the other skippers and boatie-people I knew seemed to have extremely active social calendars. One friend of mine, a South American gentleman, was so busy in this respect that by early June he had to move house because Alimos Marina had become untenable. Another young Adonis of the Aegean, over whose identity I think a complete veil must be drawn, was once placed in a desperate predicament when he entered a harbour with a female companion only to find, waving from the quay, another lady who had arrived earlier than expected. Taking immediate action, he apologetically dumped the incumbent into the middle of the harbour and motored away to collect the new arrival. I can absolutely vouch for the truth of this, because I was fifty metres behind him and had the thankless task of picking the discarded lady up... it was like trying to rescue a beehive.

So, that was the situation. Everyone else was happily splashing around in the gene-pool, and I was sitting on the side with a verruca. For my reputation as much as my self-gratification, therefore, action was required.

* * *

On the face of it, I could not have been in a better place for romance. The northward advance of the sun brought beauty and nubility to Greece in swarms, and female tourists outnumbered males by about three to one. One would have thought that any man alive and possessed of teeth and hair would have been plucked off the stem like grain before locusts; but my grasshopper lifestyle, my disdain for disco tunes, my club-footed dancing, and my alienation from anything resembling current fashion apparently made me an Untouchable. The lovely creatures swept in herds across the landscape, but when they reached me they parted smoothly and flowed past without so much as a caress. It seemed that I was esteemed as a companion, but unconsidered as a swain. I do not say that there were no young ladies who can love a chap of earthy pleasures and pseudo-classical pretensions; I merely assert that they did not take holidays in Greece that spring, and as I continued to prowl the Aegean littoral on the lookout for a compatible mate I felt increasingly like the last dodo.

There was, of course, one cast-iron prospect: PeePee, who had been unable to close the deal with her Canadian prospect, still lurked around every corner, but her intentions remained possessive and procreational. What I had in mind was a series of romantic dalliances with willowy nymphs, not perpetuity with a maternal pile-driver. Whenever I saw her alone, I climbed trees to keep out of her way. However, with this single exception, I was now ready to consider almost any application, even, as Billy the Bard so eloquently had it, 'Be she as foul as was Florentius' love... with as many diseases as two-and-fifty horses'. (There. You see the problem?)

One evening I was at George's Cafe in Poros when a skipper I knew asked me to join him with a group of ladies. Frankly, I didn't much like the chap but I was prepared to prostitute myself for the sake of an introduction... the ladies he had acquired were just a trifle elephants, and I was hopeful that one of them might not be averse to another one. I shelved my objections to Chris the Charismatically Challenged and slithered on over.

It quickly became obvious that Chris was taking advantage of his wife's absence to indulge a whim for adultery; and it also became evident that the target of his affections was the golden girl of the group, a lady who quickly dispelled any enlightened thought about blondes being unfairly represented in popular culture. A refrigerator could have given her 20 IQ points and still beaten her comprehensively completing The Beano crossword. But she was evidently Chris's drinking vessel of infused herbs, which neither surprised nor concerned me.

I was left with a choice of two ladies, one apparently dying of malnutrition and the other so covered in tattoos that she could have stripped naked and laid an ambush in the Louvre. They were nice legs, though, so I gave it my best shot. This transpired to be one Trish, an English actress. (Out of work, naturally.)

Of Trish's tattoos, apparently the ones on her arms were the result of a recent theatrical performance, and were temporary. (Fortunately, or she would have been limited to roles in productions about Hell's Angels or the Maori Wars.) The only indelible one was a fantastic face which peered behind her over the belt of her jeans… it turned out to be a dragon tattooed across her back, but at first I took it to be a crocodile looking out of the crack of her arse. On balance, I liked that.

Our conversation proceeded most satisfactorily, with the rapid discovery of a mutual love of Shakespeare (what a pleasure to speak of The Bard with an interlocutor who did not think I was talking about a fishing-rod manufacturer) and moved with encouraging despatch to the tickling-each-others-palm stage… I confess a very real attraction grew on me. However, just as things seemed to be progressing magnificently, she suddenly broke down completely and out came the story. Her husband had dumped her for her best friend a few weeks previously. The rest of the night was spent walking and talking on the beach, trying to dry the tears.

Trish left for England the next day, leaving me very sure that I wanted to see her again, whenever she felt able to do so. She said she'd call… but, as Hamlet has it, the rest was silence. I went ruefully back to work.

* * *

Of course, cheerful memoires such as this modest tome must have at least some happy endings. One day, when I was in the boatyard in Aegina collecting a yacht, Spiros called me urgently.

"Can you get back to Poros tonight? I have two tour operators coming from Sweden this evening. They are interested in a skippered flotilla, four or five boats. I need you to meet them tonight, take them to dinner, and then tomorrow take them out for a couple of days, to show them some of the ports and bays. And if that all goes well, then you'll be the lead-skipper for the first flotilla, if you like."

I did like, and I liked even more that evening when I was introduced to Karlotta & Inge, who turned out to be eminently and charmingly feminine.

Karlotta was a handsome and somewhat Olympian lady, tall and full-figured, with an eternal smile and clouds of black hair so capricious that it seemed to re-style itself every time the wind changed. Inge was an elf, a delightful Scandinavian elf, blue-eyed and petite beneath a blonde page-boy coiffeur. Both had a lively sense of humour, and they spoke that faultless, accent-less, pristine, advanced English which can never be imitated by an

Englishman, even at the 'old' BBC. They were vivacious, absolutely delightful and not one iota diminished in my admiration by the probability that they were both about a decade older than me.

Naturally, one had to be professional. For all I knew these ladies were married, or in relationships. They were travelling on business, and I had no grounds to think that either of them was interested in romance. They were also, of course, potential clients... both for Spiros and myself. One could not take liberties in such a situation. I did not, therefore, make the adolescent mistake of falling in love with both Karlotta and Inge immediately... I considered the matter maturely, with care and objectivity, for at least a couple of minutes.

I dined them at the Delfini, a favourite taverna set half way up the broad steps which lead from the South Quay up to the main square. The tables were set out in a narrow alley, immaculately whitewashed and overhung with jasmine and bougainvillea. Being on the steps, even the Greeks did not ride motorbikes in the area, so there was no unwelcome noise to pollute the homely, relaxing murmur of conversation, the tinkle of cutlery and the plinking of the ubiquitous 'usual suspects' Greek tunes. Brightly-lit boutiques lined the steps, tourists passed up and down, the wine was crisp and satisfying, and the food was as good as anywhere in town. It was a wonderful evening, full of light, and laughter, and bright eyes.

In the cool of the following morning I collected a large bag of prawns, caught close to the nearby island of Angistri and so fresh that some were still moving, and some decent white wine from the market before meeting my Swedessess at Petro's. After watching them deal enthusiastically with melon, yoghurt and honey I piled our bags aboard *Mucky Duck,* which had returned from her excursion in the Dodecanese.

We had a bit of a schedule to keep if we intended to see as much of the proposed flotilla itinerary as possible in two and a half days, so I motored fast in the morning calm to Hydra. Here I put the ladies ashore for about an hour, so that they could get a quick taste of the place.

As soon as they returned we pushed on to Pondikonisi Island at the west end of Hydra. I anchored the boat, in immaculate, glass-clear water over a rocky bottom, and let the ladies snorkel with the fish, which they did in true Scandinavian style, stripping naked without the least self-consciousness. I busied myself preparing an early lunch to limit the drool. They didn't dress for lunch, but there at least I could pretend to be slavering over the prawns.

They didn't see any reason to dress again for the sail over to the Peloponnesian coast, either. I left Pondikonisi just after midday, and we picked up the *Bouka Doura* wind from the sou'-sou'-east as soon as we cleared the end of Hydra. *Mucky Duck* loved a close-reach, and we turned a ruler-straight furrow through the rocky islets around Trikeri and then across the open sea to Kiparissi. As always, the wind slowly increased through the afternoon, the ladies shrieking with delighted protest as the weather bow whipped spray across their naked hides. Now, it is not the intention of the author to turn this book into a prurient exposition of erotic ephemera... a *Fifty Grades of Spray*... and so I shall leave the reader to imagine for themselves the effects of cool spray on naked breasts and bare skin, and thus also, indirectly, on said author; but by the time we arrived in Kiparissi I was having trouble seeing straight.

Enervated by their day on the water, my passengers were positively bubbling with enthusiasm in Kiparissi. We went to my favourite little restaurant *Klimateria*, which had no menus and served any meal you liked so long as you wanted small fish followed by a pork chop with salad. The wine went down like water, and both of the ladies were becoming very tactile. Unless I was as mad as a box of frogs, love was definitely in the air... so much so, in fact, that I started to have some anxieties about how I should break the bad news to the unsuccessful applicant. I need not have worried... it was done for me.

Returning to the boat, Karlotta stripped again, gave me a big smile, and went for a shower. I busied myself making industrial strength G-and-Ts. Next a naked Inge slipped out of her cabin and into the shower. Funny, I thought... I didn't see Karlotta come out. She must have been quick.

Then the giggling started.

Love was indeed in the air. Specifically, in the air in the shower, and, as custom demands, there was a happy ending. But not for me... I was surplus to requirements, so I went for a beer.

After two more days of watching unprotected Swedes cavorting all over the boat, and two more nights drinking on my own to give them a bit of privacy, I arrived back in Poros where I was informed, by Mary at the Jungle Bar, that Trish, the tattooed actress, had come back and had been waiting three days for me. She had just left on the evening ferry.

* * *

I wasn't the only one to fall into the gender-assumptions error. Yiorgaki, one of the skippers from the Grave-Robber, tied up next to me in Aegina one Saturday evening, fresh out of Alimos Marina on a big Atlantic 55 boat absolutely heaving with gorgeous women. It looked like someone had bought a job-lot of unemployed cheerleaders, the boat was wriggling with attractive limbs and scraps of material stretched tightly over the most interesting shapes. Yiorgaki looked like the cat who not only got the cream but inherited the dairy to boot. Whilst his crew were getting ready for the evening, he sat on the cabin-top and chatted with me. Between his legs was a bathroom window, in which I simply could not help noticing one of his goddesses combing her hair.

"Po, po, po!" He exulted delightedly; "Po po PO!!!" He put down his beer and used both hands to delineate in the air a figure which Mae West would have considered Rubinesque.

"You see?" he crowed, in a hoarse whisper, "You see them? *Kouklakia*! Dolls! Twelve of them!"

"Shhh!" I admonished him… the combing in the window below him had slowed to a crawl, and the head was tilting as if listening. She might have been, but Yiorgaki wasn't.

"Ten days we have, ten days!" He exulted. "And no mens! I gonna get one of thems for sure!" He winked hideously. "Maybe two, heh?"

My eyes flickered up the mast. From one yard-arm flew several national flags… Australian, New Zealand, Canadian and American.

From the other flew a rainbow flag.

I almost laughed out loud, he was so smugly sure of himself.

"What's that flag up there?" I asked innocently, pointing out the seven kaleidoscopic bars undulating lazily in the breeze. At that moment, the head in the bathroom between his legs turned and frantically motioned me to silence, one palm waving in negation whilst the other hand laid a finger on lips pouting a silent 'shhh!'.

Yiorgaki looked up for a few minutes, and shrugged.

"Dunno," he admitted carelessly. "One of those South American places, innit?"

"That's it!" I agreed, and the head in the window gave me a wink and blew me a kiss.

Yiorgaki disappeared to take a shower shortly after, just about managing to pack himself and his self-satisfaction into his tiny cabin in the bows of the boat. When he had gone, the girl who had been in the window appeared and spoke with a broad Aussie accent.

"Thanks, Mate!" she purred, "…He's been trippin' over his tongue all day. Y'won't tell him, will ya? This is going to be SOOOO much fun!"

I gave her a wink and she responded with a thumbs-up.

"Dinkum!" she said, which delighted me: I had never actually heard an Aussie say 'dinkum' before.

"Your name isn't Shiela, is it?" I asked.

She laughed. "Na, it's Bruce!"

We both laughed.

About two weeks later, I was walking past Stavros' *kafeneion* in Poros when I met Yiorgaki coming the other way. He did not acknowledge me by so much as a flicker, but turning to the astounded Stavros and his clients announced, in a ringing voice which reached the peaks of Poros and echoed back from the Peloponnesian shore, "This man is a veeery BEEEG bastard!"

So, that worked out very nicely!

* * *

Green Dragon was not an easy boat to sail. As modern as this morning, she was light, beamy and so insubstantial that, when I looked in the cockpit lockers on the side where the sun was shining, I could see the water-level through the fibreglass of her hull. Going downwind she skied fast but skittishly, and going upwind she bounced off every short Mediterranean wave and either stopped dead or fell off to leeward. I didn't like her one little bit, but charterers did… she had three double cabins, each with an en suite shower and head, a big saloon, an enormous cockpit and she looked flashy. The other thing her charterers apparently liked was Kos, so to Kos I went. There wasn't anyone available to go with me, but *Green Dragon* boasted an auto-pilot so Spiros and I greedily split the wage for the crew between us and I went on my own.

I don't really enjoy sailing alone. I am too gregarious by nature for one thing, and for another, I tend to make very different decisions when there is only myself to consider; decisions which I wouldn't be comfortable making under scrutiny. Left to my own devices I become rather experimental and I have frequently been left feeling very glad that there is no-one else around to watch me cleaning egg off my face. I am on record as having admitted, frequently, that I do not sail alone because I end up in bad company.

Despite recognising my unsuitability for solo sailing, however, I was willing enough to take *Green Dragon*, a boat I did not esteem, the two hundred-odd miles to Kos, for money. Many of my decisions are influenced by what one might call the fluidity of the situation, and this was yet another example; but for once the liquid in question wasn't alcohol, but rather testosterone.

The Poros waterfront was a very public forum where secrets were few and where professional seafarers and young yacht-jockeys, motor boat drivers and fishermen all rubbed shoulders in the kafeneions and competed, even when unconscious of the fact. It was not an environment that set much store in caution, so when one was asked to do something, one did it. If it worked, one affected a nonchalant modesty; if it did not, one had ready to hand all sorts of reasons why it was the fault of the proposer, the elements, the design of the boat, that bloke over there, or, in fact, any other person or thing under the sun, rather than the perpetrator. It was, I suppose, a bit like living in a gladiator's school... one really didn't want to be second best. So off I went to Kos, perfectly happy simply to have an opportunity to showcase my casual attitude to single-handed passages and blithely supposing that 'someone' would help me to tie up at the other end.

* * *

I left Poros before the dawn, puttering down the harbour in a twilight enhanced by a sinking moon. All around me, quite by chance but seeming to salute the nobility of my solo quest, were an escort of little boats whose rudimentary exhausts riveted the morning quiet as their ancient engines drove them out in quest of the morning fish. Greeks have a deep distrust of exhausts... anything that mutes the sound is under extreme suspicion of equally emasculating the engine. Fishing boats, motorbikes and pump engine exhaust systems are routinely eviscerated or discarded altogether.

Once clear of the channel I brought in my fenders and then, increasing the engine revolutions, I bid farewell to my fisher escort with a series of grave salutes as *Green Dragon* accelerated.

Setting course to the west-south-west, I passed Modhi Island at the east end of Poros and gradually began to feel the tickle of northerly breeze in my beard. By the time the east was orange-gold I had the engine off, the main sail and genoa drawing pleasantly, and *Green Dragon* chuckling contentedly as she ran out from the land.

The direct route from Poros to the island of Kos, which lies in the Southern Dodecanese islands hard against the Turkish coast, runs close to the western Cycladic island of Kythnos then just north of the large, central island of Naxos, and the distance is about one hundred and eighty-five nautical miles.

In Greece, however, the shortest distance from anywhere to anywhere else is rarely a straight line, and the canny Aegean sailor will only consider this direct route if the wind is confidently expected to be from the south. In any other conditions at all he is wise to be as alert as a mouse in a cattery, for the Aegean is a capricious creature and exceedingly prone to northerly winds which can be much stronger than forecast where they funnel between the high, rugged islands. Anyone who doubts this need only take a look at the Cycladic scenery, which is almost devoid of trees; and those that do manage to cling to the friable soil are either sheltered from the North or else they are stunted, blasted freaks, fantastically deformed and permanently bent away from relentless Boreas.

In the South Aegean, the part which lies below the narrowest point linked by the islands of Evvoia, Andros, Tinos, Ikaria and Samos, the wind is not uniformly northerly, however. In the central Aegean it blows from very close to true north, but at the western side it is deflected by the Peloponnesian coast and blows more from the north-east. Similarly, on the eastern side, it tends to follow the Turkish coast and blow from the north-west. A diagram of the prevailing winds over Homer's Wine-Dark Sea looks a little like an inverted Prince-Of-Wales feathers.

The knowledgeable sailor can make good use of this. By leaving the Peloponnese coast on a south-easterly heading he can keep the wind on his port beam, allowing him to enjoy an exhilarating close-reach at a good speed instead of beating hard and uncomfortably to maintain the direct track. If he passes close to Sifnos and then under Paros and Naxos he will also avoid the worst of the large seas which develop in the open area north of those islands. As he crosses the Aegean, the wind will normally back steadily from north-easterly through northerly, until he clears the island of Amorgos; and then the wind goes slowly into the north-west. This means that, by keeping the wind a little forward of the beam all the way, he can cross the Aegean at good speed in a relatively comfortable arc, gleefully trading about twenty nautical miles of extra distance for speed, comfort and fun. We called this southerly passage 'The Gentleman's Route', and it has the added advantage that, if you wish to stop on the way, there is much greater choice... Serifos and Sifnos, Dhespotico, the Small Cyclades, Amorgos, Levitha, Kinaross, and Astipalea are all ideally on the route, whilst Milos, Folegandros, Sikinos, Ios and even Nisiros are just a little further south.

With all the above in mind, and further impelled by the knowledge that *Green Dragon* was too buoyant to make easy progress on a hard beat, I shaped my course east-south-east for Sifnos, and settled down to enjoy the sixty-five mile sail. My progress was modest at the outset, but I was not worried... my local knowledge was developing fast, and I was also confident that the wind would increase by one or two points on the Beaufort scale when I passed my old friend Agios Yeorgios. To my intense satisfaction, it proved exactly so; and thus, about six in the evening, having enjoyed a leisurely sail all morning and a spanking, eight-knot close-reach most of the afternoon, I brought *Green Dragon* into the long inlet on Sifnos which leads to the main ferry port of Kamares.

Rounding the light on Akra Kokkala, I was suddenly a busy man. There were the sails to douse, and as I removed canvas* the skittish *Green Dragon* was too inconstant in her movements for her auto-pilot to handle. This meant that I had to go back to the cockpit periodically and steady her up again. Then I rigged fenders in case there was a chance to go alongside, and prepared some mooring-lines.

All this I did between frequent pauses to admire the scenery, as the bay is a fabulous one indeed. Both sides are majestic, rocky slopes or crags, predominantly grey but shot with sandy-coloured outcrops and here and there threaded with gleaming green or coffee-toned swirls of minerals, rising almost five hundred metres on either hand. The highest peaks are tipped with chalky monasteries, the head of the bay is rimmed with the brilliantly white, cubic

---

* Alright... terelyne. But it doesn't have the same ring to it.

Cycladic houses, and the Cycladic sky overhead is usually a pristine, cloudless powder-blue. It is a spectacular arrival.

Noticing during these scans of the scenery that a ferry was about to depart from the port I edged *Green Dragon* closer to the northern shore of the bay and got on with my preparations for mooring. I had just unlashed the anchor when I heard, very close by, a strident voice.

Looking quickly ahead I saw nothing close, and a rapid scan of the shoreline revealed nothing... I was looking, of course, for one of the omnipresent fishing boats which are almost universally painted white. Not seeing anything I was turning to look offshore when the voice came again, this time sounding angry and now definitely inshore of me.

Turning back to the rocks, I perceived at last a darker slab of stone low to the water, upon which were a number of gesturing figures. All seemed to be uniformly dressed, all very animated. My heart sank as I apprehended that these appeared to be officials in uniform, and they didn't seem very happy with me. What on earth they were all doing standing on a flat rock in the middle of nowhere puzzled me extremely.

I looked around for a church... Greeks seem to measure piety in terms of how inaccessible a place they can build a church, and the only explanation I could imagine for a horde of officials to be marooned on a desolate rock had to involve religion. I saw no sign of a church, however... and then I noticed, on top of the rock, a strangely smooth column. My mind, fed delusions of adequacy at an early age by an 'O'-level* in geology, had just formed the thought 'that must be a weathered basaltic intrusion' when a man emerged out of the top of it.

'OK,' I thought, '...so it is quite a talented weathered basaltic intrusion.'

But, do you know, it wasn't a weathered basaltic intrusion of any kind, talented, hollow, or custom-built. It was a submarine.

Once I realised what I was looking at, it sort of 'materialised', appearing so clearly that I could not understand how I had missed it in the first place. The hull and fin were a mottled mix of light and dark grey, which gave it an element of camouflage, but now the outline was quite clear against the lighter rock behind. Her bow was a smooth hump, her stern sloped down into the sea

---

* Grade D

and her fin was a square block topped with several protrusions. I was within fifty metres of the beast, so close that I could now see the bubble and haze of her generator exhaust; and definitely so close that I could not plausibly ignore the gestures of her crew, who were clearly ordering me to come closer.

Bugger, I thought.

I had good reason to be concerned, because Greeks are pretty paranoid when it comes to their armed forces. Any military or naval installation has large signs warning against photography, and these rules are enforced with scant respect for *habeas corpus*. Even at the naval school in Poros, which consisted of no more than classrooms, old buildings and a mothballed World War Two destroyer, the click of a camera-shutter would bring the normally lethargic sentries out onto the street with fixed bayonet, truncheon and the snarling ferocity of dogs after a postman. A foreigner getting within a hundred metres of what was obviously an active, operational, modern submarine was likely to be particularly vexatious to the uniformed mind.

Throttling back and taking my time to turn towards the submarine, my mind raced. What would they do to me? No doubt there would be some minimum distance within which I should not approach, of which I was utterly unaware. I faced, at the very least, the confiscation of the film on my camera... and now the thought occurred that this posed another problem, since I didn't *have* a camera. I was officially on holiday, and who goes on holiday without taking a few snap-shots? My fertile imagination conjured up images of grim-faced MPs ripping *Green Dragon* to pieces to find a hidden camera, or alleging that I had thrown it overboard to conceal my guilt. I could imagine courts charging me with entry into prohibited areas, failure to keep a safe lookout, illegal fishing and anything else that came to the official mind short of poisoning the hamster in the national zoological gardens. Yes, I know, I am paranoid... but I don't think I am *sufficiently* paranoid.

As I approached the submarine, my mind waxed increasingly pessimistic. In Greek law, all offences are liable to jail terms. Sentences of less than two years can usually be 'bought off', effectively being commuted to a fine. Now, I am not a habitual offender, and anyway the Greek police tended to be as tolerant and relaxed as the nation generally; it was hard to get them sufficiently annoyed to fill in papers unless one made an effort. It required violence, or public disrespect for the nation, authorities or the church, to move Plodopoulos to action. Although I was learning actively every day about all aspects of life in Greece, I had somehow omitted to research how to irritate The Fuzz, and the consequence of this omission was that I had not the slightest idea how heavy a fine might be; but my lifestyle was somewhat hand-to-mouth and I very much doubted whether I had enough money in the country to pay the standard bung for high-level espionage. Sending money from England took over two weeks, and even if they allowed the condemned man a phone-call home I didn't much fancy spending that time in a Greek slammer.

With all this negative energy bouncing about between my ears, I pulled *Green Dragon* up close to the starboard side of the submarine. I could now see that she had an anchor out forward, and her stern was secured with two long lines to the rocks astern of her. Two men, who had obviously just secured them, were swimming powerfully back. I did my best to look as disinterested in the vessel as possible, in particular averting my gaze from any antennae or anything else that might appear sensitive. A man in officer's epaulettes was shouting at me in Greek, and I understood him to be calling me alongside.

I have a penis, which means that I like techy stuff; and submarines are about as techy as it gets. I had also, in my tanker officer persona, refuelled a few submarines in my time. This meant that I knew a little about them... not enough to steal one, or even make an informed choice about buying one, but certainly enough to know that they don't have a 'conning tower', they have a 'fin'. I also knew that this one was a conventional diesel/electric type, and by the looks of it probably built in Germany or Sweden. And I was aware that it wouldn't be the best idea in the world to try to put a yacht alongside one, because of the ballast tanks.

The bit of a submarine one sees is mainly the casing, which is quite narrow; but their external ballast tanks extend out sideways from this some way under the water. Putting a sailing boat alongside would probably result in the keel and ballast tank making contact below the waterline. That doesn't do the yacht much good, and it certainly won't raise the value of the submarine either... modern subs are often covered with rubber 'anechoic' tiles which absorb sound and sonar signals, and a yacht keel would probably chisel them off like a paint-scraper. Not wishing to add sabotage of a front-line naval asset to the list of crimes I was about to be accused of, I didn't want to go alongside. But I also didn't want anyone to know that I knew about anechoic tiles, or, indeed, anything at all about submarines; so I played a bit dumb. The officer evidently bought it, as he suddenly switched language.

"Do you speak English?" he called.

Not much point in denying that… they'd probably have my passport within the next five minutes. So I confessed myself a son of Albion, and waited, resolutely straight and stoical, for them to throw the book, or possibly the whole library, at me.

The officer signalled me to wait and turned to speak up to another imposing-looking chap on the top of the fin. I could not hear the brief conversation, but I gathered from the body language that an agreement had been reached before my tormentor turned back to me.

"Are you aware," he said sternly, adopting a pugnacious stance by putting his fists on his hips and lowering his chin so that his glare ricocheted off the underside of his eyebrows, "…That there is an exclusion zone around warships, which you have entered without permission?"

"Is there?" I asked, attempting to sound astounded by this news. "No, I didn't… but in any case, I didn't see you" Then I improvised desperately. "Excellent camouflage, I must say…"

The officer was visibly, massively, extravagantly unimpressed.

"You will have to come alongside. I must put two men on board you."

Oh, bloody hell. The officer's English was dreadfully fluent, there was no plausible way of creatively misunderstanding this. Glumly throwing out a couple of fenders I started to move *Green Dragon* towards the bow of the submarine, where the ballast tanks hopefully weren't as wide. As I did so, I contemplated making a run for it. After all, I couldn't see a gun, and I reckoned you'd have to be pretty good to hit a yacht with a torpedo. Unless they happened to have Sean Connery or Jürgen Prochnow on board, I should be away and gone. But, sadly, there was a port police station in Kamares, and most of them have radios and fast inflatable boats; and even if they didn't take direct action, *Green Dragon* had a registration number clearly marked on her stern… it would be like beating someone to death with your social security file, and then leaving the murder weapon at the scene of the crime. I reluctantly discarded the Hornblower option.

"I'll try to come alongside your bow" I told him, and a couple of capable looking sailors trotted purposefully forward. This turned out to be a good thing, because, at this point, a small *spilliade* ruffled the water and, before I could do anything to prevent it, *Green Dragon*'s stern swung in and gave the sub's bow a shrewd thump which would have been a lot shrewder had the brawny arms not been ready to catch her. A petty officer and a rating, looking horribly official in what the Royal Navy would call 'number eight uniform' complete with caps, leapt nimbly aboard.

"You must proceed to the harbour, and take these men with you." announced the officer.

Morosely, I tried to manoeuvre away, but the *spilliades* were feeling playful. I tried every trick I knew for what seemed like an hour, and was in fact a rather embarrassing couple of minutes, to get that yacht away from that sub, only to be defeated by little gusts of wind which patted me back against the mottled grey hull like a cat playing with a hapless mouse. Every time I landed alongside again was a separate collision, and although these were again mitigated by the hands of the crew on the deck, I had a mental image of each separate impact representing an individual act of sabotage in the eyes of the Greek Navy. I believe that there is an anti-submarine weapon called a hedgehog, but this may have been the first recorded instance of a woodpecker in the genre.

Finally I managed to get clear, and we set off down the approach to Kamares, a spectacular entry which would normally have captivated me. Now, however, I had no eyes for it. I made a couple of nervous attempts to talk to the two sailors, but they appeared unable to see or hear me. They sat each side of the hatch, swapping cigarettes and low chatter with the most unnerving lack of concern for my presence or plight.

I swung *Green Dragon* around the end of the main breakwater, hoping there would be no room to tie up. Port full. Sorry, chaps, did my best. Just hop off at the end of the pier and I'll be on my way. Pip pip! Mind the dolphins down there! But of course, there was plenty of room. Almost the whole length of the inner side of the quay was empty, and plenty of places on the south side of the harbour were also available. Gloomily noticing that there was a telegraph pole next to a whitewashed wall at the root of the breakwater which could almost have been made for a firing-squad, I easily secured *Green Dragon* alongside.

My two guards watched this performance with mild interest, and the sailor went so far as to pass me a rope when I asked. Then they climbed onto the dock.

"Thank you very much" said the petty officer, politely. He offered me a cigarette.

"The last cigarette?" I asked him, bitterly, in Greek. He looked puzzled, and flipped open the pack to show the contents.

"No. I have plenty!" He offered them again.

"I don't smoke."

"Ah. *Endaxi.** Anyway, thank you."

They walked away. What the hell was going on? I called after them.

"What do I do now?"

They considered this carefully, and then the petty officer shrugged.

"Anything you like," he told me, and they departed for the town.

I didn't have a clue what to do… I watched them carefully to see if they went to the port police to report me, but they continued into town at a leisurely stroll, deeply engaged in conversation.

Well, bull-by-the-horns time, it seemed. Let's find out once and for all. Collecting my papers, I marched determinedly into the port police office to declare my entry. Would I be arrested? Nope. A thoroughly polite and smart young man gravely calculated that I owed forty-eight drachmae for staying overnight (a sum which would barely pay for all the ink he used filling in the complex receipt) and bad me a cheery 'good evening'. As fast as possible without damaging property, I left in search of it.

At the head of the bay of Kamares is a sweeping beach fringed with trees and restaurants where I sat, wriggling my bare feet luxuriously in the sand, whilst keeping a leery eye on *Green Dragon* for anything that resembled a uniform. When an hour, and a number of gin-and-tonics, had passed, I began to breathe a little easier.

The setting was truly beautiful, the last of the light lingered in the western sky and the heights of the mountains were tinged with the rosy caress of the parting sun. A pristine white church was illuminated like a Disney attraction opposite me on the north side of the bay, and all around, above the warm, yellowish glow of the restaurants, reared spectacular mountains.

It was still early in the season, but the tourists were here in modest numbers, so Kamares was pleasantly alive with people and muted music. It

---

* OK.

was utterly delightful, and only the sense that the sleek, death-dealing, sinister shadow lurking under the cliffs still had dastardly intentions for me detracted from my pleasure.

By the last of the light I saw the two sailors, conspicuous in their white-topped caps, boarding a passenger caïque. Some boys passed down a number of cardboard boxes, and they set off out of the harbour again. Had I been mentally scarred just so that they could get some bloody groceries? Or were they going to return home, report that the port police had done nothing, and set the grim-looking officer again on the path of retribution? Well, I have a procedure for these tense and uncertain situations. As an old captain of mine once remarked, when bailing me from a Chilean calaboose, "Always try to go to jail with a full stomach, Son." It remains excellent advice, and I ordered lavishly.

Sifnos is renowned for its cookery, and one of its specialities is their local version of the ubiquitous Greek salad. They add capers and use a local soft cheese called *myzythra*, which is deliciously salty, creamy, and has a delightfully sensual texture. Together with a charcoal-grilled *kalamari*, a *pylino** of luscious *moussaka* and a copious dose of muscle-relaxant, it set me up splendidly for a prolonged spell in chokey, but the beadle remained ostentatiously absent. I began to think that I had heard the last of it… but just in case, I decided to leave very early in the morning. I had intended to get going at first light anyway; now I decided to have another couple of gins, get turned-in, and be away before daylight.

I lazed in that beach cafe, nursing my frosted glass and marvelling at the effect of a rising moon, just past the full, on the overhanging cliffs above me.

The moon's declination must have been somewhat northerly, as it shone onto the spectacular folds and spurs of the south side of the bay rimming every ridge with blue-white light and plunging every chasm into pitchy shade. When people ask me what are the most beautiful sights I have seen in Greece, that night always comes to mind. The light of the full moon on the mountains of Kamares… see that, and you are a huge step closer to dying content. The light was also bright enough to show me the tourist-caïque chugging in full of sailors in their best uniforms, but after an initial consternation I realised that they were just coming in for a night in the town, and relaxed again before my

---

* A pylino is an individual, oven-cooked dish which may be of various types. It takes its name from the earthenware baking-pot in which it is both cooked and brought to table.

apprehension had registered on my laundry-bill. With great reluctance I dragged myself away from the glorious moonscape, set my alarm-clock for four A.M. and rolled into my pit.

* * *

I had thought to awake before officialdom, but no matter how early you rise, you can't beat a man who has not been to bed. As I emerged into my cockpit just after four in the morning, the still-vivid moonshine showed me four uniformed figures on the dock next to the *Green Dragon*. The second glance showed that one of them was the officer of the day before.

"Ah! Good morning!" He beamed. "I am so glad to see you are awake… I would not like to wake you."

His grin, in my befuddled and guilty state of mind, reminded me of the Gestapo officer in *The Great Escape*… you know, the one in the leather jacket who says "Your German is excellent, Herr Bartlett. And also, I hear, your French. Your arms *up*, please!"

For an instant I thought, 'Here it comes!' and seconds later I thought, 'Bloody hell! Middle of the night, no-one around to see… what the hell *is* this?'

"We were wondering," asked the spokesman in his really excellent English, "if you would be so kind to take us back to our ship? We are sailing in two hours."

All was great bonhomie as we puttered up the moon-drenched bay towards the submarine. The officers had enjoyed a night amongst the tourist girls in the bars, their uniforms being of the utmost service to them in this environment, and they quite candidly admitted that they had been having such a splendid time that they had missed the last boat back. They had, in fact, been sufficiently desperate to 'borrow' a boat had it been necessary to get them back in time… delaying military operations for debauchery, I do understand, is frowned upon in the more elite units, and in contemplating such irregularities these chaps were no doubt just being ordinarily sub-servient… but a lift back was a much less contentious way of resolving their dilemma. They were generous with their thanks.

"All very well," I growled as we approached the dark, menacing shadow below the cliffs, "But you scared the living daylights out of me with that stunt yesterday. I've been waiting to be arrested all night!"

They looked sympathetic, but also smug. Greeks anywhere love putting one over on someone, and enjoying a clever solution to a problem is a core national value. Even deep gratitude isn't going to stop them glorying in it a little.

"Sorry," relied the linguist, as sincerely as he could through his smirk, "But the Captain told me to organise some souvlakis for the crew. It just seemed the quickest and easiest way to get a couple of guys into town."

So that was what had been in the cardboard boxes. I had been traumatised so that a Greek submarine crew could enjoy a pork lolly.

I deposited my debauchees, giving the submarine another couple of clouts in the process, received more fulsome thanks which included a friendly wave from the official-looking character who was again surveying the world from the top of the fin, and departed with the glow of dawn at my back. Turning southwards out of Kamares Bay, I headed under Sifnos and eastwards towards Amorgos.

An hour later, as I motored along the rocky Sifniot coast in the morning calm and munched a bacon butty, a steel cylinder slid vertically out of the water barely ten metres to starboard. I was half expecting it. The lens of the periscope turned towards me, and then it dipped gravely, two times, below the water in salute. I waved back. It dipped a third time, and was seen no more. Leaping to the rail I looked down into the blue depths and thought I saw a shadow moving away to seaward.

How very friendly, I thought, considering I had crashed into them. Truly, one does meet a better class of people in collisions.

CHAPTER EIGHT

SALVAGING PRIDE

A spot of harry-roughers... great hydrofoil journeys of the world... malodour-de-mer... techniques for rough weather... what to do when they don't work... blowing for a tug... how to tow if you can't do it properly... the bun-fight at the Omega Kappa corral... philotimo... an unlikely explanation accepted... the reward of virtue.

In terms of my reputation I may not have been achieving much on the romantic front, but my Barnacle Billy-ness was about to have an opportunity to exhibit itself.

Lochinvar had been struggling. She was a good-looking boat, a Gib-Sea 106 with a very sweet sheer, and she was a capable sailor; but she was not designed for the bloody-minded conditions we had encountered together over the last two days.

Firstly we had beat thirty-five miles to windward into a relentless north-north-east, driving over steep, short, slamming seas, which are so typical of the Eastern Mediterranean, under a treble-reefed main and half a genoa. That had been rough, and wet, and very tiring; and yet we had made headway, and the exhilaration of bucketing over the ramping, slab-sided, thuggish waves had still held some charm. The astringent spray, the whipping freshness of the air, the profound, cathedral-vaulted, cobalt lustre of the deep, deep sea as we clove into it, combined with the sheer achievement of making progress would be compelling memories long after the aches, the chill, the hunger and the weariness had been forgotten. The second half of the trip, however, was one of those sailing experiences which make one wish that one had lived one's entire life up a mountain, and bred vampires for a hobby.

146

The call had come a couple of days earlier, when Spiros had managed to trap me at about four in the morning at the Jungle Bar, where I was just having a last glass with the owners, Stathis and Mary, as they put the shutters up. Mary was mixing the gins as Stathis and I carried two last clients, overcome by their exertions, outside and arranged them comfortably in the municipal flowerbeds to pass the rest of the night. Jingle, jangle.

"Julian! Phone!"

I knew what would happen, but I picked it up anyway. And I said yes. (I always said 'yes' in any case, but after a pleasant evening with Dr Tanqueray I would probably have volunteered to take a petrol-tanker to Dunkirk). Then I packed a bag, forestalled a hangover with a heart-attack breakfast at George's Cafe, and caught the first Flying Dolphin to Monemvasia. It had been blowing a stiff northerly for a week, and Spiros had a boat stuck at the bottom of the Peloponnese. Fifty-five miles, give or take… it would be a bit of a punch to get back, certainly, but all the same I considered it money for old rope. I blithely assured Spiros that I'd have the boat back the following night. I was a pillock.

There was a Flying Dolphin hydrofoil link down to Monemvasia. One had to get to Spetses, change onto another boat which went down to Plaka Leonidhion on the Peloponnese, and then wait for the service from Navplion which touched at Tyros, Plaka, Kiparissi, Gerakas and Monemvasia before it rounded Akra Malea and made its furthest-south in either Neapolis or Gythion. It was an excellent service… sadly now long discontinued… which opened up many wonderful, isolated bucolic havens along the Eastern Peloponnese by making, in a few hours, a trip that, by road, would have taken all day and half of the night; and yet, if there was any weather it was not a voyage for the faint-of-heart. It was even less so for the faint-of-stomach!

Two and a half hours to Leonidion followed by another two to Monemvasia was a long time to sit in a sealed tube which smelled faintly of diesel, especially with the sea that had been kicked up by a week of anemos-ity; for the hydrofoils rolled sluggishly in the quartering seas, stalling on the backs of waves and racing down the fronts, and the ponderous, slow and unpredictable motion had many a passenger intensely occupied trying to re-pack their breakfasts in bags which were neither sufficiently large nor waterproof for the purpose. Blame it on the excesses of the previous night I could and did, but whatever the reason, the fact was that, after a lifetime in boats and ten years at sea professionally, even I was not immune. Monemvasia is a magnificent, towering, vertiginous pillar of ruby-hued rock crowned with the spectacular ruins of a mighty acropolis, but by the time I arrived on the old stone jetty, which juts out of the ancient causeway joining this eminence to the mainland, my eagerness to disembark had nothing whatever to do with enjoying the view.

The apologetic clients who were leaving *Lochinvar* met me off the hydrofoil and handed over the keys. I cursed them for this consideration, as it meant I had to keep my rebellious digestive system in check whilst I appeared saltily immune for the benefit of the punters. Fortunately, after tailing off into silence as they took horrified stock of the condition of the refugees disembarking from the contraption, they hurried away to cancel their tickets on the afternoon return service and look for a bus.

I proceeded with all despatch to the rather wonderful pizza restaurant under the great rock-face and settled my stomach with a calezone and a flagon or two of icy amber elixir. Then I checked out the boat, had a couple of hours sleep, made a pack of sarnies to last me the night, and set forth to battle the elements.

* * *

Thus it was that I came to be regretting the siren-call of the oceans, and it was all my own fault; firstly, in general, for saying 'yes' without due consideration, and secondly, in particular, for the route I had taken. I was coming north to Poros from Monemvasia, at the bottom of the Peloponnesian coast, against a north-north-easterly gale, and it had seemed to me that I might get some respite from the seas if I passed west of Hydra, using that high, rocky island as a breakwater.

Smugly confident in my 'local knowledge', I had allowed for the nonsense which Greek wind gets up to whenever it meets a rock and I expected to find, as I sailed into the narrow gap between Hydra and Ermioni, that that the wind would simply turn to follow the Hydra Strait and blow dead against me. However, I suspected the seas would be much higher in the open water east of Hydra, and I took it as the least-worst option. What I had not predicted was that, in the confines of the Hydra Strait, the sea built even higher. It was bad enough beating into that, but then the wind died altogether.

Delivery-skippers in Greece either become adept at making way against the wind, or they give up entirely. People pay to sail downwind, but most of us don't sail back up unless we are well remunerated for it. Some folks leave their boats at the downwind end of their voyage by pre-arrangement, and some are simply overcome by the elements; but the fact is that boats accumulate downwind and have to be brought back up for the next client. The majority of deliveries are against the wind, and anyone of any brain soon develops a strategy.

Normally when faced with head seas and winds, one either sailed close-hauled or else one flattened the main sail with a reef and motored on a course which just allowed the sail to be kept full. That way a fair, if uncomfortable, speed could be maintained.

Today, however, the wind having died away to leave only the high, spiteful sea, I had been forced to lower the mainsail to prevent it flogging itself to death in the pitching and rolling. All attempts to change course and angle across the seas had failed, because I lost ground as I gained speed. The boat was needed in Poros, so I didn't want to take shelter until the sea dropped. I had endured most of the night slamming into the detestable and undiminishing chop, unable to prepare a hot meal* and feeling as if I had spent a month on the dodgems.

Lochinvar was game. With resolution and tenacity she slammed and pitched into the chunky, white-maned, anarchic swells which hissed down the Hydra Strait, her engine purring stoically despite being alternately stood on its gearbox or fly-wheel, but she was going nowhere. Every time *Lochinvar* hit one, her engine had to drive her up a steep hill, which slowed her down; every time the wave passed by, she briefly accelerated and then dug her bows in to the trough behind it, so that her buoyancy almost stopped her dead. It was like playing American football… short sprint, crashing stop. I was thoroughly sick of the business.

---

* I don't know about you, but sandwiches have a fatal flaw for me. I get very bored waiting for them. I can wait hours… days, even… for a meal which has to be prepared and which exists, so to speak, only in potentia: but food in existence exerts a magnetism beyond all hope of resistance. However I justify the deed… be it 'they'll get stale', or 'I might not have time later'… if it is ready to eat then eaten it shall most assuredly be. I would be a complete liability in a lifeboat.

Most of the morning I had watched Tselevinia creeping closer, moving no faster than an arthritic tectonic plate, knowing that Poros was just the other side of Dharditsa and that, in a direct line, I was barely six miles from home, shelter, ice-cold beer and my bed, and the relief as I finally nosed into the Tselevinia channel was as palpable as walking under a waterfall. Emerging on the other side of the passage to run north-west to Poros, the boat took the high swell on her starboard side. Rolling her zincs out, but no longer held back by the impact of waves from ahead, *Lochinvar* swooped over the heaped beam seas and raced towards home. I had already decided on the pepper steak at Mouraghio Taverna and could just about taste that beer.

The seas were, not to mince words, bloody awful. Generated by a full blow in the Aegean they hooked westwards at Cape Sounion and hit the lower Saronic from the east-north-east. As they smashed on the sheer, rocky coast, they created back-waves which radiated out and even a mile from the land these conflicted with the next waves coming in, making them higher and steeper. I reckoned some of them were touching three metres, and I kept a good way offshore, partly to avoid the worst of them and partly to give me time to get sails on in case I had an engine problem.

In the eastern approach to Poros lies an island, Bourtzi. It is a low, rocky dome, perhaps fifteen metres high and two hundred metres long, and it is crowned with a turreted, defensive wall, like a small castle. I was watching it keenly as the thrashing white water all about it clearly showed that the waves were still potent even this far into the entrance. Foam frothed around the island like spittle on a maniac's lips, and from this an occasional spout of white erupted to reach almost as high as the foot of the walls as the massive energy of the seas vented itself on impassive rock. And then, in that anarchy of tortured seas, I clearly saw a flash of blue which was far too light to be natural.

It took me some moments, in the chaotic, bucking world of *Lochinvar's* cockpit, to lay my hands on the binoculars. It took a lot longer to snatch a reliable glimpse of the waters in front of the island, but eventually I had some sort of focus. A moment later I caught a fleeting sight of a coral-blue fishing boat rearing her bow over an advancing comber. A man was clinging to the net-winding gear.

I immediately flung the helm over and headed down towards the island. There was no time to be lost, as the boat seemed to be already perilously close to the rocks. I could only assume that the engine had failed… not even a fisherman, a breed of men who are definitive risk-takers, would conceivably be in that position by choice… and if the boat touched those rocks in such waves she would go to pieces in moments. In that sea there could be no chance for anyone aboard. I needed to get that fellow off, and quickly.

As I roared in, with the waves scooting me forward, I got a long rope out of the locker and attached it firmly to the lifebuoy. I didn't think there was any chance of getting the fisherman on board directly in such a chaotic sea, so my plan was to stop head-to-weather just by him and recover him over the stern using the lifebuoy and rope. I longed to call for help, but the VHF radio was in the chart-space, and I couldn't leave the tiller. Anyway, the fishing boat would be on the rocks long before I could even explain the situation, never mind receive any assistance.

The motion became increasingly wild as I neared the rocks, and now the man on the fishing boat could be clearly seen when she rose at the same time as *Lochinvar*. I recognised him, had seen him on the dock… he was an enormous, dark-skinned, bare-footed, gypsy-ish character, balding with an extravagant comb-over, whose belly spilled with contemptuous ease out of whatever garment he employed to contain it. I assumed he lived on the boat, as he certainly slept on it most nights, and I didn't know his name but had privately dubbed him The Wild Man of the Sea. Now he clung to the net-winder with one hand and the cabin with the other, looking rapidly from me to the rocks and back.

I swung *Lochinvar* around, rolling what felt like about forty degrees in the process, and began to edge towards the capering fishing boat. It looked, I noted with alarm, rather sluggish and I had an idea it was already taking in water. I lobbed the lifebuoy right next to the gunwale, and shouted to the fisherman to jump for it. Waves coming in slapped into waves rebounding from the rocks, the spray and dollops of green water flew, and the malevolent deep crunch and rush of waves on the nearby island eclipsed the engine-noise. I had to keep looking at my rev-counter to reassure myself that the engine was still running, and that, consequently, I wasn't about to die.

I expected the Wild Man to jump for the lifebuoy, but he fished it out with a hook.

'Fair enough,' I thought, 'he probably can't swim… it is surprising how many traditional seamen can't. He'll put it on and then jump.'

But then I saw him untying the lifebuoy from the rope.

I was, I confess, just a trifle irritated by this. It was irrational of me, I admit, especially in light of my constant failure to attract a mate, but I had a touching fondness for life; and I was aware at that mine was currently entirely dependent on the game little engine, so puny that I could not even hear it over the greedy gobbling of the ravening waves, pounding its little alloy heart out down in *Lochinvar's* bilges. One hiccup, one bubble in the fuel system, and I would, very briefly, be garnish on the serrated, stony flanks of Bourtzi. I roared at the bloody idiot, telling him to jump, but he blithely ignored me. And then, with a stone in my heart and liquid soap in my intestines, I realised what he was doing.

He was tying the bloody rope to his boat!

Aghast, I howled my disagreement at him. I could see no way under the firmament that *Lochinvar* could tow that hefty, dead-weight and probably waterlogged boat out of that watery bedlam. But he evidently disagreed. Indeed, he appeared to repose such utopian faith in his salvation that he calmly sat down on the drive-mechanism for the net-winder and gave every indication of taking a well-earned rest.

What was I going to do? Cast him adrift to die? Cursing and blaspheming, I secured my end of the line and started to manoeuvre to take up the strain on the tow.

The trickiest part of towing is taking up the strain on the tow-line. The towed vessel is, initially, stationary and it is easy to put the strain on the line too fast and break it. The best way to get the tow moving is to move to the side, as she will turn more readily than she will move bodily through the water and so there is less resistance to getting her moving. Then, as she begins to turn, it takes less energy to convert a turn into forward motion than it does simply to start pulling a dead-weight. One can come in line and start to pull her with much less chance of breaking the towing gear.

This I began to do now, and it took me some hour-long minutes to crab across and take the strain. These minutes, tense in any case, were made no easier by the roaring and gesticulating of the Wild Man who was defeating even the thunder of inexorable nature in exercising his inalienable Hellenic right to tell me I was doing it all wrong. By the time I had the engine up to full revolutions and pulling directly offshore, I was angry enough... terrified enough, come to that... to have shut him up with an iron bar if I could have reached.

To judge by his language, the Wild Man found my failure to follow his instructions as infuriating as I found his interference; but even if he had known what he was talking about, and even if I could have understood it, I was towing from the stern... this is very difficult, as the towing vessel has great difficulty turning, and the stern is perpetually dragged in the direction of the tow. The tow-line really needs to be connected in the middle of the towing boat. I partly compensated for this by shifting the weight of the tow from one quarter to the other, as required, using a line from the cockpit winches.

After much adjustment, all conducted to the constant litany of contradictory advice and instructions, I ended up heading diagonally away from the island, with the tow secured to the port quarter of *Lochinvar,* and tried to edge my *ménage* slowly to the westward and the shelter of the Poros entrance without losing ground back towards the seething cauldron of malevolent energy which raged at the island's flanks.

The fishing boat had come partly in line and appeared to have stopped her drift towards the rocks, but I could do no more than that. *Lochinvar's* engine was about thirty horse-power, if I remember correctly, and completely inadequate for this task. Thinking back, I suspect that it was as much the back-wash of the waves as *Lochinvar's* engine that kept the fishing boat off those fatal rocks; and yet, oh so slowly, I began to drag my salvage, inch by excruciating inch, sideways across the rock-face of the island. Every time I looked back I took a marker on the island... a bush, a fold in the rock... and watched the plunging bulk of the fishing boat creep past it. I rode the throttle, trying to damp out the snatches on the tow-line, but on occasion got it wrong. Then the line would snap taut with a 'twang' and hum like a harp string; the snatch pulled *Lochinvar's* stern round, and my heart stopped for a few minutes as I waited for the line to part. Then, when it didn't, I had to wrestle us back on course.

We were not moving away from the rocks; on the contrary, in fact, I think we were slowly losing ground towards them. But infinitesimally we were moving sideways, and after what seemed like a decade, I could make out that the stern of the fishing boat had just, marginally, somehow, cleared the end of the island.

Between the island and the channel into Poros there is another outcrop of rock. Being reasonably confident that I could clear this, especially as the seas had subsided somewhat as we got closer in, I managed to turn more towards shelter and then I even rolled out some genoa. Supplemented by the sail, the engine was now moving the heavy fishing boat a little better, and I was heading for the entrance to the port.

And then The Wild Man of the Sea let the bloody rope go!

I stopped my prop, rolled up my genoa, and heaved in the slack line. The Wild Man ignored me completely, and was trying to rig a large, unwieldy pair of oars... a hopeless task, even in the lesser seas at the entrance to the channel. The boat drifted quickly towards the rocks to leeward, where the man himself now might survive but the seas were still capable of destroying the boat. I approached the loony again, and offered him the rope.

He declined.

"Go get my friend!" he roared in Greek. He used *áde,* which is an impolite imperative for 'go', and did not volunteer who his friend was, or where he might be found.

I managed to construct a few terse sentences in Greek which, if they were correct, should have informed him that if he didn't take the line, he would lose his boat. He played the stoic for a while, until his boat shook with an impact on something below the water; and then, with ill-grace and bad temper, he re-secured the line and I pulled him again offshore.

As soon as I got him inside the blessed calm of the channel, he cast off again and tried to row. Even now he could not make way, but he was safe now... he drifted gently aground on the mud on the Galatas side of the channel, and at that point turned his back emphatically towards me and settled down to watch the mainland. I left him to it. With my keel I couldn't get near him there anyway, even if he had wanted my help... and he certainly didn't.

I knew what it had all been about, of course. The fellow was worried that I would claim salvage on his boat.

Greeks have their own ideas about salvage. The basic principle internationally is that a successful salvor, one who has prevented the loss of a vessel and re-delivered it to the owner in a safe place and condition, can claim up to half of the value of the vessel and cargo salvaged. It is a generous award, which is intended to encourage people to do their utmost to save property, and the most commonly used agreement is 'Lloyds Open Form'. The Greeks, masters of one of the world's pre-eminent shipping industries and as sharp the scythe of Death in enforcing their rights under maritime law internationally, know this as well as anyone in the world; and yet, they are peculiarly blind to salvage laws when they happen within their own jurisdiction. Within Greece, the universal belief is simply, 'I saved it, it's mine!'

There are a lot of things about salvage which everybody in Greece 'knows'. Most of them have no basis that I am aware in anyone's maritime law, but that doesn't matter, because Everybody Knows. There are various theories about towing other boats, such as whose rope is used, or what agreements are made, or where the salvage takes place, which never appeared in any of my shipmasters law courses but which are all solidly established as case-law in the high court of the *kafeneion*, and they make the complexities of European Legislation look like the Ten Commandments by comparison; but what I can tell you, without any fear of inaccuracy, is that if you get towed by a Greek in Greece you are almost certain to have your boat impounded and the lawyers will be booking their kids into Eton.

This, then, was the reason for the Wild Man's apparent ingratitude; and, since the boat was almost certainly all he possessed, I considered his position perfectly understandable... well, I did once I had downed a couple of cold beers and wrestled my heart-rate back into double figures.

I totally ignored the whole matter and didn't mention it to anyone; not out of modesty... this was Poros, and a main road overlooks Bourtzi Island; I did not for one second believe that the drama on the rocks had gone un-noticed, or un-remarked... but simply because I thought that it best became me as a Brit and a professional seaman to say nothing. So I ignored it.

Later in the day I saw the Wild Man being towed off the mud and back to the quay by a water-taxi. Over the next few days, in the mornings, he took up the heavy oars and rowed up the sheltered bay to fish, and in the afternoons he sat morosely contemplating a mediocre catch of tiny fish and his silent engine. He religiously failed to make eye contact when I passed by, I made no initiatives myself, and there the matter rested for a few days, and it was about midday perhaps three days later when the Wild Man cracked.

I was pottering on the dock where, having stopped to chat with some charterers I had met on my peregrinations, our discussions carried us into The

Snail's souvlaki joint for one of those impromptu Poros paralia lunches. The Snail was a wonderful Poros waterfront character, a bear-like maniac with a permanent grin and a truly magical gift for roasting meat. Humorously passionate about absolutely everything he loved, which principally included his family, his nation, his church, his island, fresh local ingredients in his cooking, Olympiakos and Liverpool football clubs, his friends and good whisky, he was largely dismissive of everything else. He ran his *souvlatsidiko* with a ribald eccentricity which Basil Fawlty would have considered bizarre, exuding bonhomie with Stentorian force.

Retaining his nickname from his schooldays, from whence he also retained his charming wife, The Snail was avuncular to tourists, boisterously offensive to those he loved and darkly menacing to those he did not. When Olympiakos or the Greek national team won, he was not above launching whole stacks of plates over the pavement. His grilled meat was tasty and juicy, and his oven-roasts were so tender that they abandoned the bone at the mere sight of the fork. I gradually found myself spending more time in The Snailery than I did at my own room. As I was simultaneously holding forth to my chartering acquaintances and addressing one of The Snail's legendary pork chops, there hove into view a desperate crew consisting of The Wild One himself, Big Savvas and a water-taxi driver called Fotis. It was plainly an assembly constituted to air grievances.

The Wild Man, of course, was the injured party. Fotis, I remembered, had spent time in Australia, so he presumably appeared as interpreter. Glancing nervously at Big Savvas's shovel-sized hands and towering physique, I didn't even want to think about what his function was! All three had evidently taken nourishment before visiting, for they were somewhat unsteady, universally unkempt and decidedly belligerent. Glancing around, I was dismayed to find that The Snail had disappeared on an errand... probably to have a quick, refreshing glass with the butcher, as was his wont. Pity. I could have done with the support of a fraternally-biased grizzly.

To the discomfort of the people I was sitting with, the Wild Man began to state the case for the plaintiff most forcefully.

"Go on!" He roared. "Take it! Take my boat! Take the food from the mouths of my children! Take the legacy of my father! Take it! Go to the port police and just take it! Why do you torture me? You are an animal, a monster! Why do you do this to me?"

To gain a moment or two to think, I affected to have no idea what he was talking about. I surmised that word had gone around that he had been saved by the English sailor and that, fearing that he would have no defence if I made a salvage claim, he had got stoked up and the angst had overflowed. By his understanding of the law, the boat simply became mine, or he had to pay me the full value.

I was not, of course, in the slightest bit interested in his boat. The thought of salvage had never crossed my mind until I realised why he had been behaving the way he had; but, even if I had been mean enough to try to take his boat, or mad enough to risk alienating the whole waterfront community, I reckoned it wasn't worth much more than the equivalent weight of firewood anyway. I had helped the guy out, that was enough for me, but if I was to gain anything out of the affair at all, I was perfectly content that it should be the good opinion of the seafaring community. Well, that, and, of course, my skin intact! And since passions were clearly running very high, I obviously had to handle this carefully.

Greek hospitality to the stranger is legendary, but even legends have their limits. The nation, despite the enormous historical and existential presence it has in the world, is still less than two hundred years old, and one hundred and fifty of those years have been spent in struggle. From the achievement of independence in 1831 to the assimilation of the eastern islands from Italy in 1945, Greece has gradually expanded to assimilate those regions where the dominant... almost the only... culture is Greek. War after war, diplomacy and treaties have gradually brought the Ionian Islands, Epirus, Thrace and Salonika, Crete and finally the Dodecanese within her current boundaries. The struggle with Turkey resulted in a population exchange in the 1920s, Muslims being deported east and Greeks expelled from Asia Minor in reply. This is deeply preserved in the national consciousness, and in the Asian influences in the anarchic, melancholy music of Rebetiko.

Even since the settlement of the current borders, Greece has known unusual political upheaval as monarchists, Venizelist republicans, democrats, communists and military dictators succeeded each other. In the 1950s the country suffered a hideous civil war, and the last military government was only overthrown as recently as 1974. The legacy of these struggles and experiences has left Greeks a little insecure, with a keen sense of injustice and an inbred propensity for revolution, and the foreigner makes light of these at his peril. The same qualities which make Greeks spontaneously joyful and generous can just as quickly make them powerfully resentful if the stimulus is there.

Another thing I had learned in my time in the country was the importance of personal respect. People, especially men, have their pride and this is a no-go area. Northern Europeans often don't understand this well... British people in particular, perhaps because our culture tends to self-deprecation, are apt to underestimate the value of persona... but if you are going to live amongst Greeks then ignoring people's dignity is not a good way to find positive experiences.

In Greece there is a concept called *philotimo*, which translates directly as 'love of honour', but is in fact very difficult to characterize. It is an indistinct quality, and one can have serious arguments attempting to define it, but it seems to me to be a code of conduct, a way of life. It may be expressed in treatment of others, response under adversity, generosity, manners, deportment, and many other ways. The term may also be used to refer to a person's pride, in so far as it refers to their relations with others, and, by extension, to the wounding of that pride. Hurting someone's *philotimo* has the potential to attract a robust response!

My normal means of deflecting anger is with humour, but any attempt at wit, at this moment, would have been an astoundingly bad idea... these chaps were stoked on booze, inflamed by every injustice since the fall of Constantinople, and sensitive that, by their own beliefs and customs, they were in the wrong. If I misjudged this now, I'd be eating my lunch from a hose-pipe up my bum.

Since my detractors were already hyperbolic, I decided that was the language to speak. Calling on my (considerable!) flair for over-acting, I affected utter perplexity.

"Your boat?" I asked, as if in wonder, "What would I do with your boat?" Fotis was really quite fluent.

"You think, just because you tow his boat, you have right to take it? It is the boat of his grandfather!" (I could believe that) "It is the boat that feeds his children!" (I was less inclined to believe that... I had never seen him with any children, and he was the sort of chap, to be frank, that one wouldn't expect to see in the gene-pool unless the chlorination plant was on the blink) "You think, just because you were passing by, that you have the right to take this from him? He not need your help... he is seaman. Son of seaman. He know."

I raised my hands, palms outward, in pacification.

"I am not going to take his boat. I don't want his boat."

"Ha!" exclaimed Fotis, triumphantly, looking around to ensure that this admission had been registered by witnesses. And then his look changed to consternation.

"What?" he demanded.

"I am not going to take his boat. You are talking about salvage money, yes? I don't want it."

Fotis was having trouble with this.

"Why?" he eventually asked, in evident amazement.

My reply was delayed as the Wild Man, comprehending that the conversation had taken an unexpected turn, demanded to be updated in Greek. When I finally got my say, I struck a noble pose and said rather pontifically, "I am a seaman. He is a seaman. We are brothers."

This was translated, and apparently found to have some value. Pursed lips and shrugs indicated that, yes, this might be so, possibly...

"Our enemy is the sea, not each other. We must fight our enemy together. This time, I was able to help you. I do not need money to make me help my brother."

This was accepted. This was hyperbole, and it was also touching on their core beliefs. I was almost speaking their language now.

"Next time," I added wickedly, deciding that I had deflected the worst of the ill-feeling, "Perhaps I will be in danger, and my brother will be as generous to me."

The reaction of the three men to this made it clear that I could expect no such thing. Fotis and the Wild Man started like horses bitten by a snake at the idea, and then looked shifty. Big Savvas, on the other hand, loved it. He roared with laughter and clapped both of his companions hard on the shoulder. Big, big joke! I took care not to smile, but relief flooded through me. If nothing else, I now had the muscle on my side. By keeping my face straight I had, well, kept my face straight! The three of them departed, Savvas perfectly happily and the other two throwing puzzled look over their shoulders as they went.

As far as I was concerned, the matter was closed; but about three days later I was on a boat all on my own, right at the end of the quay. It was a hot afternoon, everyone else was off the streets, and so I was slightly alarmed to see all three men making straight for me. I began edging my hand close to a winch-handle just in case things got ugly, but stopped when I saw the grins on their faces.

The Wild Man was bobbing and smiling like a chap trying to please a child, and Fotis announced grandly that, to thank me for my help, I was invited to the Wild Man's family home for dinner. There would be, I was informed, his brother's famous *tsipouro* and... all expressed reverence and awe at this point... his mother's famous fish soup.

They came to get me that evening, all three of them. We took ouzo at the Blue Ouzerie near Petros' cafe and then walked up into the back streets of the town. Rounding the shoulder of the hill we entered the Brinia neighbourhood, very high up and looking west to the sleeping lady, and here entered a yard above and behind a faded, jaded little house. The yard was untidy, littered here and there with fish-boxes and piled nets, but we lifted a tin table and some chairs out onto the track above and seated ourselves to face towards the setting sun. The rocky peak of Sphaeria behind us was fringed with pines which scented the air, and the view was spectacular.

The tsipouro was an acquired taste, being quite the fieriest and most peppery of its kind that I had yet encountered, but Big Savvas had some pieces of octopus on a small grill, and these tempered the unsophisticated liquor somewhat. I was soon happy enough. I listened gravely as the Wild Man explained, through Fotis, the history and provenance of his boat, and particularly of its treasured single-cylinder engine. He then told me, in detail, how he had never really been in danger off Bourtzi Island, and how he would have handled the matter if I had not arrived. I nodded sagely, as one sea brother to another, whilst he explained the virtues of local knowledge.

Fotis then regaled me with accounts of his time in Australia, and Big Savvas retold, from his own viewpoint, some anecdotes from my pig-roast. For my part, I told them of the Lake District mountains where I had been brought up... *Patrida*, or homeland, is always a subject of interest to Greeks... and explained how I had come to Greece. I did this, as far as my ability allowed, in Greek, which evidently pleased them despite my undoubted mangling of the language. We were a companionable bunch.

Finally a bent, aged lady in a once-black dress which had turned grey with sun and washing appeared in an upstairs window of the house below us and uttered a screech like a banshee who has just had a tax-demand. Big Savvas galloped down to the house and returned with an enormous, battered aluminium pan, climbing with infinite care so as not a drop of the cherished soup should be spilled.

He set it down, and an enormous ladle was used to entirely fill my bowl. Everybody watched as I tried it.

To be honest, my eyes had watered as soon as Savvas took the lid off. It smelled, pungently, of fish... not cooked fish, just fish. The sort of smell you get walking through a fish-market when they have just closed for the day but not yet hosed-down. The soup itself looked like a patch of sea in which a shark had just finished lunch, an opaque, greyish, lack-lustre fluid in which suspicious objects floated, and from which things like fins and bones protruded. I had about as much desire to taste it as I would have had to lick a dustbin clean.

Have courage, I thought, it will be delicious. There are lots of things like this in ethnic cooking... they look and smell repulsive, and taste delicious.

Not, unfortunately, in this case. If did not stretch credulity too far, I would assure the reader that it tasted even worse than it looked. Worse even than the Wild Man looked.

Of course, everyone was watching, and so I called again on my aforementioned powers of acting. Yum, yum, congrats to Mum. Delicious. I gradually emptied the bowl, gagging on scales, bones, and things whose texture made me close my usually vivid imagination down with a clang like a tank-hatch slamming shut. Suddenly the toxic tsipouro tasted infinitely better, and I took to imbibing it at a worrisome rate in an attempt to negate the foul, fishy filth.

Finally I managed to finish it, and of course, I said it was delicious, and of course, they gave me more. I'll tell you one thing... I wouldn't risk another soup like that to save a passenger liner full of naked, nubile nymphomaniac millionairesses: the next time the Wild Man is stuck on a lee-shore in a gale, and I happen to be the only passerby, he dies!

CHAPTER NINE

TAKING THE HEAT

In which the heat is on… Greeks coping with Dog Days… the eternal flame… and how to put it out… how to enjoy Pserimos… briefly to Amorgos… collecting tortoises… familiar paths… disreputation… a trysting we shall go… and quickly come home again… the sage counsel of Dr Manolis… poor recompense.

The year was beginning to advance into summer by now, and in those days before climate change Greece used to get very, very hot indeed about the middle of June. Temperatures would soar into the low- or even mid-forties, and at the first mention of *kavsona,* or heat wave, the country took on a siege mentality.

There was very little air conditioning in private houses, most relying on thick walls and window-shutters to keep the heat out. Even without access to weather forecasts one knew when the sun was coming… the streets filled with people carrying large fans; fans which, with the certainty of people who knew that they had seen the last cloud in May and would not feel rain until at least September, they mounted in the open air with no concern about weatherproofing. Some of the kafeneions erected enormous, oscillating fans with water-nozzles attached, which blasted a fine mist across the clientele… I stayed clear of those; it was cooling, to be sure, but seemed to me the best imaginable way of catching legionnaire's disease, and it felt like being backed-into by a hovercraft.

Direct sunlight was detested. People walked on the shaded side of the street. If forced into the sun they accelerated and held any impromptu sun protection over their heads… briefcases, shopping-bags, newspapers, cardboard boxes, even buckets. In their gardens, vines which covered many pergolas were not yet sufficiently in bloom to provide complete shadow. To supply the want, the most ingenious sunshades were deployed... bed sheets, old sails, lorry tarpaulins, bamboo fencing... as the normally house-proud Greeks abandoned order and neatness entirely in their fervour to avoid the sun. On the waterfront in Poros there was one house that had a military parachute which hung from a balcony, making the place look like a scene out of *The Longest Day*. Finally, as the heat began to peak, the authorities would sent the school kids home and open the air-conditioned schools for old folks.

The anatomy of a hot day was very precisely regulated. Work began early. Business and trade was well in hand by eight o'clock, and the housewives swept, washed and whitewashed energetically. The afternoon meal was often prepared in a personalised *tapsi,* or baking tray, and the kids could be seen taking these to the bakery to be cooked in their oven... even the blistering heat of June will not induce most Greeks to forgo a substantial *yevma,* or midday meal, but only a madman would create heat in his own house.

By about ten o'clock the sun began to bite, and activity slackened. Most deliveries, the re-stocking of shops, bars and restaurants was now complete, and the fishermen had sold the night's catch, washed down their boats, and were spending the proceeds in the *kafeneion*. Doors and shutters, opened to admit the cool of the morning, slammed shut as the heat rose. Awnings were rolled down, water was sprayed around the courtyards, and people scuttled along the shady side of the road to complete their business in town as early as possible.

By midday the Greeks were only to be seen at their place of work or under a shady awning, and by two p.m. all indigenous life-forms disappeared. From then until the sun sank in the west, most people stayed inside or retreated around their houses, keeping in the deepest shade.

After the midday meal came the *mesimerino,* the midday siesta which fell heavily across the land, stopping it like a careless princess's kingdom in a fairytale. Traffic and all music ceased. Dogs and cats evaporated, livestock stood stone-still under the trees. Only the insects thrived... the chirp of the crickets and the rasp of the cicadas crescendoed as the temperature peaked.

Not until the shadows lengthened did the enchantment break. The first activity would be housewives spraying water around their courtyards and balconies to lay the dust and temper the heat; then the workers returned to their toil and the more fortunate went to the beach, there to float contentedly in the cooling sea under enormous, wide-brimmed sun hats. At the end of the quay in Poros lay a set of steps into the sea were all the old ladies of the town used to cool off in the evening. Utterly impervious to the procession of ferries, hydrofoils, yachts and motor boats passing just metres away from them, they floated contentedly under their prophylactic headgear, looking like large mushrooms growing in a paddy-field.

All this was in the towns, of course... the beaches were hives of activity. Tourists were here for the sun and they indulged to satiety, swimming, water-sporting, eating and drinking, and laying themselves out in the blasting rays, as if attempting to one-up the pork they had just had for lunch.

I was somewhat surprised to find how well I handled this warmth. As a seaman I was tolerant of abnormal heat, and could put up with almost any extreme for however long it took; but I didn't usually like high temperatures. I found myself, however, positively enjoying this blast-furnace weather in a way that I never had done in, say, Singapore, or the Persian Gulf.

I think it was the dryness of the heat... there was very little humidity, even in the early hours, and the warmth seemed somehow therapeutic. I would borrow a motorbike and go up into the forests of Poros, or Lemonodassos, or Aegina, breathing deep the pervading scent of pine sap and feeling the wholesome blast of heat radiated from the rocks as I passed them. I seemed to feel it reaching my bones. At times I could feel every individual hair in my nose singeing when I inhaled, which I had only ever felt before in a sauna.

I loved to swim, and to feel the salt drying on my body. I never sunbathe... that requires patience and the ability to do nothing, qualities which I have never possessed or aspired to... but I was perfectly happy to work in the heat of the day and feel the sun on my skin that way. The Greeks thought I was deranged. I liked their heat. They didn't.

* * *

The locals and I may have disagreed about many of the effects of the high temperatures, but on one aspect of it we were in complete accord. Only a loony likes a forest fire.

The land was drying out quickly now, flowers dying and grass bleaching so that, day by day, the greenery was changing to the colour of straw. Baked dry and turned to tinder by the heat of June, the land was ready to blaze at the merest spark and lumbering red-and-yellow firefighting aircraft were now routine features of the otherwise pristine blue sky. Despite the regularity with which their distinctive tractor-engine growl was heard, they never failed to turn the head of every Greek.

Fire was a universal fear, and when the fire planes were seen or heard all conversation would cease as everyone made his own assessment... were they alone, and thus hopefully just patrolling, or were they in company, which usually meant they were heading for a fire? If together, were they heading upwind? This might mean that the fire could be moving towards the watcher. Or were they going downwind, where the fire would move away? Could smoke be seen?

All too frequently the 'planes could be seen working nearby. They were Canadair seaplanes which loaded firefighting water by scooping from the sea, and very often the calm waters of the Bay of Poros would be used for loading the aircraft. The port police boat would clear vessels out of the area whilst the ungainly aircraft banked in over the Methana isthmus and lowered themselves gingerly to the surface.

One quickly learned to spot the veteran crews, who remained fully in flight and merely skimmed the sea with their loading scoops, lifting smoothly back into the air again after about thirty seconds half-enveloped in spray. The less experienced landed completely, their aircraft settling deep in the water and throwing up a great moustache of bow wave; then they taxied fast to fill their tanks before opening their engines with an angry bellow and waddling awkwardly back into the air. Even someone who knew nothing of aircraft could discern the difference in their performance between the almost insouciant banking as they came in empty and the earnest, straightforward effort of heaving their heavy bellies aloft.

Sometimes I was close enough to the fire to watch the aircraft at the point of release, and here too one got a stark reminder of the weight they were carrying. There was usually high ground which served as a height reference, and it was clear to see how the 'planes leapt higher as the cloud of water spewed out behind them.

There was a fascination in watching them work, of course, and many of the foreign visitors treated the spectacle of aircraft skimming the water to load up and then dropping their loads as an entertainment, and at times even expressed disappointment when the fire was out and the 'show' ended. It said a lot for the forbearance of the Greeks, whose houses, families, communities, orchards and livelihood were at risk, that I never saw any of them react negatively to this thoughtless behaviour.

One day that summer I was passing Methana when the fire planes were working a fire perilously close to the harbour at the southern edge of the town. The flatter land close to the sea had been mostly extinguished, and one could see that the fire engines had moved in to deal with the last scattered areas of flame; but Methana is a volcano, so the slopes quickly become sheer but are also fertile. There was a lot of greenery even on the steepest surfaces, and the fire was still going strongly in areas where the aircraft could not pass close enough above to water-bomb it effectively, and where no fire-engine could go. I thought there was no way to prevent it burning the whole face of the mountain, until I saw a fire plane bumbling in from seaward towards the filthy, orange face of the fire.

The aircraft clattered close over my head, trailing faint twin tails of dirty-blue exhaust from its engines, so slow that it seemed to hang in the air and so close that I could see lines of rivets in the hull and a few leaking traces of water from its scoop. Its red-and-yellow colour scheme was muted, grimed with dust and smoke; patches of bare aluminium showed here and there, the engines were stained with streaks of exhaust. The air shuddered to the clatter of bizarrely industrial sounding engines… these always remind me more of a bulldozer with a dodgy silencer than aero engines. The aircraft looked and sounded like a flying tractor; battered, over-worked, about as aeronautical as a blacksmith's back yard, but it also looked earnest, implacable and indestructible. I was irresistibly reminded of Henry V and his 'warriors for the working day'

I watched where the 'plane was going in puzzlement at first, and then with a growing sense of alarm, for it seemed to be flying obliquely towards the cliff, rising slowly as it went. It was almost the same height as the fire and, as it got closer and closer to the roiling smoke and clutching flames, I had a dreadful thought that the controls had failed, and that the aircraft was going to smash into that blazing rock-face. Then, at the last moment, it banked steeply and began to turn, and seconds later, in amazement, I watched as the cloud of water exploded out of the 'plane's belly and flew sideways under the impetus of the turn to spread out over the face of the rock. I saw the flames recoil, the dirty smoke turn to grey steam, and the aircraft, still banking steeply as it cleared the mountain, sink back to the sea to collect another load.

I saw two 'planes dump probably ten loads of water on that mountain in the same fashion that afternoon, and I remember thinking that anyone who treasured images of the Greeks as inept or indolent could learn a lot from the spectacle.

I also remember, very sadly, an occasion when a fire plane crashed at the end of a long day fighting enormous fires in the Peloponnese. The lament for the crew was nationwide, and powerful. Every television channel, every newspaper carried the news as a headline, editorial and feature; everyone knew the names of the dead flyers. It felt as if the entire country had lost a pair of beloved cousins. It was a deeply moving tribute, and I thought it a revealing comment both on the fear of fire and the unity of the nation.

* * *

Pserimos was an island I had not so far visited, so when tasked to bring back a catamaran from thence I went with double willingness: both to discover and also to take a little respite in the rather cooler temperatures of the Aegean.

The voyage there, on a large, old English Channel ferry, was not a lot of fun… it took about fifteen hours for the venerable hulk to make the two-hundred-odd miles from Piraeus to Kos, and at this time of year the overcrowding was starting to get beyond a joke. In addition, the wind had fallen uncharacteristically quiet, and at times the light airs carried the exhaust fumes forward at exactly the same speed as the ship, driving everyone from the decks.

From Kos I caught a day-trip caïque, a rather splendid yellow-and-varnish affair with an enormous, carved eagle in front of the wheel, to Pserimos. I arrived mid-morning, and my catamaran was due in the evening.

Pserimos is a small island lying between Kos and Kalymnos, and barely four miles from the Turkish coast. The caïque deposited me in the main harbour... although calling anything so small a 'main' harbour is possibly the worst descriptive phrase since 'civil servant'... and I can't say that I was overwhelmed. The beach was, however... in fact, I didn't even know there *was* a beach until a large lady went for a swim. The entire tourist population of the Dodecanese appeared to be engaged in a competition to see how many people could fit on one foreshore, and the tavernas were so packed that I had to sit on the wall to drink my beer; so, cursing the Guinness Book of Records, I wandered away from the sea, found a quieter, local *kafeneion*, and spent the afternoon cat-napping over a book.

Descending to the port again at about six in the evening, I was astounded by the change. The noisy arse of the last day-trip boat was just disappearing round the corner, and the only people on the beach were busily raking it clean for the morrow. The tavernas had a pleasant quota of customers, just enough to give a little atmosphere. The little bay looked south-west to a lowering sun framed between the flanks of Kos and Kalymnos, the odd fishing boat puttered idly, and the place could not have been more tranquil or delightful.

A catamaran, which I presumed to be mine, could be seen miles out to sea, so I took a half-kilo of wine in a taverna and spent an hour thoroughly enjoying this delightful little Aegean backwater. I also absorbed an important lesson which I am happy to share with you now: The lesson is... if you like traditional and peaceful surroundings, stay in Pserimos, and visit Kalymnos and Kos by day, NOT the other way around!

The boat, when she finally arrived, was a rather odd looking craft about thirty feet long with the mast set well aft, and she rejoiced in the name of *Mon Goose*. My only experience with catamarans to that point had been sailing Hobie Cats in Australia and Honolulu, and I had been hoping for some of the same sort of exhilaration from the current voyage, but I realised as she came to anchor that I was probably going to be disappointed: *Mon Goose* was privately owned, and she was so loaded with stuff that she sat at the anchorage looking like Steptoe's yard at high tide. Bicycles, barbeques, spare anchors, dinghies, outboard-motors, fuel-cans and even a shopping-trolley were festooned about her decks, and she sat in the water in a solid, determined way which tended to suggest that her interior was probably much the same.

The aquatic pack-rats who part-owned this raft were a genial couple, he broad Lancashire and she equally profoundly Northern Irish, and they were heading back to England for their daughter's wedding. My task was to take their pride-and-joy back to Poros, where another set of the boat's co-owners would expect her in about three days.

'Oh, good,' I thought: 'So there's no hurry... just sixty miles a day, on my own, with no wind, in a boat with the hydrodynamics of an ice-berg.' And then I found out about the engine... a single thirty horse-power unit which acted on a 'leg'... a propeller which was lifted out of the water when not in use. I had heard that many catamarans are not too good at sailing close to the wind, and I suspected that this one wouldn't be able to motor to windward either; it was going to be like pushing a haystack through treacle with a cocktail-muddler.

"Yer shoulda sin 'er in Biscay!" exulted her proud owner. "Eleven knots, she wur deuin'!!"

I managed to smother my retort, which was that I didn't think she could do eleven knots even if she sailed over Niagara Falls.

Blind as the proud owners may have been to the true nature of their boat, however, but they were hospitality personified and made me embarrassingly welcome for the night. Madame laboured mightily in the red-hot galley to produce for us enormous plates of sausage-and-mash with Bisto gravy. The potatoes were further enriched with cheese, onion and butter, a concoction which she called 'Champ', and pronounced to be a great favourite in Ulster. Quite possibly it is, with the freshness of the North Atlantic whistling through your letterbox, but in the baking remnants of a windless June day in the Aegean it was like trying to eat an anvil. The couple's good will, however, was so palpable that I did it the best justice I could, whilst my nose wrinkled under the caress of the delicate scent of fresh fish grilling in the tavernas. Then they made me a bed in a forward cabin. Mrs Mon Goose asked me if I was warm enough, and offered me a blanket, forsooth! I was amazed that she didn't offer to tuck me in.

I got rid of them late morning, driven almost to violence by their kindly "Oh, Ah know what I 'aven't shown yer..." and "Feel free t'elp yerself from't larder." Finally, they climbed onto the day-tripper, and I raced back to *Mon Goose* and hoiked the anchor up before they could swim back to tell me how the can-opener worked. It was sixty-odd miles to Katapola in Amorgos, and I had already lost about six hours.

I should have had a good northerly wind on the beam, but there wasn't a breath of wind to help me. The engine would rev no higher than twenty-two hundred RPM, and *Mon Goose* barely managed five knots.

It was just getting light again as I came in to Katapola. I had been up all night, and spent two hours of that with my head in the engine compartment, cleaning the fuel filter and bleeding the fuel system. The maximum RPM of the engine had steadily fallen until, at sixteen hundred revs and with the engine beginning to overheat, I knew that I had to do something. The fuel filter looked as if it had last been cleaned shortly after the conversion from coal, and the wildlife I evicted from the water strainer would have stocked a respectable aquarium.

That done, the engine perked up enormously, reaching a little over three thousand revs; but unfortunately, her prop wasn't deep enough in the water, and all I did at full throttle was aerate the ocean. We compromised at about two thousand eight hundred, when the boat managed about six knots, and that, I figured, was all I could hope for.

In Katapola I had breakfast with the drunks and night-owls at the all-night café, and watched the day dawn on that remarkable, high and craggy island. Amorgos is your true Cycladic isle, mountainous and remote, fringed with some incredible beaches and garlanded with tortuous roads which cling to precipices and peaks as they loop and swirl from one white, cubic village to another. I would love to have stayed a day, but the stern duty of a skipper demanded sacrifice. Putting all thought of personal indulgence from me, I managed to button hole the fuel truck nice and early. Then I set off to the ferry office.

On the way, I met Charlie and a lady-friend. *Aquafrolic* was in town, and I stopped for a quick coffee and a catch-up.

"Can't stay long," I warned, "I've got to get going again."

"You look loike you'm needin' some sleep, moi lad!" protested Charlie.

"I'll get it on the way."

"You got any crew?" he asked, peering at *Mon Goose* for any other signs of life.

"Not yet," I replied, "I'm just going for a tortoise."

"Tortoise?" Charlie and his lady looked at me with sudden concern, and I hastened to assured them that I hadn't gone doolalli with the heat. I was not talking about the proverbially slow, reptilian kind of tortoise, the kind which looks like a Cornish pasty with legs. There are plenty of those in Greece too, but the sort of tortoise I was after was a girl with a backpack.

* * *

'Tortoises' crawled all over Greece, and in those days they were predominantly female. Enormous packs, which eclipsed their owners so effectively that, from behind, they looked like nylon bags with shapely legs, were to be seen queuing for ferries and busses, tramping in and out of towns, and waiting at airports. For breakfast they congregated around the cheapest bakeries, and for other meals they sought out souvlaki-joints. In the afternoon they slept under trees at the beach. In the evening they looked for shower facilities, often making do with the beach wash-offs, or bathed in streams. At night they often sat around in the parks, the town squares, or returned to the beaches, where they drank retsina and played guitars. Sometimes they took the cheaper pension accommodations on offer, frequently they slept on over-night ferries to the next island, and in high summer many slept rough. On popular islands, like Santorini, Mykonos and Paros, there were people who had given up drinking after seeing a stampede of luggage sweeping majestically across the harbour front.

According to my fairly thorough observations, there were three grades of tortoise. The lowest was a Grade Three, and this was a part-time tortoise, a 'wannabe'. The first characteristic of a Grade Three was the newness of the pack… it would be still bright, with few scuff-marks. In many cases a Grade Three might not even be a real backpack at all, merely a suitcase or grip with shoulder-straps. Grade Threes were only capable of short periods disconnected from society, and they clinked as they walked because their packs were full of cosmetics and labour-saving devices which needed plugging-in to civilisation frequently. Grade Threes had hairdos, and only roughed it between hostels or *pensions*. They wore trainers, carried stereos, called their parents twice a week, and possessed dated return airline tickets. They generally didn't tortoise for more than a month at a time.

Grade Twos were sterner stuff. A Grade Two tortoise was an independent beast, capable of washing its hair in the sea and roughing it for up to a fortnight at a time. The pack told its own story, faded, scuffed and stained, and often spattered with brag-flags and badges advertising where it had been and where it came from. These bags did not clink, unless they had cooking utensils strapped to the outside. They had useful attachments such as rain-covers, or sleeping mats.

Grade Twos brushed their hair straight and tied it back in a pony-tail. They wore hiking boots, some carried musical instruments, and they might stay out most of the summer; but their stay was finite; they eked out their pennies skilfully, and went home when the money ran out. They acknowledged the existence of family by sending a postcard once a week, and usually only called home for birthdays; but they knew that somewhere, if they really needed it, there was a credit card which would fly them home.

Grade Two Tortoises could sleep rough, but they looked for a laundrette once a fortnight, and you could still see the outline of a hair-dryer somewhere in the pack.

No such effeminacies... if that is a real word... were to be found on a Grade One Tortoise, however. Grade Ones were hard women. Boadicea would have minded her P's and Q's around a Grade One.

A Grade One Tortoise was a resolute, self-sufficient, self-assured and self-sustaining professional traveller of experience and resource. The Grade One pack was tough and utilitarian, with locks on every pocket, waterproofed and worn high on the back. It was not adorned with boastful stickers or national symbols... the pack itself proclaimed its provenance, and the prime-mover usually considered herself a Citizen of the World. Grade Ones bathed in the sea, rinsed off with a bottle of water, and dripped dry; they washed clothes in streams or whenever a kindly soul offered facilities; they acknowledged no support system, slept rough without a thought, and when the weather became intolerable they simply moved on to somewhere more clement.

Many Grade Ones cultivated skills with which they could earn a living on the road, and some of these were predictably feminine... hair dressing, jewellery making, bar tending, fortune telling, music making, fruit picking; but Grade Ones didn't go much on stereotypes and I also met mechanics, paramedics, offshore-workers, a helicopter pilot, dog trainers, and a good few capable boat crew. I think quite a few of them taught survival techniques to the SAS.

* * *

I found my tortoises sitting by the ferry ticket office, waiting for it to open. Three of them, Grade Two-C's by my estimation… newly promoted from Grade Three, with slightly faded genuine back packs and still displaying traces of styling in their hair. Their stickers proclaimed them to be Swiss, and their brag-flags suggested that they had travelled thus far via France, Italy, Yugoslavia and Turkey.

The process of engaging my crew was expeditious, to say the least. I asked where they were going; they said Piraeus, because they wanted to go to Epidavros. I asked how much the ferry ticket was; they said three thousand drachs. I told them that I could take them as far as Poros on a boat for free, and from there they could get a bus to Epidavros for a hundred drachs; they shouldered their packs and fell in line behind me.

I suppose that it was about five minutes after leaving Charlie's boat that I passed it going the other way with my three chelonians. The look on his face made my week. I bought some grub at the supermarket and we left straight away.

I was a bit grimy after my night in the engine room, so I motored out of the harbour, stopped to jump over the side and scrubbed up a bit, and then I headed *Mon Goose* for the distant shape of Irakleia. I set the auto-pilot.

"Just before we hit that island, or if any other boat comes close, or if the engine alarm sounds, wake me up. Don't touch anything", I said, and with that I collapsed on the saloon couch and I instantly fell unconscious.

I awoke in some confusion on an unfamiliar couch, with a hand on my shoulder, and a strange, smiling and rather lovely face bending over me. There was singing. There were also bare breasts, large ones. I had been very deeply asleep, and it took me rather longer than it should have to orientate myself.

"Ve are almost at ze island," said the large, naked breasts. Or possibly it was the smiling face.

I emerged into the sunlight to a cheerful rendition of 'Michael Row The Boat Ashore'. My crew were very comfortably installed, it seemed. They had stripped down to bikini bottoms, found a few beers and one had a guitar fired-up. The sea about us was still flat and benign, the engine purred smoothly, Skinnousa was to starboard and the wedge-shape of Irakleia was close ahead, just where I had hoped it would be. I have woken up in worse circumstances.

They were called Herta, Gerta and Berta... well, actually, they probably weren't, but it was something like that... and they were an attractive bunch, each in a very different way. Herta was slim, fair and could drive a guitar. Gerta, plump and dark, had an angelic voice. Berta was statuesque. And, of course, had talking breasts. They offered me a cold beer, and all of a sudden I couldn't quite see why I was in such a hurry to get to Poros.

"Let's go into Irakleia for lunch" I suggested. So we did.

I was welcomed back at the goat and spaghetti restaurant with open arms, and the fact that I had left with one girl and come back with three was the subject of many raised eyebrows and 'Po, po, PO's'. I felt quite the king, sitting like a local under the huge tree in the restaurant forecourt, holding forth to my old acquaintances and my new acolytes.

They didn't have any goat-spaghetti on the go this time, so we just had a meat *poikilia* and a few cans of wine. After a couple of hours we simply moved on again.

We cleared the harbour and headed west-north-west towards Sifnos with a fresh stock of cold beer, and I thought, as Gerta put some sun-block on my shoulders and asked me to do the same for her, what a wonderful life this was: dropping in at familiar islands, meeting friends old and new, lunch here, dinner there, a tortoise or two, a guitar to sing along with, and I was actually being paid for this. Even without being surrounded by naked breasts, I would have had few complaints.

By early evening, I had, however, noticed one thing about my nereids; all their songs seemed to be spiritual ones. At first I barely noticed, and then I supposed that they were simply popular guitar melodies, but as 'Michael Row The Boat Ashore was followed by Oh You'll Never Go To Heaven, Morning Has Broken, Amazing Grace and the like, it eventually dawned on me that there was a religious thread. As far as I could understand their Switzerdeutsch, their German songs were spiritual too. Even the secular songs they knew were hearty, healthy wholesome numbers like The Happy Wanderer, and nothing even slightly risqué. Eventually, emboldened by the evening beers, I mentioned this, and those three pretty girls, sitting almost naked with their beers, informed me that this was a valedictory holiday, as they were going to enter a holy order together when they returned home.

"Ve vill gif ourselves to Gott," smiled Berta.

"Does he really need all three of you?" I demanded, possibly a little petulantly. That amused them, but they seemed to think he did.

By nine o'clock that night we were just north of Sifnos and making excellent time, so I decided that we would stop for a late dinner in Serifos... on consideration, I bore my crew no malice for preferring spiritual to earthly pleasures, which I thought pretty noble of me... and my reward for such altruism was rich indeed; for, as we crossed from Sifnos to Serifos over a glass-flat sea, the water alongside *Mon Goose* suddenly flashed streaks of ice-green and blue. The dolphins I had seen with Clemmie were with us again, and this time they were illuminated by some of the most magnificent bio-luminescence I had ever seen.

Blessing the auto-pilot, we all piled up forward to watch the playful mammals race past our bows, curve back and come again, trailing phosphorescence from their flanks and fins as they wove and dodged each other. The girls almost cried with joy as the sleek backs broke the surface so close that we could feel the spray of their exhalations on our skin.

Anchored in Serifos, we swam to a beach taverna where the girls continued to chatter excitedly about the dolphins over dinner. The restaurant took a relaxed view of dripping wet people in swimsuits turning up for dinner at midnight, making no comment other than the rather practically suggestion that we dried our money on a nearby lamp.

We swam back, got under way again at about three A.M., took it in turns to sleep through the morning, and a little after midday we were anchored close to Poros near Bourtzi Island, which was rather more inviting than the day of my encounter with the Wild Man. There we swam and the girls had a wash before going in to Poros, and so we were all frolicking mother-naked in the cockpit, passing the shower-hose and the shampoo around, when a large boat passed close by; in its stern I saw Yiorgaki, he of the boatful of playful lesbians, giving me a particularly exasperated stare as his respectable, elderly clients looked pointedly elsewhere.

Later I walked the girls up to the ferry quay, where we had a farewell drink and a salad at George's Cafe. Then I received a huge kiss from each one, and put them on a *varkaki*, the taxi-boat to Galatas. Half of Poros, of course, had seen this little display, and this was no accident.

Walking back to tidy up *Mon Goose* I found Gina and Andrea having a drink at Stavros' cafe, and joined them.

"So, who were the ladies?" they asked me archly. I shrugged.

"Picked 'em up in Amorgos. Just crew for the trip, so I could get some kip."

"Oh, yeah? Just crew? Yiorgaki, says you were all butt-naked and chucking water at each other!"

"As a matter of fact," I said, "They were apprentice nuns."

Andrea snorted ouzo down her nose, and Gina said, "Yeah! Right!"

A few minutes later, Yiorgaki himself walked past. This time he shouted, "Thees man is veeery beeeg LUCKY bastard!"

As I had fully intended, no-one believed a word I had said. My reputation was safe for a while.

* * *

About the beginning of July I finally found myself at liberty for a few days in Poros. *Mucky Duck* was again mine, as I had just delivered her back from another excursion, this time to the Ionian. I had three days before setting off to Corfu to bring another boat down to the Saronic… three whole days, on a holiday island which I knew well, and a boat at my command. Fully intending to make hay whilst the sun shone, I repaired immediately to the Jungle Bar.

I am a pub- or cafe-lover rather than a bar-fly, as a rule. I like conversation rather than music, people watching more than dancing; but needs must. Noisy disco bars are no sort of pleasure to a musical diplodocus like me, but it was becoming quite obvious from the lack of approachable ladies in my habitual haunts that, if I was ever to be kissed again, I would have to try the rhythm method; and if, in the pursuit of romance, I occasionally had to embrace pop culture, then the Jungle Bar was an establishment I could tolerate. In fact, in a Stockholm syndrome sort of a way, I almost came to enjoy it after a time.

The Jungle lay far down the South Quay of Poros and was somewhat less purile than most of the bars. It avoided the most egregious of disco tunes… no-one met anyone at the candy store, no salutations were offered to silver linings, the velocity of summer loving passed entirely without comment and people could look elsewhere for assistance spelling 'disco'. Most importantly, Stathis, who acted as the DJ, was a sparing as possible with Lionel Ritchie. From my point of view, this was utterly critical.

'Helloooooo, is it meeeee you're looking fooooor?'

'Indeed it is!' said Julian, as he levelled the flamethrower...

I didn't avoid this sort of music because I didn't like it myself... anyone who has dealt regularly with Nigerian port authorities or Suez Canal bumboatmen can put up with almost any amount of incessant, repetitive acoustic violence... but rather because I didn't think I could communicate with someone who did.

Stathis was a frustrated heavy metal headbanger, but he knew his clientele wanted rhythm and he managed to supply it in a manner which he found just barely acceptable, eking out the essential disco numbers with heavier stuff which increased in frequency as the evening progressed. I didn't exactly come to like it, but I did develop quite a tolerance, especially since it seemed to attract a clientele which I thought I might have an outside chance of doing business with. On the evening in question I struck pay dirt at about ten p.m.

Hèloise was French, and looked it. She had all the usual womanly features... hair, arms, legs, curves... in pleasing proportion and style, and no doubt I could describe them if I put my mind to it; but her immortally imprinted and defining feature was her mouth, which was wide with charmingly bowed and rounded lips permanently elevated at the corners in a gentle, mischievous, pouty smile. Coupled with her slightly hooded dark eyes, that enigmatic mouth gave her a teasing, amused, mysterious character that fascinated and enthralled. You could have put that mouth on the face of a camel chewing rotten cabbage and I'd still have wanted to kiss it.

She was simply, elegantly dressed in a blouse and short, tight skirt, her collar was worn wide open to frame and emphasise a graceful neck, and any cosmetics that might have been in use were discrete about their business. She couldn't have looked more French if she had been wearing a Phrygian cap, carrying a tricolour and leading musketeers over the barricades of a revolting *arrondissement* with her left boob hanging out.

I introduced myself as a '*Rosbif'*, * which amused her straight away. She had an elfin, Audrey Hepburn charm which utterly enslaved me, and a droll sense

---

* Roast Beef... French slang for an Englishman. Some of these Froggies have a bit of a nerve.

of humour which found apparently endless contentment in my whimsical French.*

To my utter delight, Hèloise was only too delighted to escape from the music, and what cared I if it was only so that she could listen more attentively to my linguistic howlers? She was gorgeous, and fun, and I was prepared to make any end of an ass of myself if it kept me in her company. I would have juggled hedgehogs to make her laugh.

We found a comfortable seat in one of the kafeneions, where I managed to delight her with the combination of tsipouro and vanilla ice cream… an inspired blend… and when she leaned forward earnestly in her chair, her chin cupped in her palms, giggling at my jokes, she made me feel that I was the luckiest chap alive.

The moon swam high over Dharditsa, and the surface of the bay sparkled under its silver caress. The mountains around the bay showed clear in the moonlight and the residual heat of the day was a balm. The ambience was perfect for my nefarious purposes, and I was mentally shuffling through a number of carefully prepared 'spontaneous' suggestions which, hopefully, would entice this bewitching creature to a more discrete venue. They all seemed hopelessly cheesy and utterly transparent, however, and translating them into my sort of French would in any case probably render them either incomprehensible or offensive. But the French are skilled in these matters, and I have often found them tolerant and supportive of *Rosbifs* when they struggle to be romantic†. When it became evident that my fecklessness was going to ruin the night if left unchecked, Hèloise gently took my hand between both of hers, looked straight at me and purred, in English with an accent as sweet as an angel's blessing, "Tonight Ah will like to sweem naked."

---

* It is a funny thing, but I have often heard tell that French people, addressed in their own language by a foreigner, have a rather rude propensity to change abruptly to English. It is never so with me, I must say… they seemed fascinated by my French, and hang on my every word.

† Once, at a French airport, I was waiting for a lady with some flowers and a bottle of champagne. A great number of passing women pointed me out to their husbands, who strangely either couldn't make me out or else didn't seem very pleased with me. Eventually, one such lady dragged her grumpy swain over to my table, said "Bravo! Formidable!" and asked me where I was from. When I replied "Angleterre", she recoiled in amazement, crying, "C'est pas possible! Les Anglais sont pas romantiques!"

Taken completely off balance by her straightforwardness, I degenerated into drooling idiocy and asked her, quiet seriously, "Have you got your costume with you?"

Fortunately, she thought this was the wittiest thing she had ever head. She threw back her head, accentuating the slim delicacy of her neck, and emitted a throaty, sexy peal of laughter which instantly earned me the undying hatred of every heterosexual man within earshot. Then she peered briefly down into the open neck of her loose blouse, plucking it forward with both hands and pursing those lovely lips as if considering the matter, and chuckled, "Ah seenk Ah 'ave everysing Ah need!"

My wits returned. The entire pantheon of Olympus appeared to be on my side tonight... not only were my companion and the conditions perfect, but *Mucky Duck* was lying at the end of the quay, and I knew that Spiros would not object if I borrowed her for seductive purposes. Like most Greeks, he was an incurable romantic, and would instantly forgive such a liberty. And if, with a boat at my command and such idyllic conditions in such a beautiful place, I could not woo this lovely, spirited girl, then it was probably of Darwinian importance to human development that my genes should be banned from the pool.

"Would you like to take the boat? We can go to a bay."

Her eyes glistened.

"You 'ave a boat? *Formidable! Ça sera parfait!*"

And so, shortly later, we puttered out of the east end of the channel to pass close to the little fortification on Bourtzi Island. There, finding the sea benign and a gentle northerly wind blowing, I decided on a whim to run down to Tselevinia and anchor in the aquarium-clear water behind Spathi island.

Mucky Duck sailed well enough on just the genoa so I killed the engine and we chattered happily as the Aegean chuckled under the forefoot. The mountains slipped past our starboard side. Hèloise took the wheel, and I sat close to enjoy her perfume and show her how to get the best out of the boat.

I suppose it was about two o'clock in the morning when we sailed into Spathi, where I was delighted to find only one other yacht. We ghosted through the anchorage under sail, disdaining to shatter the peace with the engine, and the gentle ripple of water around the bow merged with the shushing of wavelets on the shore and the intermittent whooping of a scops owl. I anchored us right down at the west end of the little passage, a discrete distance from the other vessel.

I dropped the swimming ladder on the transom, and turned to find Hèloise stepping out of her skirt, utterly composed and without an iota of self-consciousness. She slipped off her knickers with a delightful wriggle, and tossed them at me with a naughty chortle; next she carefully unbuttoned her blouse and removed it slowly. She held it in front of herself, and looked thoughtfully at it for a moment; then she struck a pose. Resting her left hand casually on the enthralling curve of her hip she transferred her weight onto her left leg, giving full definition to her waist and thigh. Her head turned sideways with the chin down, the eyes up and that private half-smile, and she looked at that blouse as if saying goodbye to a beloved but difficult child she was anticipating having a rest from. Then she drew the blouse away to her right, her wrist cocked back and her little finger extended, and followed it with her eyes as she revealed herself to me. For a moment she froze like that, apparently concentrating on the blouse, and for a fleeting instant I shared my cockpit not with Gallic flesh-and-blood but with the alabaster perfection of Ancient Greece, an image worthy of Phidias. I had never seen anything so graceful in all my life. Then she dropped the garment, looked at me sidelong, nodded in apparent acceptance of my stunned, wordless homage, gave me a cheeky grin, and plunged headfirst into the blue-black water.

Her pale, graceful flanks sparkled with bright flashes of bio-luminescence, and I stood mesmerised by the scissoring rhythms of her body as she drove herself adroitly through the sparkling sea.

My mind… what there was of it still at my own command, at any rate… was peripherally aware that a chap of any understanding at all now needed to display equal style and poise. But somehow, communications between the brain and the outlying regions couldn't quite get on the same bicycle that evening. I was only wearing shorts and a shirt, but I felt like a mummy trying to get out of its windings, and when I did finally succeed I managed to hit the water like a windmill toppling off a dyke. I surfaced facing completely the wrong way, with Hèloise's delighted, ringing laughter challenging the immensity of the ocean and the sky directly behind me.

I dived again, driving myself deep, found the indistinct translucence of her body above me and rose slowly to surface again face to face. We trod water for a moment, then our hands met. I pulled her gently to me, and put my arms around her.

She head butted me sharply, and let out a piercing scream.

I recoiled in horror. The scream cleft the peace of the night, rebounded from the rocks and echoed on and on forever, bouncing from the cliffs to the island and back. My mind churned with terrible thoughts… had I somehow hurt her? Had I misread the welcoming signs? Was this… black thought indeed, but things had seemed rather too good to be true… some form of entrapment? And would that bloody scream never die? I didn't know whether to help her or stay the hell away, and I also craned my neck to see if the other boat had taken any notice.

It seemed to take an age, but really it was only seconds before Hèloise swam towards me again. Initially I backed off, but she was almost weeping apologies.

"*Pardonnez moi! Oh, mon pauvre… non, non,* not your fault… *oh! C'est agonie! S'il t'plait, je doit monter. Je dois sortir… oh, oh!*"

She was obviously in considerable pain, and my thought… my discreditably relieved thought… was that she had been stung by a jelly-fish. I took her hand, drew her quickly to the bathing ladder, and cursed the fates as I thought how much I would have enjoyed watching her rise from the sea in any other circumstances.

When I followed her into the cockpit I found her standing, dancing from one foot to the other in great agitation, and in answer to my questions she turned away from me, indicating her back. The moonlight made the problem instantly clear… her buttocks were starkly pale against the darker shade of her back. She was terribly sunburned.

I laid her face down on a towel on the cockpit bench, got a torch and took a look. She was *bien cuit* from the waist to the nape of her neck, and on her shoulders the skin had blistered. No bloody wonder she had been leaning forward in her chair at the *kafeneion*… it now seemed unlikely to have been due to my personal magnetism.

Some of the blisters were open, which I must have done when I put my arms around her, and obviously the salt water was causing her a lot of pain. She was quiet now, but quite rigid and she lay on her elbows with her fingers in her mouth and eyes closed.

I opened a fresh bottle of mineral water and did my best to irrigate the open wounds clear of salt, which apparently gave her some relief. Then I opened the medical box, where I was relieved to find a number of sterile dressings and some painkillers. I put a towel in the ice-box to cool, then administered two tablets to try to ease the pain. I gently dressed the open wounds with the cool sterile dressings, and covered the rest of her back with the cold towel to try to take the heat out of her skin… I could feel it radiating, and when I put the cold towel on, as gently as I could, Hèloïse exhaled so sharply that I thought for a moment it was the towel sizzling. Then I started the engine, hoiked up the anchor, and gave *Mucky Duck*'s game little Perkins engine the spanking of its life as I raced back to Poros. I was concerned about infection getting into the open blisters

All the way back Hèloise apologised, fully aware of how high my hopes had been raised and touchingly remorseful for my abyssal disappointment. She confessed she had felt 'a leetle sore' after her day in a canoe, but had thought it would go away. I moored *Mucky Duck* on the North Quay and helped the poor girl to dress and walk her to the naval base, where there was a doctor on duty.

"You are so sure I need zee docteur?" She asked. "Eet ees feeling a leetle better now… ees it so bad?"

"Yes, it is," I assured her. "I am a *Rosbif,* remember? So are you. I know one when I see one."

The doctor on duty was one Dr Manolis, whom I had already met when assisting one of Spiro's clients. On that occasion he had seemed a very charming and soothing sort, and so I was glad to find him here now; but I soon changed my mind. Our first encounter had been just after his mid-morning ouzo. Freshly disturbed to deal with self-inflicted injuries in the early hours he was not quite such a tolerant creature, and as he dressed Hèloise's wounds he muttered discontentedly. His tone was soothing and did not distress Hèloise, but his words were stilettos and my Greek was unfortunately good enough to understand quite a lot of it.

"*Gamoti illithea! Val' tin sta malaka karvouna, yiati ochi?* " he crooned in a soothing, reassuring tone. "Fucking idiot! Put her on the bloody barbeque, why don't you? She doesn't need medicine, she needs mustard and a bloody salad! What were you after? A fuck or a pork chop?"

A truly sensitive doctor might have asked me to leave the room whilst a lady patient was naked under his care, but Manolis was only just warming to his theme and I suppose he assumed we were an item, so he was quite happy to keep me where I could be an effective butt for his censure. Hèloise seemed to think the combination of his deceptively soothing tone and my presence comforting, so I sighed and put up with him ranting at me, constantly and in the most gentle voice, for not taking better care of my girlfriends.

This, of course, was hideously unjust... I hadn't even met Hèloise until after the sun had set... but when an aggrieved Greek is in advice-giving mode you might as well try to reverse Niagara as reason with him. I stoically endured his castigation for ignorance of solar puissance, lack of education, general stupidity, wilful destruction of the Greek tourist industry and for blatant being a foreigner. His nurse, a pimply young national serviceman, had to leave the room after a while, and could be heard giggling round by the lavatories.

Finally Dr Manolis covered Hèloise with a gown, sat her the wrong way round in a chair so that she could lean forward onto the backrest, and connected her to a saline drip.

"Does the lady speak English?" he asked.

I said she was French. He raised an eyebrow, and asked me in Greek, "Is that why you did this to her? Wasn't Waterloo enough?"

He then switched effortlessly into excellent French, and told her she could go home when the drip was empty. He scribbled a prescription, told her to drink plenty of water, to stay out of the sun, and away from idiots. With that, he went emphatically back to bed.

I took my wounded conquest back to her room at Kanali, and spent the rest of the day popping in to check that she was alright. That evening we ventured as far as the restaurant opposite her apartment and then I walked her chastely back to her door. Before she bad me goodnight, Hèloise gripped my shirt-front in her fists and, drawing my face down to hers, went earnestly to work on me with that soft, sweet mouth. The long, profound and eloquent kiss was one of the most amazing I ever knew; and all it did was torture me with the knowledge of the far greater delights I had been denied by faithless, fickle fate.

The next morning I borrowed a little motorbike and took my Gallic goddess and her bag to the Flying Dolphin... about four minutes of tantalising torment as she put her arms around my waist* and laid her cheek and breasts against my back. Then, with one more kiss, she went home to Normandy.

---

* They almost reached.

My sole consolation from the whole affair was a postcard from Villedieu-Les-Poeles about a fortnight later on which Hèloise had recorded her apologies and eternal thanks to '*un vrai gentilhomme Anglais*'.

Gentleman? That was one misapprehension I fully intended to correct whenever we met again... but of course, we never did. Nuns and *Nons*. Oh, how those Gods must have laughed!

CHAPTER TEN

UNACUSTOMMED AS I AM...

The sterling qualities of Ermioni mud... entertainment cordiale*... I observe an accident from a distance for a change... a damsel in dis-dress... I pass a rigorous interview... customs of the sea... the obliging Porto Xeli... view halloo!!!... woman overboard.*

True to my Second Law of Nautical Recreation, I met Bron through a collision, but there was nothing iniquitous in this. It is my habitual policy always to maintain that accidents aren't my fault, but on this occasion my denial was built on firmer foundations than usual; I was in a taverna when it occurred.

The harbour at Ermioni is noted for its 'holding'... that is to say, the tenaciousness of its mud. Ask any real sailor what he thinks about a port, and he won't tell you about the restaurants, or the berthing fees, or even about the wildlife on the village beach: He will tell you about the 'shelter' and the 'holding'. 'Shelter' is the direction from which, and the extent to which, a boat in the harbour is protected from wind and waves and 'holding' is the adhesive properties of the seabed which keeps it there. And in Ermioni the holding is about as good as it gets... the seabed is an obstinate, possessive sludge which cherishes anchors as a dog does a bone... it snaffles them with the speed of a striking snake, buries them deep, and forgets where it put them.

Ermioni is the on the Peloponnese coast opposite Hydra. The port nestles in the armpit of a narrow spit of land which projects eastward out of the mainland, rather as a thumb projects from a hand, forming a long, narrow bay against the adjacent coast. The harbour, closed off by a concrete mole at the seaward end, looks to have almost perfect all-round protection, and from the open sea this is so; and yet Ermioni cannot be said to have all-round shelter, because when the wind goes into the north-west it tears down the mountains of Didyma and drives white-capped waves pell-mell across the closed end of the bay to hit the mole from the inside.[*]

There is an open quay on the south side of the peninsula which can sometimes be used in northerlies, but no-one really wants to be on an open quay in any strong wind and so, in all except the strongest blows, boats tend to use the harbour and rely on the bulldog-grip of the Ermioni mud to keep them off the mole. And keep them off the mole it does, for if you once get your anchor into that seabed, you will break your chain before you dislodge the pick. You might say that Ermioni is, at bottom, a gripping place to visit.

It was a hot day, bright and clear, but the problematic north-wester was blowing. It was not yet strong enough to be a worry, but it was already a bit of a pest... some of the 'bullets' coming down off the hills were sufficiently powerful to set white caps skimming over the bay and the boats in the harbour jostled and swung as the gusts hit.

This was a matter of very little concern to me as I didn't have a boat; I had come down by ferry to fix a genoa-winch on one of Spiros' smaller yachts and, having failed spectacularly to do so... it was an old aluminium winch, and one of the castings had dissolved beyond any hope of repair... I was buying the clients a consolatory lunch at the *ouzeri* on the waterfront whilst Spiros hustled around Alimos trying to find a replacement which he could put on a hydrofoil.

The clients were a very pleasant bunch, a young French couple with four kids; a serious girl of about fourteen, and three boys who were presumably at liberty only because they were still below the age of criminal responsibility. The family's dismay at the delay quickly evaporated when plied with *mezes* and cold refreshments, and, like Hèloise before them, they apparently found listening to my French to be one of the high points of their holiday[†].

I enjoy entertaining, at least when I can plausibly claim to be unaware that it is for the wrong reason, and so was thoroughly enjoying my filibustering when a large sailing boat of about forty feet entered the harbour looking for a place.

---

[*] There is now a breakwater to reduce the sea from this direction, which helps somewhat, but that wasn't yet built in the eighties.

[†] I confess that, for many years, I thought La Vie En Rose was a song about a pink aeroplane.

A chap on the front of the new arrival prepared the anchor, slacking the chain and then poking with his foot to persuade the reluctant lump of iron to slide out over the roller. Unfortunately, it seems he forgot to put the brake on again, because when the anchor did finally move it grasped the concept of gravity with such alacrity that, by the time the anchor man had hurriedly applied the pawl, it had obviously reached the bottom of the harbour. The boat was still doing about five knots. At that speed, and on such a short scope of chain, an anchor would normally simply have bounced along the seabed, but not in Ermioni. The greedy, glutinous gunk seized that anchor like a politician seizing an excuse, and the yacht stood on its nose.

There was a horribly expensive sounding bang and something took off from the foredeck, curving through the air to end in an ice-bright splash; the yacht pitched steeply forward, then back, then swung rapidly round about ninety degrees, so that the wind came full on her starboard side. The helmsman abandoned the wheel and joined two or three people on the far side poking desperately at something in the water.

Listing slightly and left to her own devices, the boat drifted sideways and landed with an audible 'crunch' across the bow of Spiros' boat. As the wind piped up again she started to grind her port side on our bow-roller, and the world was treated to a rare display of Blatchley attempting to run, grinding up through the gears in the style... and I am eternally grateful to the clients who were kind enough to share their image with me... of a drunken yeti trying to catch the last bus home.

Arriving on board Spiros' boat, I grabbed a couple of fenders and started trying to limit the damage. The parents were preoccupied with their three young storm-troopers, and whatever was in the water on the other side of the other boat was still engrossing her entire crew. The resources at my disposal, therefore, consisted of the girl, who spoke not a word of English.

Spiros' boat was fine, as only the bow-roller was in contact with the larger boat, but the new arrival already had some spectacular scratches on her side. I managed by main force to exert enough pressure on her shrouds to permit my apprentice to slide a fender in horizontally, and then hopped over the pulpit onto the other deck. My intention was to see whether there was enough anchor chain deployed to heave the boat clear; however, I too quickly became primarily concerned with the thing in the water, because it turned out to be a rather attractive young lady.

The rest of the crew were apparently trying to lift the lass by main force, but they weren't achieving much beyond annoying the victim considerably. The bathing ladder at the stern was masked by a caïque, so I quickly made an improvised foot-step by tying a bowline in the end of the genoa sheet and dropping it over the side. Adjusting the height of the loop to water-level, I secured it to a winch at the foot of the mast, and using this as a step the reluctant mermaid managed to get a grip of the toe rail. Bending low, I took her hands one by one and heaved upwards.

She was a willowy creature and rose easily enough, the pressure of her body on mine causing my T-shirt to ride up, until I had her hands level with my ears. In this indecorous position we were locked for a moment, as she felt for a foothold on the toe-rail, and it was at exactly this point that the upward strain on her arms popped her breasts neatly out of her strapless sundress.

Suddenly sharply aware of a dramatic change in the texture of that part of the lady which was now firmly in contact with my belly, I nearly choked as I stifled a snort of amusement and lifted my eyes heavenward in a vain attempt to pretend I hadn't noticed. I doubt if it conveyed much conviction. And, on further consideration, if it did, it may have been received with mixed emotions.

We were now in something of an *impasse*. I couldn't… either physically or morally… lift her any higher; and she was having trouble getting a foothold. I couldn't drag her inboard, as the lifeline was between us. So I hung on, feeling the strength starting to ebb in my arms but increasingly aware of rather more pleasurable sensations in my belly as she jiggled and wriggled, trying to get a leg over the railing.

I don't know how long we indulged in this bizarre embrace, with myself considering whether it might not be the best thing all round if I were to lob her back in the harbour; but just before my strength failed me the helmsman insinuated himself into our *ménage*. Grabbing the lady's leg and lifting it over the rail, he sort of rotated both of us until the she could sit on the cabin-top. Everyone else, the boat's crew, the French family and a couple of fishermen, were sniggering. I feigned interest in something at the top of the mast, until the victim said wryly, "You can look now!"

I did, cautiously. Tried to make eye contact only, and never came close. Her top was back in place, but one could see why it had failed... frankly, it was working for its living.

"Thank you very much!"

She was fully aware of my flickering gaze, and indulged me with a wicked grin and a tiny wiggle of her recaptured appendages. The voice was dainty, cheeky and Welsh.

"Worth saving, I hope?"

I deliberately misunderstood that.

"Who knows, you might find a cure for cancer one day!"

"I might indeed... if someone was smuggling it. I'm a customs officer, see."

They all laughed. British customs officers to a man, on a works outing.

Using a line from the next mole we dragged Her Majesty's Finest off Spiros' boat, and got their anchor set. This had to be done using the cockpit winches, as their windlass had disintegrated in the unequal fight with the Ermioni mud... the shiny bit which I had seen arcing into the harbour was the pawl. I had a look at the toothless remains with Bron, my erstwhile dancing partner, and Geoff, the skipper.

There was nothing to be done. The cast metal of the winch-body had fractured where the pawl attached, also detaching one end of the brake-band. It was a hand-powered winch, and without the pawl it couldn't heave in. Geoff asked me if I could explain it to the charter company, as he didn't know all the names. The company was in England.

In those days in Greece, making international phone calls was an arcane art. You went either to the O.T.E., the telephone company, or more commonly, to a *periptero*... a street-side kiosk. There was an exaggerated displaying of metres being reset to zero, and then you started dialling. Here was where a person of nervous disposition with urgent business could easily run barking mad.

The phones were pulse-dial types, and the occasions on which the call went through on the first dialling could be counted on the fingers of Admiral Nelson's right hand. There were various theories on how best to defeat the system... some advocated speed but the general wisdom was that you should dial each number at the very instant that the last click of the preceding number sounded. That worked as often as anything else, if you could count fast enough.

Time of day was important too… in the early evening, when the Greeks were awake and the tourists were just back from the beach, you might as well try to talk to the Pharaohs across the Styx as your mum in Chipping Sodbury, and a three-page fax could end up costing fractionally more than a first-folio Shakespeare. But on a good day, in the afternoon when people were mostly eating, resting or sun bathing, you might get through on the sixth or seventh attempt.

When I did make it, my response was a breezy, laconic, mannered voice with just a hint of West Country about it which claimed to belong to one Rory Carteret and asked me "To whom am I speaking, please?"

I think it was the first time I had ever been 'whom'ed' by a telephone.

I explained my mission, and described the problem. Mr Carteret displayed a good practical knowledge of the windlass in question, and in a staccato exchange of questions and answers we efficiently established that the winch had nothing further to offer the general progress of mankind unless it became a door stop.

"Thank you so much for helping, and forgive me asking, but are you a professional skipper?"

I replied, with the utmost complacence, that I was, and that appeared to be the end of the interview.

"I wonder, if I can get a new windlass to you, would you be available to fit it for them, and get them on their way as soon as possible? We would of course pay you for your time, and any travel."

I said that I would.

"We have an associate in Alimos Marina who should be able to get a windlass today… can you take down a couple of telephone numbers?"

I jotted down the first one, and found myself looking at the very familiar series of digits which connected one… quite often… with Lefteris' souvlaki shop on Amfitheas Street. This was followed inevitably by the Alimos hotel bar. I was therefore completely prepared when the associate turned out to be none other than the ubiquitous and multi-functional Spiros Thallasodoros.

"Don't worry," I assured Mr Carteret, "I know Spiros. In fact, I'm expecting him to call me within the hour."

"Well, that's a result!" enthused the telephone. "If you know Spiros, I can just send your money via him."

"If it's all the same to you," I hastily interjected, "I'd rather you just sent a cheque to my home address in UK."

The bellow of laughter which erupted from the handset turned heads across the road.

"Ah! I see that you DO know Spiros!" it chortled. "Okey doke, pip pip, job's a jaffa, drop me a line if there are any problems." He gave me a fax number, signed off with a hearty 'Toodle-oo!' and hung up.

Spiros managed to send me a 'new' winch for the French family's boat by an afternoon hydrofoil, and by early evening I had installed and tested it. They were free to continue, and set off immediately for the nearby island of Dokos to spend the night in a bay. The anchor winch, though, proved harder to find, and by the time Spiros had located a suitable replacement there were no more ferries to Ermioni that day. It was agreed that he would send it instead by taxi to the mainland harbour of Porto Xeli, about fifteen miles further down the coast, and I should take a hotel for the night, sail down with the boat in the morning, and fit the winch in the afternoon. And thus it was that I sailed the next morning with a boat load of my mortal enemies.

* * *

The British Merchant Navy has been at war with Her Majesty's Customs and Excise service since about quarter-past nine on the morning of the day the very first excise-man put on his uniform, and the subsequent hundreds of years of incessant mutual antagonism have transformed a rational, proportionate contest into fervent tribal combat in which no blow is too low, no stratagem too vile and no victory too Pyrrhic.

As in any worthwhile sectarian feud, the origins, long obscured by time and distorted by chauvinist rhetoric, have become utterly insignificant. The war is perpetuated for its own sake... and just for the fun of it, here is the British sailor's point of view.

Some seamen probably were... and probably still are... smugglers in the full moral sense of the word: conscienceless, evil-minded criminals bringing in saleable quantities of dutiable or prohibited goods for illicit gain or nefarious purposes. We didn't know them, we had never met them, we didn't approve of them, and anyway they were probably foreigners. And that, we strongly felt, was where Customs ought to have been spending their time... rummaging foreigners.

We, of course, were not smugglers... bringing home a few thousand fags or a couple of hundred Havanas to smoke on leave... well, that isn't smuggling, is it? Or dropping off a couple of cases of spirits for the landlord of the King's Head? Or taking home a few stereos for the family? A sailor was away from home for months, years sometimes, so it was only fair that he could bring more swag back to the country; after all, in those days people could go to the continent for a day-trip and return with a larger European Union duty-free haul than we could bring back after a year in the Pacific. It stood to reason we had to be allowed some latitude, we were a special case and clearly the excise laws weren't intended for *us*.

Then there were things like Citizens Band radios, which were prohibited in Britain despite the fact that everyone under the age of thirty had one in his car... it was for safety, wasn't it, and how else was one supposed to get them if they were not available in the shops?

H. M. Customs, regrettably, took a divergent view on all these issues, and far from exempting us from their attentions they seemed rather to circle like vultures over a wounded buffalo at the first glimpse of a Red Ensign coming up the river. They insisted on treating us... *us!*... like criminals, and plagued us so zealously that it seemed they hardly bothered with foreign ships at all. Oh, it was enough to make the blood boil! Why couldn't they spend their valuable time annoying dishonest foreigners, for Pete's sake? Purely in the spirit of teaching the swine a lesson, sailors considered it a moral duty to put one over The Revenue.

Intense as it was, however, this battle was fought on a narrow front. The relationship between seamen and the customs officials in British airports, for instance, was nothing short of cordial. There, excise-men seemed to have some sympathy for sailors who had been away for months at a time, and in turn the seamen couldn't get too outrageous as they were limited to what they could physically carry. At airports we made our profession obvious, and many were the tales of generous, lenient treatment.

However, when Jolly Jack turns up on a ship in a British sea-port he has the extravagantly honeycombed bowels of an entire vessel in which to hide his plunder, and cranes to offload it, and there he is greeted not by indulgent, avuncular well-wishers in collars and ties, but rather is confronted by the 'Black Gang'. Officially known as a Rummage Squad, this is a grim platoon of humourless professional snoops, heavily armed with flashlights, sniffer dogs, bristling tool belts, mirrors-on-sticks and an assortment of electronic wotsits. Frankly, you could find more mercy in a firing-squad.

Ships were dirty places in those days, and those who sought to uphold the command 'England expects that every man will pay his duty' wore black overalls to hide the grime they accumulated when fossicking in the crannies of vessels; but there wasn't a British sailor alive who didn't devoutly believe that the Black Gang were named not for the colour or their dress, but for that of their hearts. And of all the rummage squads on the British coast, the hearts of the Liverpool Black Gang were, by common consent, considered to be the most Stygian.

Merchant Navy folklore has it that Liverpool is where they train the youngsters; where the most malevolent and remorseless older hands impart their low cunning to, and expunge all vestige of trust or decency from, the recruits. Over dinner I learned that my new shipmates were all members of the Liverpool Black Gang.

* * *

The harbour of Ermioni is only a short walk over the ridge of the town from the South Quay, and here the restaurants have a charming view of the sunset over the mountains of the Peloponnese mainland. To this panorama I led my party, an action which grieved the owner of a hotel and restaurant in the harbour so much that he chased me up the road and tried to remonstrate. The only thing his performance achieved was losing him my custom as a lodger as well, and on the way up the hill I engaged a room at a small *pension* up in the town… I didn't even bother to look at the room, having no baggage or toiletries to leave, and the proprietor gave no indication that he found this at all unusual. Without even asking my name he pocketed his modest fee and handed me a key with a grave nod of thanks.

We ate juicy, grilled kalamari, crisp chips and a village salad, washed it down with a few *kanatas* of decent rosé and skirted playfully around the subject of smuggling as the sun set flaming orange and then blood-red behind the serrated skyline of the Peloponnese.

In the taverna I sat next to Bron by chance, and we chattered away quite happily… she was new to sailing, but loving every minute of it, and full of questions. She was as chirpy as a chaffinch, black haired and dark eyed, and when we moved to the subsequent *kafeneion* there was nothing chance about my sitting next to her again; I held her chair for her, and claimed the adjacent one with all the tact of a prop forward approaching the bar after a hard game.

By the end of the night Bron was leaning towards me sufficiently that I was regretting not having had time for a shower, smiling a lot and twirling a finger playfully in a strand of hair over her ear. Her tinkling laughter rang like a bicycle-bell through the subdued murmur of the evening. I had the highest of hopes... and the profoundest of falls, because at the witching-hour she gathered her paraphernalia, gave me a sisterly peck on the cheek and, with the other two girls in the crew, she Cinderella'ed into the night. The gents stayed somewhat longer, and over the late-night drinks the talk turned increasingly to our common enmity. We chuckled far into the night at tales of smuggling done, and smuggling dished.

I longed to tell the tale of Captain... well, no names, no pack-drill; but anyway, a shipmaster I once sailed with. On the day when he left the ship to go on leave, his wife came to collect him. Entering the dock gates, of course, she was not an object of suspicion... smugglers go away from ships, not towards them, after all... and no-one looked in her handbag. On the way out, she stopped the car at the gate and the back was duly inspected, revealing nothing more than the captain's suitcase and a normal allowance of duty-frees. A quick look was taken under the bonnet, and a customs officer took the spare tyre off the back door and bounced it a couple of times, to make sure it was not packed with something illicit. Finally a couple of mirrors were waggled under the vehicle briefly before the car was waved through. The captain's wife pulled the Land Rover expertly out onto the road and disappeared in the general direction of Yorkshire.

If a customs officer *had* searched her handbag on the way in, he would have found a pair of vehicle registration plates. He might also have noticed that she had arrived in a taxi.

I didn't tell that one... I might want to use it myself some day; but we did find some tales we could laugh at. I told them of the time we had managed to get four cases of Four Bells navy rum[*] ashore and onto the Gladstone Dock quay in their very own bailiwick of Liverpool. At the inopportune arrival of

---

[*] At that time an export-only brand, much prized amongst a sea-going clientele and for which knowing harbour-side publicans would pay handsomely. When I first went to sea, the duty-free price was eighty-four pence a bottle, so spectacular profits could accrue.

the dreaded blue mini-van with the portcullis emblem on the door, we had swiftly stacked the boxes on a convenient pallet so that it looked like cargo waiting to be loaded. By the time the van cruised suspiciously by, we were innocently having a smoke and a chat. Turning again as it disappeared we were just in time to see our booze being lifted high into the air and swung into number four hatch, where it was duly placed in the bonded locker and sealed. We were about forty quid… a month's pay for an apprentice… out of pocket, and some lucky swine in Papua New Guinea was roughly two months away from a very pleasant surprise.

Another tale concerned a 'channel fever' party. In those days of long contracts on ships, channel fever was the madness which gripped British seamen when the English Channel hove in view and the imminence of family, home and leisure changed people's natures dramatically. Its effects varied from person to person… some became withdrawn, others effervescent, but few remained unaffected once 'a dose of the channels' took hold.

Once upon a time, safely tied up in the King George Dock in Hull after a nine-month trip to the South Pacific and back, a boisterous party had been celebrating the climax of the channel fever outbreak in the Fourth Engineer's cabin whilst awaiting the bus bringing our reliefs. We were in ebullient mood, and when a customs officer in his Great Escape 'ferret' overalls appeared we gave him a good amount of cheerful cheek.

The customs man ignored us stonily, and stepped amongst us, peering thoughtfully at the pipes running through the top of the cabin. Then he departed. We hooted disparagingly at his back but moments later he returned, indicating a pipe about four inches in diameter with his heavy screwdriver.

"What's this pipe, then?" he demanded. We peered at it, shrugging… it was a bit odd, as it had rings around it at intervals.

"Looks like ventilation," said the Fourth Engineer unconcernedly.

"Well, it doesn't go through the bulkhead!" said the now gleeful customs officer. "Funny ventilation trunk, that!"

We filed out into the next cabin, and sure enough… no pipe. The Fourth was looking concerned now… it was his cabin.

"I dunno…" he said; but that customs officer… not lacking, it must be said, in a sense of the theatrical, peeled his lips back in a Hannibal Lecter grin, raised his eyebrows, placed his hands on the suspicious tube, paused a moment for full effect, and gave it a sharp tug. It split in two places and a shower of cigarettes fell to the deck. The 'pipe' was a series of circular tins of cigarettes, stuck together lid-to-base, and given several coats of paint.

"Whose are these, then?" enquired the delighted official.

"They're not mine! I don't even smoke!" protested the Fourth, who had a ticket for a train home that afternoon and was rapidly becoming aware that the station which figured in his immediate future was more likely to contain policemen than trains.

"Well, sir, I suppose you were meaning to sell them, then? I'm afraid we take an even dimmer view of that."

He called down the alleyway, "Bob! You got a minute?" and then enjoyed the Fourth's incoherent and utterly unconvincing protestations for a few moments until a grizzled crew-cut wrapped around a cynical grin appeared in the doorway.

"Ah! What have we here, then?" it growled jovially. "Ahh, I see… a little something we forgot to put on the crew declaration, is it?"

"They ain't bloody mine!" muttered the Fourth disconsolately, but he was running out of conviction… or, more likely, running into one.

"No, no, of course not… someone just put them up in your cabin, gave them three or four coats of paint… coats of *smelly* paint… without you knowing a thing about it, didn't they?" said Grizzly, sympathetically. "Could happen to anyone, that could."

He paused a moment, and then scooped up one of the tins and a handful of the cigarettes. He peered intelligently into the former, sniffed the latter, and then gently crumbled one of the gaspers between thumb and forefinger. It disintegrated into dry dust.

"Tins of fifty Gold Flake," he announced, confidently. "They haven't made them for almost twenty years, I should think. They've probably been there since the ship was new… this isn't smuggling, it's bloody tomb-robbing! You have a good leave, son."

They both disappeared, looking unbearably smug and displaying an intolerable jollity in the swing of their torches.

We all, of course, knew the matches story. It is a bit of an old classic. Back in those days, ship's engine-rooms still often had water swilling around in the bilges. No-one wanted to get involved with that… very nasty business, all kinds of muck and sharp edges lurked in there... so the ship's engineers liked to use the bilge to conceal bottles of spirits. They would wrap a piece of lead around the bottle to make sure it sank, and then attach a match to the neck using fishing line. A customs man looking into the bilge would see only an innocent match floating, if he saw anything at all, and the bottle could easily be retrieved by picking up the match and pulling the fishing line. The problem was, this had been going on for quite a while, and the trick wasn't as novel as it had once been. Customs men like a joke as much as anyone else, so whenever they saw a sliver of wood floating in a bilge they emptied in another two or three packs of Swan Vestas and wandered off grinning, leaving a blaspheming tribe of furious engineers wading around in knee-deep filth picking up hundreds of matches one after another to save their investments.

A good night was had by all, and many risible tales were told of victories and defeats in the interminable war. And the guard was never completely lowered, and notes were being taken.

* * *

The next morning we breakfasted on board... a further trial to the grumpy restaurateur, who now looked as if he was fixing my face indelibly in his memory and consigning it to his personal seventh level of Hell. Then we departed early with a modest northerly wind.

We bubbled steadily through the narrow passage between the mainland and the island of Dokos and lost the wind half way to Spetses. Bron was again very attentive, and she and the other two girls took the opportunity to learn a bit of sailing until the breeze failed; then we continued with navigation... lessons which the men also attended to, but in a slantendicular manner, whilst earnestly giving the impression of being engrossed in something far away. Through all this, Bron was very close by my side and frequently laid her hand on my arm... all very promising stuff, and despite her lamented early departure the night before my hopes rekindled that she was not indifferent to me. My own partiality could, of course, be taken for granted; I have a sociable nature and quite often develop a liking for girls, even those who have not massaged my belly with their breasts.

We had a quick swim in one of the lovely, fir-scented, sylvan bays which line the entrance to Porto Xeli, and were tied up by lunchtime.

I had never been in Porto Xeli* before. It is set in low, rolling hills on the mainland of the Peloponnese, facing south across the straits to Spetses; and although it has neither the charming Mediterranean architecture of that island nor the grandeur of the nearby coast, it quickly revealed itself to be a homely place.

Little could be seen of the port from seaward, as it is entered by a deep channel whose edges are scalloped with a number of gorgeous bays set in vibrantly green woodland. The coast in the approaches to the entrance was liberally adorned with villas, many of them palatial affairs boasting helipads and berths for enormous yachts, from which the great and wealthy of many nations enjoyed, doubtlessly with extreme comfort and complaisance, the view over Spetses and down the Arcadian coast. This set our expectations for Porto Xeli to be a chic, Saint Tropez-style bijou-sort of a place like Hydra or Spetses… expectations which couldn't have been more wrong.

Emerging from the verdant, rural charm of the channel, Porto Xeli opened out as a large, almost circular bay around which the town sprawled; a hotchpotch of construction styles ranging from substantial, square hotel-blocks to traditional ceramic-tiled cottages. The anarchic architecture was accentuated by a number of rooftop advertising hoardings which would have looked more at home in Athens, or even Times Square, than in a Greek port. The surrounding land was not high and sloped gently, so once the delightful wooded entrance channel was behind us there was little green or spectacular to be seen, just buildings on every side. It was a very far cry from the distinctly Mediterranean styles of the adjacent islands, and possibly even a disappointment at first sight; but a church here, a Greek flag there and a scattering of tiled roofs gave it a sufficiently local, if rather urban, flavour.

Despite the utilitarian nature of the place, however, a yachtsman entering Porto Xeli quickly developed a sense of belonging, for the bay obviously offered perfect shelter and it seemed to be almost filled with pleasure craft. There were many boats in the anchorage, butterfly-bright sailing dinghies

---

* Pronounced Pórto Heli, with a guttural 'H'.

scissored the surface of the bay, speed-boats fizzed in and out, and the immensely long quay was well-populated with everything from fishing boats through massive luxury yachts to charter -boats. And Porto Xeli also has 'good holding'. Very good holding. In fact, if Ermioni's mud may be termed possessive, then that of Porto Xeli is obsessive-compulsive.

The waterfront was a substantial open park area, with cut grass and a good number of mature trees, and was inhabited by a boisterous pack of large stray dogs who happily adopted us as we explored and foraged for lunch. The town appeared, above all, to be alive, and once we tied up and got ashore a few more characteristics of Porto Xeli become evident.

Our first impression was of bakeries, supermarkets, fishing tackle shops, modern styled *kafeneions* and, above all, estate agents. Property sales showrooms and architects offices seemed to be everywhere. The wide street was a perfect sun-trap which amplified the power of the sunshine until it baked a man's bones, and all traffic along the waterfront took place in the shade of the trees at the edge of the grassy park. In this shade there lurked a series of hulking *peripteros*, kiosks with a yearning for *lebensraum*, which had flung out awnings, magazine racks and refrigerators in all directions until they more resembled Bedouin encampments than mere booths.

Porto Xeli was something of a service centre, it seemed: it lay at the heart of a rolling, rural olive-farming district which had become a booming holiday home area, and here Greeks and foreigners alike had built their dreams and other people's nightmares amongst olive groves with spectacular views across Spetses, Ermioni or the Peloponnesian coast. Builders buzzed like bees, electricians and plumbers swarmed. Hardware shops thrived, water- and septic-tank trucks roared around the paralia day and night, and every second shop seemed to house either an architect or an estate agent.

A very wide range of offcomers had made their homes around the bays, and one consequence of this cosmopolitan populace was that the rather ordinary looking supermarkets were found to contain some rather extraordinary fare... Krug, Dom Perignon, Veuve Cliquot; some very decent Bordeaux carefully racked in temperature controlled cabinets; Brie and Camembert; prosciutto; Havana cigars. These were unheard of luxuries in the normal Greek supermarkets of the time, and I emerged deliriously from one emporium clutching two bottles of Bechevelle, a door-step of mature

Cheddar, four tins of English mustard powder and a carrier bag full of tinned baked beans.*

Coupled with the holiday home trade, Porto Xeli also had some decent beaches suitable for resorts and, of course, an almost perfect harbour. This made it a natural terminus for the Argo-Saronic ferries bringing people from Piraeus, an almost ideal water sports centre, and a fabulous base for a yachtsman at the heart of a magnificent cruising ground. A boat yard and several chandleries prospered, and what they didn't have could usually arrive from Athens by ferry or taxi the same day, if ordered before lunch. Porto Xeli, slightly scruffy, unpretentious, infinitely obliging and noticeably cheaper than the islands, appeared to us to be onto a very good thing.

There were a number of respectable looking eateries about the town. We finally settled for an *ovelistirio*… a restaurant which specialises in cooking on a charcoal grill… slightly raised up above the north end of the quay with a shady tree to sit under and a pleasant view across the bustling harbour. By night, it seemed, they had fine things to offer. A whole roast sucking pig was turning dreamily on the grill, and we were enthusiastically shown joints of lamb roasting in the ovens; but the lunch fare was cooked-to-order. The sight of the word *loukaniko* on the menu prompted a grateful memory of that reassuring meal on the Piraeus waterfront some months earlier, and on a whim I chose sausages.

Now, even my mother, I think, would tend to the view that the sight of me enjoying sausages is not one which could inspire anyone (except a hungry dog) to love me; but nevertheless it is a fact that, after lunch, when the crew took the dinghy and buzzed off in search of a beach, Bron decided to remain with me and pass me spanners and cold refreshments whilst I wrested the old windlass out of its tenacious silicon bed and fitted the new one.

When the rest of the gang returned we were absent without leave in one of the cafes, and by the time Geoff had tracked us down we were suspiciously close together over an aperitif, giggling without due care and attention at each other's stories. I had been extolling the virtues of the nearby Peloponnesian coast, and a plan was hatching; Bron was intending to ask her compatriots if

---

*   Out of consideration for my fellow man, I don't eat baked beans myself; but other Brits
    in Greece used to long for them, and they were scarce. As currency within the ex-pat
    community, they were the equivalent of bullion.

I could accompany the expedition for another day or so as a 'guide' whilst we got to know each other better. It was a proposal of most infinite charm and appeal; but, in a dogged continuance of my ill-fortune in the pursuit of romance, one which never saw the light of day.

"There you are!" cried Geoff, "I just tried the winch... works fine, thanks!"

"The Merchant Navy is delighted to be of assistance!"

"I've just spoken to Rory," continued Geoff; "He's asked me to settle up with you here... cuts out the middle man, I s'pose. We'll end up paying it anyway, as we bust the winch."

This was a most refreshing and welcome initiative, and I graciously accepted a gratifyingly substantial fistful of thousand drachma notes.

"Rory also asked if you could give him a call as soon as possible," added Geoff, and signalled for a waiter.

I got through on the thirteenth attempt.

"Thanks very much, the client's very happy!" enthused Rory, "Now, listen, if you are interested, I have another job for you."

I steeled myself to decline. With the prospect of a couple of days with a Welsh enchantress in prospect, I wasn't about to be deflected by the opportunity to earn five thousand drachmae for fixing someone's toilet... known in the yachting business as 'going through the motions'. But it wasn't a repair job; it was a charter.

A charter. And not just any charter, but a rescue... a family, caught by strong weather in the Aegean, were in need of a skipper as soon as could be arranged. Make a good job of this one, Rory promised, and more would follow. By going, I would not only be indulging my penchant for helping people but taking a huge leap along the path from being a jobbing boat-bum to a gainfully employed charter skipper. I had to go... but those bloody Gods had me again. Another fascinating woman was about to sail the opposite way out of my life, leaving no more than a whisp of scent and a Wirral phone-number.

CHAPTER ELEVEN

EN-DEERING MYSELF

In which we find Fourni... an upright family... a corrupt official... nefarious negotiations... civic atrocities... Hellenic dance, a critical summary... the debauch of the Righteous... En-Deering myself... who laughs last?

Fourni is not easy to get to. Having callously deserted my paramour on a distant shore I packed my gear in Poros and endured a fond farewell from Kyria Fotini, who was so enraptured by a house guest for the whole summer who paid monthly in advance that she appeared to have adopted me. Then I caught the old pantouffle *Apostolos P* up to Piraeus and once again found myself on the creaking old ferry to Samos.

A strong northerly wind was blowing in the Aegean, as it very often does, and the ageing ship rolled extravagantly as she passed the gaps between the islands, through which the seas rolled down all the way from the Thracian coast.

Keeping as far as I could from the many unwell tourists, I eventually landed again in Vathi, which I had last seen through a haze of roasting lamb- and goat- fumes on Easter Sunday. From there I went by bus through the resin-scented pine forests on the mountains of Samos to the little south coast port of Milopotamus, and finally on a tiny, 2-car ferry which corkscrewed alarmingly down to Fourni.

It had taken me a while simply to find Fourni on a chart. It is situated just to the south of the gap between Samos and Ikaria, close to the Turkish coast. A Rorsach blob of an archipelago, it is composed of two principle islands which are so close to each other that, at first glance, they appear to be one fantastically-shaped one. To my eccentric imagination, Fourni appears on a map as having the shape of a lobster, a long central body linked by thin arms to two bulky claws. The port lies approximately in the lobster's left ear-hole, facing west to see what he has picked up in his left clipper.

The approaches to the port form an unusually spacious anchorage by Aegean standards. There is decent shelter, good holding and good depth in the lee of Akra Paleomilos, and this makes the isolated Fourni Islands an unlikely haven for a large fishing fleet... and by that I do not mean the picturesque, gaily-painted little *caïques* of the part-time fishermen which cannot be kept off the postcards. Fourni is home to serious, open water boats, a mixture of large traditional *caïques* and modern steel designs, all with powerful, up-to-date deck equipment and massive nets, uniformly scarred and stained by constant confrontation with the elements.

The appearance of this workaday armada in so rugged, wild and unspoiled an environment was a bit of a shock to me, but the town, behind a charming beach lined with trees, was a pristine delight. Not until I landed did I realise that the shore was lined with large freezer-stores; for they were low, flat-roofed, white-painted structures set about with trees and they fitted in amazingly well with the quaint, traditional village behind.

There was a single jetty in front of the town, one side of which was reserved for fishing boats to unload, and on the other lay two yachts. One of these was the one I had come to find... a forty-foot Sun Fizz containing the family of one Dr Deering.

It seemed to me that Dr Deering, a bespectacled, medium sized chap with thinning sandy hair and a light complexion which had been turned classic crayfish-orange by the sun, couldn't quite make up his mind whether he was pleased to see me or not. Certainly, if I expected to be hailed as a saviour, I was quickly disabused of the idea, for my greeting was a perfunctory, business-like affair; polite but impersonal. His handshake had the softness of a man who goes out of his way to emphasise that he is intellectual planes above alpha male knuckle-crushing contests: civilised, scientific, analytical, remote. I regret to say that it did him little good... skippering and alpha male behaviour are a bit like party political broadcasts and nausea... you rarely get one without the other. By the time I had interpreted the handshake, he was already massaging the blood back into his fingers and looking at me as if I had escaped from the high security wing of a zoo.

The good doctor (of chemistry, I was quickly informed, presumably in case I was secreting a festering boil about my person) spoke clipped English with a hint of a Midlands accent to it. His good lady had a pleasing, matronly appearance, a soft Scots accent, and was equally reserved. The family was completed by two pretty girls, both in their late-teens, who were so obviously 'on-their-best-behaviour' that they could have given deportment lessons to the guards outside Buckingham Palace.

All of the family were about as formally dressed as anyone can be in the Greek sunshine… pressed khaki shirts and neat shorts, matching sun hats; Dr and Mrs D wore sandals with socks, and the girls were in the same style, but with slightly brighter blouses and track shoes.

They also all looked fairly fit. This latter was hardly a surprise… it didn't take much imagination to see this particular socio-economic co-habiting group doing calisthenics together every morning. I had a mental impression of the Von Trapp family crossing the Alps, slapping their *lederhosen* and singing uplifting songs about sexually-deprived practitioners of animal husbandry.

We sat down around the cockpit table, and they offered me an orange juice. Now, our destination was Lavrion, which lay on the outside of the Attic peninsula close to Athens, and so the voyage ahead of me involved crossing about a hundred and twenty miles of the Aegean Sea. At first glance, given the prevailing weather and time frame, it was not a daunting prospect; but when I was offered an orange juice at six in the evening, Lavrion suddenly became Paris, Fourni became Moscow, and I felt like Napoleon!

My brief from Rory was that there had been a bit of a bad experience somewhere on the holiday, which had resulted in my call up. They were good clients who had chartered several times in the quieter areas and seasons, and had felt ready to try the central Aegean; Rory wanted them back safely and in time, but most of all he wanted me to try to restore a bit of confidence… he didn't want to lose the custom.

With this in mind I tried to break the ice by being bright and breezy, to instil confidence by downplaying the difficulties, and I outlined a minimum stress, maximum scenery route to get us back to Lavrion as painlessly as possible. I had spent considerable time on the ferry working this out with the aid of the pilot book, and it included as little upwind sailing as possible and lots of white churches with blue domes. And Dr D wasn't having any of it.

"We shall go to Patmos tomorrow," he announced firmly, "I would like to leave early, and be there before noon. I particularly wish to see the Monastery of Saint John the Theologian, and the Cave of the Apocalypse. Then we shall need two nights in Mykonos, in order to have enough time to fully explore Delos. One night in Naxos should be sufficient I *think*... the harbour is said to be uncomfortable, in any case... and then we need to go to Paros to see the Church of a Hundred Doors."

Well, that was five of his eight days, and it would leave him a long way downwind of Lavrion and barely half way home. The thing was perfectly possible, even with the current forecast for the strong northerlies to continue or even strengthen, but it was not easy. Tomorrow's run to Patmos was twenty miles due south with the wind behind us, but the day after we would have to beat up to Mykonos, a run of over sixty miles through all the sea and wind coming through the gap between Ikaria and Tinos. Then we would surrender all our hard won northing to go down to Naxos and Paros, and have only three days to climb up to Lavrion again... the last day of it crossing the notorious Kavo Doro strait where the sea again runs big between Andros and Evia. In the forecast weather, it wasn't a trip for faint hearts, or for restoring bruised confidences.

I tried to moderate expectations, suggesting that Paros could be visited by ferry from Syros without going so far south, but the adult D's were firmly insistent and the girls had no say, so I smiled sweetly and said 'OK'.

"We did want to go to Santorini too," remarked Mrs D airily, "but one of my secretaries went there last year and she said it was frightfully touristy."

Thank all the Gods for one of Mrs D's secretary, I thought... Santorini is another fifty-odd miles south of Paros... getting back from there in this wind would have made the Anabasis look like taking the Jack Russell to the nearest lamp post.

There was no spare cabin, so I installed myself in the saloon and got cleaned up after my travel whilst the family went for a swim exactly in the manner I would have expected... all cleaving the water purposefully, no splashing or sky-larking. Then we ambled up the single street of Fourni, which slopes gently up away from the quay, lined with traditional, white-washed, flat-roofed houses and an abundance of fragrant orange trees. Great, hungry gulls eyed us speculatively as we walked, and cicadas rasped like football rattles.

An excellent and healthy dinner of fresh fish and salad was consumed at a delightful little taverna, and for a moment my spirits rose as Dr D ordered a bottle of wine; but sadly, he was suckered-in by a fancy label, and it wasn't so much a *chateau* as a *chat eau*. Even in my deprived condition I was quite grateful when it turned out that the girls were also indulged with a glass, so my share of it didn't amount to much. I was uncharacteristically stoical when there was no suggestion of a second bottle.

After the family went to bed, I found a half kilo of decent Samian table wine to lay the ghost of the dinnertime filth. Then I called Rory and let him know what was going on... I didn't want him thinking I had led them into evil ways, but he was quite relaxed about it.

"OK, chum. Do what you can to make it easy for them. 'Preesh the call! Toodle-oo!" Click. I noted that I wasn't being 'whomed' any more, which seemed, on consideration over the last of the wine, to be a good thing... it sounded as if I was already a part of Rory's team. As I enjoyed that thought, I noticed that people were stringing flags from the trees as if for a festival.

* * *

The next morning I walked up the street again to the port police office, a single room set far enough into the town to prevent the occupant from seeing anything in the port which might alarm or disturb him. I had slightly ticklish business to transact... I had to get myself entered on the crew list, but I couldn't do that as a skipper; foreigners were not officially allowed to skipper in Greece.

At that time, probably seventy-five per cent of the skippers in Greece were foreigners, and the authorities knew it perfectly well. The mainland ports of Alimos and Lavrion were chock-a-block with men... and a few women... of all nationalities; some highly regarded and retained by large charter companies, some working from contract to contract, and very, very many trying to break in to the market. I had been fortunate to slide in as serendipitously as I did. There were a good few Greek skippers too, of course, but the majority were *xeni*.[*]

Some thought the industry would have collapsed without the incomers, others thought not; but there certainly was plenty of work for the established

---

[*]   Foreigners

skippers, and it did seem that they were filling a need and bringing a lot of money in to the country. The authorities ignored the rules or not, as it best suited them… and since inactivity was always an attractive prospect in a hot country, it usually best suited them to do nothing; but some lip-service still had to be granted.

The way this was managed was simply to put the skipper on a bareboat charter crew list as one of the charterers, even if it meant a Kalahari Bushman sailing with a family of Eskimos; and if, for example, a port police official in Alimos Marina happened to notice that he had just signed the same skipper out for the twentieth time in one season… well, coincidences happen. Many people ridiculed the bureaucracy for stupidity, but anyone who thought they were pulling the wool over the authorities' eyes was very much mistaken: those port policemen never seemed to do very much, but I was often in the port police offices, and as I started to learn the language I quickly became aware that they were well attuned to waterfront gossip. They generally knew who was who… as those characters who carried any dubious activities beyond reasonable limits were apt to find out.

Getting the skipper on the charter crew list at the beginning of the charter was done by the boat's owner or agent, and was never a problem; but joining the vessel as skipper half way through the charter might make an official suspicious. Greek civil servants didn't do much, but then they didn't get paid much either; their lifetime goal was early retirement on a secure pension, which could be seriously affected by missing promotions. They didn't like irregularities… they then had to make decisions, for which they could be held accountable; so I was being a little cautious as I approached the very young port policeman in the flag-decked Fourni office with a concocted story about being a family friend joining the party and a notarised letter from the boat's owner.

The port policeman was not only very young; he was also very smart in his pristine white uniform, very merry and very cheerful. At his elbow was a carafe of something which looked like, but certainly wasn't, water, and he had his feet up on the desk, holding forth volubly to a couple of girls and two or three other men who looked like fishermen.

As I was posing as a family friend joining the holiday I thought it best not to speak any Greek, but the policeman spoke (for those days) unusually good English. He regarded me speculatively, gestured me to a chair, and then sucked his teeth thoughtfully as he flipped through the papers. After a moment or two he filled a small glass from the carafe and pushed it across the desk to me with a friendly smile.

"Drink!" He invited me. "Today is our saint's day. The church, and also my girlfriend."

He gestured towards the two girls without distinguishing one from the other… maybe he couldn't, because they appeared to be sisters and neither could I… and I cheerfully toasted his apparent polygamy. As I had expected, the drink was *tsipouro*. He nodded his appreciation as I drank it off in one, and refilled it; then he went back to the papers. Whether it was the booze or just natural ability, he had unusual presence for such a young and junior chap.

I could see a frown developing as he flipped the papers back and forth, and did my best to appear unconcerned. Then abruptly, he said to me in Greek, "When you are leaving?"

I almost answered, but just managed to stifle the reply in time. I raised my eyebrows, cocked my head and rotated my palms up to indicate non-comprehension. He smiled slightly. Then it occurred that I had responded like a Greek… a genuinely misunderstanding Brit would have said "I beg your pardon?" or "Oh! Were you talking to me?" Despite my subterfuge, I decided that he had me bang to rights.

The bright, promising future of the port police lowered his feet to the uneven flagged floor, languorously unfolded himself to an impressive height, and handed me back the papers.

"No problem, but tomorrow, Captain. Today, no sailing- too much wind. Not permitted. Please come to the party… and bring your…" he paused for a significant instant; "…Friends".

"Ah!" I replied, thinking quickly, "…But would it not be possible to sail just to Patmos? The wind will be behind us and my… friends would like to see the churches."

"*Thistichos, ochi.* Unfortunately, no. No sailing today. Bring the young ladies, they will like to dance with us." His friends nodded judiciously, as if that idea had just occurred to them. It was about as convincing as the Munich agreement.

"After all," he continued, "…You aren't in a hurry are you? You are on holiday. It is not as if you are a professional captain… that would be illegal, hah ha ha!"

He laughed to show how ridiculous such an idea would be, and then gave me a grin like an enamelled bear-trap and topped up my glass again. I smiled to signify gracious acceptance of defeat and tossed off my *tsipouro*. It made a good gesture, and also gave me a bit more courage to face Dr D with the news that the mysteries of the Cave of the Apocalypse were going to have to remain that way for another day.

He wasn't pleased. He was sitting at the chart table measuring distances, and as I broke the news to him... at least, the part about the weather restriction; I didn't chose to bother him with any discussions on the legality of my status... he pursed his lips, looked down at the chart, and severely positioned all the rulers, pencils and books in neat patterns whilst he listened to my explanation. It appeared that he had a touch of C.D.O.*

"And why can't we sail?" he enquired analytically.

I confess that I lied, but only with the noblest intentions. My function as a charter skipper, as I saw it, was to be the conduit through which he passed to pleasurable experiences, and I was doubtful whether I would improve his day to any meaningful degree by saying 'because the port policeman and his friends want to get your daughters drunk and dance with them, and probably your missus too'; so I said, "Strong weather warning."

Harbour-masters or the coastguard could indeed issue an *apagorevtiko*, which translates roughly as 'a forbidding', which prohibited vessels going to sea. It wasn't always total; often captains could sail on their own responsibility, but the policeman had not given us that option. He also had not signed me onto the crew list. Officially, we could not leave.

"But," Dr Deering reasoned, "tomorrow's forecast is exactly the same. Why can't we sail today? Or will he stop us tomorrow as well?"

I do so love being piggy-in-the-middle. In common with most people in his situation, Dr Deering did not seem to appreciate that convincing me was as useless as convincing the town hall cat.

"I don't think he'll stop us tomorrow," I replied, and then instead of adding, 'because I think he's going to have a hangover', I tried to put the best gloss on it that I could.

"The town has rather kindly invited us to the *panagyri*... it is the feast of the local saint. They are interesting folk-culture events... traditional music and dancing, local food and handicraft, and such like."

---

* It is like OCD, but with the letters in the right order.

Such a festival, known as a *glendi,* does indeed start culturally, but they tend to get somewhat more Dionysian fairly rapidly. Keeping that to myself, I stressed the cultural aspects which would precede the wassail because I was sure that would appeal to the family's apparently rather serious appetites. Or perhaps I should say, the parent's rather serious appetites, because from the corner of my eye I could see the two daughters perking up remarkably at the mention of dancing. It was also egging the pudding somewhat to say that the town had invited us, but I thought it might incline them to accept rather than appear impolite.

"Well, I think it sounds delightful!" enthused Mrs D, to my relief. So we went to the *glendi.*

* * *

It started at the church, and it didn't start well. The little building was already full to bursting, so there was no opportunity to examine the icons or frescoes, to Dr D's dismay. We were kept outside the church with the village menfolk, most of whom preferred to remain in the open air and engage in spirited conversation. The singing was melodic and unexpectedly accomplished for such a small community, but unfortunately was relayed to the listeners outside by a particularly execrable loudspeaker system which howled and rasped, at times, like a soul in torment going through a liquidiser. To converse over this racket the men naturally had to shout, and it was pretty much a cacophony even before the bells got going.

After that, the local dignitaries all took it in turns to make speeches... I don't suppose this is different in villages in any culture; those who make their way up the organisational ladder love to orate, but if they were any good at it at all they would have progressed beyond village politics. It is a pit of mediocrity from which there is no escape... turgid text delivered in mumbles with abysmal timing, punctuated by blessed lulls as the microphone drifts away from the speaker and then by harsh bellows or outraged screeches as it is brought back. And ever and anon, the hideous uncertainty of never knowing whether the fifth page which was just turned on the speakers notepad is the merciful last, or merely the end of the introduction; or, indeed, how many more assistant deputy vice-busybodies have yet to eat the air.

Through this we all stood more or less stoically. Dr and Mrs D seemed mildly restless, but the girls and I were in much deeper agony. Periodically the dapper port policeman, who stood just outside the church with two ordinary policemen, would turn around and smile at me, as though to say "If I've got to sit through this, you can bloody well have some too!" I smiled back and tried not to make it too obvious that I was wishing him in the pit of nether hell.

In fact, when I am bored to tears in speeches, churches, meetings or wherever, I have a self-preservation technique: I block out the sound and start running through Shakespearian soliloquies in my head. That evening I was Macbeth and, had that port policemen but known it, for about an hour he was the King of Scotland.

But eventually it ended, as all good things must. Now came the procession, the icon of the saint being solemnly escorted up and down the street by the priests and the three men in uniform. Some followed in the train, others stood to provide the audience. A pleasing proportion of one to the other was achieved, apparently entirely by chance. The icon was rehoused in the church, and the music began.

Now, I like Greece. It would not be going too far to say that I love the country. I certainly love its people. I have a deep regard for its history, its customs, and its values. And I like its music and dancing too... but I could wish that they would occasionally change the record.

The first twenty minutes of a Greek dance are very fine indeed. The costumes, wherever they are from in the country, are magnificent, and the grace of the dancers is enchanting. The music is fascinating; a wild, harsh mix of melody and cacophony which speaks eloquently of contrasts, of the juxtaposition of civilisation with a pagan past, of a land which has spent centuries at the crossroads of opposed cultures. The tunes are old; very, very old. And forgive me for suggesting it, but frankly, after the first half-hour, it's time for a new one!

The problem is, to my untutored ear at least, they all sound the same. In western culture, dance music tends to have a central theme from which it wanders away and, usually, later returns. Most traditional Greek dance music is the same phrase, over and over. By the time they start the second one I am starting to look hunted, and by the onset of the fourth I feel as if my dentist is approaching the job through the back of my head instead of the front.

Sadly, it is the same with the dancing... the grace and coordination fascinate me at the outset, but after a while, it is, after all, just people going around and around in a circle for twenty minutes. To an unchanging tune. There are wilder dances to be sure, dances with heel-slapping and jumping, with acrobatics and swirling partners, but they don't seem to occur at the local *glendies*. One gets a series of monotonously similar dances executed to monotonously similar tunes, first performed by the kids, then the older kids, then the big kids, and then by various local dance societies, and then the guest dancers. Round and round they go, always the same way it seems, and it can go on for hours and hours.

Possibly my problem with this lies in the perspective. Greek dancing, it seems to me, is certainly a celebration of national traditions but also, I feel, an expression of the dancer's feelings more than an entertainment. Perhaps it isn't really intended as a spectator sport. Or perhaps it is just me, because many others seem to enjoy it... Dr D seemed engrossed, and was busy with his camera; but his daughters appeared somewhat jaded by the fourth set, and as for Mrs D... well, she spoke well of it, but methought she did protest too much.

Having found the drinks table I was suffering as stoically as I could, and then I blessedly fell in with the island's doctor, who was happy to talk to me in French about the massacre of Psara. At least, I think it was the massacre of Psara, but with the strength of the *tsipouro*, the background noise and my French being what it is, he might equally well have been telling me about his technique for performing appendectomies with a fly-mow. It took my mind off the dancing, however, so I was enjoying the exchange when Dr D interrupted us.

"Have you seen the girls?" he asked with a slightly accusatory edge to his voice and a meaningful glance at the glass in my hand.

I had not, felt inexplicably guilty about the fact, and fought back with a manful, and mendacious, "I saw them standing behind you just a few moments ago."

He tutted and started doing gopher impressions as he sought out the fruit of his loins. I made an ostentatious show of looking in another direction, and after some fruitless scanning of the crowd I suddenly spotted them exactly where I should have looked in the first place... at the end of the dance-line, firmly attached to either side of a white uniform.

I prodded the peeved parent, wordlessly indicated his springing offspring, and re-engaged in my conversation. As I did so, the dance-line rotated sufficiently to allow me to see the middle; and there, in all her glory, with the hem of her long, narrow skirt carelessly tucked into her waistband to free her rather attractive legs, danced Mrs D, eyes and teeth flashing with pleasure as she received instructions from a couple of fishermen. Her husband clearly didn't know what to do about this, so I handed him a glass of *tsipouro*. He was so far out of his comfort-zone that he drank it.

Remarkable stuff, *tsipouro*. I doubt if it took it more than a couple of hours to transform that primly civilised academic into an exultant, scarlet-faced Neanderthal who bested two brawny fishermen at arm-wrestling outside the kafeneion… a conquest watched with delighted incredulity by his wife and younger daughter. I dare say they related the event to the older daughter later, because she was an even earlier convert to the charms of *tsipouro* and, having retrieved her almost unconscious from the solicitous care of one of the younger fishermen, I had carried her off fireman's style. By the time her father came to his triumph, she was already laid out in the saloon of the boat like Kirk Douglas in the final scene of *The Vikings*. Until early evening her mother made regular checks on her daughter's welfare, but after that it was left to me to keep an eye on the heir to the Deering overdraft as Mrs D changed into a rather less restricting skirt and abandoned her maternal duties in favour of dancing 'Good Golly Miss Molly' style until she had exhausted several partners half her age.

* * *

It was a fragile group who assembled for breakfast the next morning, one which, quite literally, did not know what had hit it. I don't suppose there was a lot of experience of dealing with blinding hangovers in that family, and I was rather touched by the way they whimpered and tried to help one other… it put me in mind of a litter of new-born pups when their mum goes out for a pee. When I prescribed gallons of sweet tea, toast, and a swim they obeyed with the blind zeal of Prussian guardsmen and showed the most touching appreciation of my solicitude. When I offered to delay the departure to Patmos until the afternoon, they looked at me as if I had just invented a cure for cancer.

The port police beast was made of sterner stuff… he was as dapper, as cheery, and as languidly assured as the previous day. He was also as good as his word, entering me into the crew list without even a smirk, and politely asked if I would be leaving immediately.

"This afternoon, I think…" I replied airily, "my friends want to go to the beach and look around a bit more."

His smile reflected off the opposite wall.

"You see!" he said with that gargantuan self-confidence which Greek men are so lavishly imbued with, "I *told* you they would like Fourni!"

* * *

Seven days later I waved the Deerings goodbye at Hellenikon Airport and headed down to the Plum Pudding Club en route to the hydrofoil back to Poros. As I nursed a cold draft beer and waited for Shergar to finish fixing a gin palace's anchor winch and join me, I reflected on the very pleasant sail we had enjoyed from Patmos. The girls had been relaxed and chirpy, Mrs D bubbly and pleasant, and even Dr D had been civility itself. He had accepted my renewed suggestion not to go south, and we had a night in Ornos Bay on the south side of Mykonos and then anchored overnight at Delos before day-hopping through Syros, Kythnos and Kea. By keeping the wind mostly on the beam we enjoyed fast, exciting passages, and compensated for the lost Church of a Hundred Doors in Paros by visiting the cathedrals of Ermoupolis, the golden beaches of west Syros as immortalised in the song *Frangosyriani*, the hot baths of Loutra and the lion of Kea.*

I puzzled over Dr Deering's sudden acquiescence, and after a while decided that it was a man thing… he had, of course, been somewhat crestfallen at having to call in a skipper, and in retrospect I suspected that my patronising 'there-there-it's-all-right-now-Julian-will-make-it-better' approach had probably made him mad enough to eviscerate me with the jam-spoon. In all probability, we would have clashed all the way through the Aegean, but for the fortunate opportunity offered by the licentious fishermen of Fourni for him to display his manly prowess at the arm-wrestling table. Once the lion had roared, however,

---

* All of which, thanks to the pilot book, I discoursed knowledgably about without ever having set eyes on them before.

and the pride had heard him, all was well again. I made a mental memo in neon… when skippering, the man of the party is likely to feel challenged: Take note and give him some opportunity to shine.

Two days later, relaxing over a long, exquisite lunch in The Snailery, I took a refreshing mouthful from my icy glass, opened a fax from Rory, and promptly sprayed the paper with cold beer.

'Congrats! Deerings delighted- have booked 10 days September & want you to skipper. 5% booking commission to you if accept. Itinerary to include 2 days Santorini, Naxos and Church of a Hundred Doors, Paros.'

Dr D, it appeared, had rather more of a sense of humour, and was not so easily diverted, as I had supposed!

CHAPTER TWELVE

SWAN-SONG

In which we meet a real working ship... and an idle one... a Ton of trouble... the Meltemi... problems with summer wind... a call to duty... paperwork... Swanning around... mechanical perfidy... Shergar shows his metal... we prevail... a recipe for a disaster... a summons... an arrival.

A large tug used to live in Poros in those days. She was a salvage tug which lurked there waiting for some unfortunate vessel to have a breakdown or a collision in the busy waters at the mouth of the Saronic; and that tug never slept. Her name was *Fengari*, which meant 'the moon', and it was appropriate for, even in the darkest hours of night, the porthole of her radio room shone out like an honest man in Parliament as the airwaves were greedily sieved for bad news.

When that news arrived, the *Fengari* erupted into a roil of activity in her determination to be the first to the casualty, and her behaviour then was less than considerate, for, with a salvage in prospect, *Fengari* considered, 'decorum' was something that happened to apples.

When something of interest emerged out of the radio, *Fengari's* master, heedless of waking the whole town, pulled his whistle-cord and didn't let it go until all his crew were on board. As the last man galloped, half clothed and awake, up her long stern gangway it would be pulled in even with him still on it, and the last lines slipped. The ship would clank and froth her way off the quay, and then, contemptuous of permission to sail or speed limits in the channel, she would select the most direct route to the 'shout', ploughing east down the straits or west along the bay, and disappear.

Anything between a day and a week later she would slip back into her berth, and the longer her absence, the smugger she looked on her return.

216

Anything more than three days, and she exuded self-satisfaction like a crocodile in an empty hippo enclosure. She would then apologise insincerely for any disruption, uncomplainingly pay any fine imposed for her antisocial behaviour and resume her sentry duty.

Poros did not resent this cavalier behaviour. In fact, the town took a slightly masochistic pride in the disruption. Above all, it was a seafaring community, and such a vital, virile connection with the vagaries of marine life was part of the fabric of the place.

Fengari was well known to me, not least because she had damned nearly trampled me underfoot during a couple of her impromptu departures, and I was well-used to her high-bowed, chalky shape sitting at the northern extremity of the ferry quay; so, when I entered from the west one day early in August, it took me a moment to realise that there were now two high, white bows on the wall.

At first I thought I was seeing double... a constant worry, given the lifestyle... but it was early in the day and I had passed a quiet night, so I conjectured that another... possibly (and I experienced a *frisson* of anticipation at the thought) a rival... tug had arrived. That theory also crumbled as I got closer, however, when I saw that the newcomer's main-deck was not open, as a tug's must be, but rather appeared to have what looked like a tenement on top of it. And she reminded me of something.

She was painted white with dark-green trim lines on her rubbing-strake and funnel, and her name, *Swan*, in the same forest-green on the bow. Something over fifty metres in length, with a rather old-fashioned upright stem, her forecastle was strangely high and long for her size. It eventually rose to a neat little enclosed bridge and then dipped back to forecastle level to accommodate a business-like funnel. The forward half of her was as seaworthy a craft as a mariner's heart could desire, but at the funnel the delight turned to dismay. From about amidships there rose a slab-like block of cabins, decorated with external galleries and stairs, which resembled nothing so much as a hijacked, twin-storey American motel. This edifice almost reached the stern, finally sinking gracelessly to a small, open poop for a few feet until the vessel ended in a flat transom hung with a large bathing platform. The accommodation did not flow with the line of the vessel, and looked almost temporary.

I had seen nothing quite like her. She looked as if someone had mated a tug with an American stern-wheel river-boat, and yet I still experienced a most irritating sense that I should know what she was. Her forward end was hauntingly familiar. I did in fact wonder if someone had welded two ends of dissimilar ships together… but that couldn't be, because, as the light shone full on her side, I saw that she was carvel-built out of wood. And with that discovery, the penny dropped… she was an old Royal Navy Ton-Class minesweeper, and someone had dumped an accommodation block on her main-deck.

The Ton-Class were ubiquitous in their day, a numerous family of ships in the British Royal Navy and built for, or sold to, a number of other navies too. Made of wood, to reduce their magnetic field, they had high bows to counter the harsh northern seas, a traditional naval capped funnel and a long, open main-deck which gave them their distinctive profile. With their double-diagonal carvel construction, they were tough as nails too… effectively double-hulled… and twin engines and rudders made them pretty manoeuvrable.

Doughty little ships, by the early eighties many had been paid off from naval service. I had seen them being used as training-ships, trawlers and static floating accommodation, but the extra accommodation puzzled me. I had never heard of them being used as passenger ships, and even if that was her purpose, she was in entirely the wrong place. She had a large Cayman Island ensign at her stern… and Greece is very restrictive about allowing foreign-flag carriers to operate in her waters. I wondered what the ship's current function could be.

The Poros waterfront did not keep secrets long, of course. *Swan* was not an inconspicuous visitor. Her high bow and accommodation block were almost as big as the *Ydra* and the *Danae*, the larger ferries which served the island, and her ensign was so big that it almost swept the quay. Her owner, Les, a larger-than-life chap with a vaguely Mid-Atlantic accent, a spade-beard, a ringing laugh, a beer-belly and more teeth than a crocodile's wedding photo, was not exactly a recluse either. The story of our new neighbour was soon out.

Purchased from the Royal Navy and fitted out for dive-chartering, *Swan* was neither fish nor fowl: the bridge and forecastle were rather as they had been in her naval service, Spartan and utilitarian, except that the cabins had double beds installed. She retained communal heads and shower compartments in the forecastle. The new accommodation block was composed of twin bunk cabins without en suite facilities… comfortable, basic housing which was adequate for divers but completely useless for normal passenger service. Underneath the cabins, the old mine-sweeping deck was enclosed in a single, long bar-restaurant furnished with plastic patio tables and chairs.

Les was quickly a familiar face in the watering-holes of the town and frequently invited parties back for impromptu barbeques. Invited to one of these, I got to know him a little and rather liked the chap… he was extremely noisy when happy, and he became happy very readily. His extrovert ways were not calculated to endear him to everyone, especially the officials he had to deal with, but I got the impression that he was a very genuine character beneath the persiflage.

Having fitted out *Swan* as a dive vessel for the Caribbean, Les had crossed swords with various official entities there and simply sailed away. On a whim, without any research on the matter, he had decided to do 'a bit of diving in Greece', and when he arrived from Gibraltar he announced to the port police that he had 'come to do some diving on the antiquities'.

Now, Greece was so sensitive on the subject of uncontrolled access to historic artefacts that diving was actually banned unless one had a government-approved dive supervisor; so Les's declaration, coupled with the casual revelation that he had fifty sets of diving equipment on board, was the equivalent of Lord Elgin returning with a back-hoe and an empty truck. Greek officialdom had a collective seizure. By the time they recovered sufficiently to make a decision what to do about this, Les's South African captain had left the country because his visa was expiring; so *Swan* sat in Poros, with all her diving equipment firmly under customs seal, and without a crew apart from her enthusiastic but highly landlubberly owner. And in Greece, July is the month when the *Meltemi* starts.

* * *

The *Meltemi* is a north wind which predominates in the months of July and August, and it can be anything between a robust sailing wind and a howling gehooligan. *Meltemi* is taken from the Turkish *Meltem,* which may have its roots in the Italian '*mal tempo*' or 'bad weather'; but the original Greek name is the

Etesian, or Annual, wind, derived from the word *etos,* a year. The two different derivations always seem to me to mirror the two culture's differing confidences on the sea.

At times, the *Meltemi* can be so severe that it almost closes down the Aegean, and at any time it makes that sea uncomfortable for all but very confident and adventurous sailors. It is also a wicked spreader of wild fire... extinguishing fires in the *Meltemi* is a Herculean endeavour. Nevertheless, it is welcome in one respect at least; it tempers the heat.

In a normal year, the *Meltemi* starts around the second week of July when, just as one begins to feel that the temperature will go on rising until the fishermen started to land ready-poached fish, the *Meltemi* begins to blow and finally tames the heat.

Strongest in the Aegean, the *Meltemi* is still significant in the Argo-Saronic; but its effect is rather different. At moderate strength out in the Aegean Islands it typically starts from a morning calm, building to force six or even more in the afternoon, and begins to die again mid-evening, leaving a lumpy sea.

I soon found that, on the Peloponnesian coast, however, it would typically rise to a stiff northerly by about midday; then the heat rising off the land started the thermal wind, and the *Meltemi* would be countered by the south-easterly *Bouka Doura.* This normally brought the wind to a calm about two o'clock, and then it reversed to blow from the south, rising to force five or six by early evening, before dropping again.

All this is jolly useful to know when getting up and down the coast in a normal *Meltemi*; but the *Meltemi* that hit Poros just after Les's captain made his adieus was the other sort, the sort which takes no prisoners. A full *Meltemi* can last a couple of days or a couple of weeks, and it is an unremitting, whistling torrent of northerly air which blows day and night, raising high, short seas in open waters and sending lethally strong *spilliades* cascading down the backs of any high ground to bedevil any water on the supposedly sheltered side. The best place to be in a full *Meltemi* is tied up firmly to the lee side of a strong pier. *Swan* got it half right.

* * *

My day started very pleasantly. Sleeping *al fresco* on my terrace, I was awoken by the earliest probing fingers of the resurgent sun, and, being sufficiently refreshed, I decided to start the day. Trotting down to Kanali Beach, I had a coffee at a beach bar and watched the searing orange orb detach itself from the eastern horizon near Agios Yeorgios.

As I plunged into the ocean to wash away the vestiges of night I heard the trumpeter of the nearby naval school saluting the raising of the flag, and then I pottered along to the all-night bakery behind the beach. This was doing a steady trade from a fifty-fifty mix of sprightly, early rising enthusiasts heading smartly out and dishevelled all-night revellers limping in, and I bought a piping-hot, fresh *spanakopita,* or spinach pie, for breakfast.

As I munched my pie, I wandered back over the canal into town, strolling along the North Quay as I noticed that the north wind was already sending reconnaissance parties of skittering flurries across the sheltered waters of the bay. Not a good day to be on the North Quay, on the windward side of the town, I noted; and then, with the complaisance that came from the fact that I didn't have a boat to worry about, I ignored the matter. When I reached The Snailery, close to the cinema, I saw the *Fengari* churning away up the bay, evidently with work in hand. This left the high starboard bow of *Swan* pretty much unsheltered from the north.

By about midday I was smugly content, sitting at George's Cafe in perfect shelter as the flag at the clock tower above me crackled and snapped in the rising wind. With an early, icy, invigorating beer in my paw I watched with compassionless complaisance whilst frequent blasts of wind hurled spray lashed the yachts and heeled them sharply over as they escaped from the North Quay, running helter-skelter round in to the shelter of the channel.

Gina and Andrea, winding down after their nocturnal shift before going to sleep on a beach, were with me. Shergar and Miss Iceland, who was back again, had joined me, and also Yiorgaki and his brother, Simos. This latter was a young Merchant Navy officer who was currently doing his national service as a sub-lieutenant in the Navy, and was the First Lieutenant of a World War Two-Vintage Fast Patrol Boat which was tied up at the naval school. In the finest Poros waterfront tradition, the combination of heat, beer and lack of immediate commitment had induced in us all a languorous detachment from care.

Into this lotus eating assembly suddenly came the bustling, pristine white figure of the Chief of the port police, an entity from whom I normally kept a polite, watchful distance. I always assumed that he knew I was working from Poros, and since he hadn't bothered me I supposed that, so far, I hadn't upset him. It was my earnest wish to keep things that way.

"*Kalimera!*"

He bad us all good morning and, without waiting for a response, he addressed me, in very fair English.

"Captain Tzoulian, please can you tell me... I believe you are First Captain,* yes? You have diploma? From British?"

I admitted that this was so. In fact, I held a British Chief Mate's certificate, but I had already passed a Liberian Master's examination for a foreign-flag vessel I had sailed on. This news seemed to please him.

"And you sail on big ship? Real ship?"

"Yes, that is my job," I told him... I was somewhat concerned about why he wanted to know this, and gave him a fiction he could reasonably accept. He nodded.

"Please can you help me? I have big problem. Is one British ship, this one *Swan*. She have to move. She have problem, and she have no captain. She need to go to anchor."

"What problem has she got?" I asked. The reply came in a flood of Greek, which Simos untangled for me.

"The anchor is dragging, and she is blocking the ferry quay. There is a ferry coming very soon. They want you to move her."

I agreed to take a look, and we all trooped around, out of the shelter of the town and awnings, into the teeth of the *Meltemi* gusting across the bay from Neorion. Things were, indeed, a bit grim.

Swan had been lying with two anchors out and her stern very professionally tied to the quay with four stern-lines and two crossed lines to brace her; but the wind on her unprotected starboard side had been too much

---

* Greek sailors do like their titles. Anyone with a boat, even one in his bath, is a Kapitanios, and this also applies to all certificated deck-officers. When working on Greek ships, everyone is calling each other 'captain'. The actual captain is known formally as the Kivernitis, literally 'governor' and synonymous with the English 'Master'. Informally, he is the Protos Kapitanios, or First Captain.

for her anchors. Her starboard cable was almost slack, and her port one was as tight as a bowstring across her bow, grinding ominously on her stem.

She had fallen to port so that she was at an angle of about thirty or forty degrees to the quay, with her port quarter grating horribly against the concrete. On her small poop-deck, Les was making a valiant but futile attempt to get a large fender into the non-existent gap.

"You are captain, you can take her to anchor, yes?" asked the port policeman, and almost turned away... he seemed to have complete confidence that this would now be done. I hastened to disappoint him.

"*Ena lepto...* Please, a moment, Captain," I said. "I can't just walk on board and take over this ship. I don't know how it works, what condition it is in. And unless they are declaring a distress, I need the permission of the owners."

Simos translated this, and the port policeman's face cleared immediately.

"No problem. Thees the owner."

He waved at Les, and shouted to him, "Hey, Meester! This man Captain. From British, same as you!"

He waved at the streaming Cayman ensign which, having a Union Flag in the corner, was all the evidence of nationality he evidently required. "Now, you go. You go now. Go anchor." And with that, off he went.

Les came down the gangway.

"Can ya help me getter outa here?" he demanded, whilst crushing my hand and looking at me as if he was buying a horse with a limp.

"Dunno," I replied, "Is everything working?"

He shrugged.

"Think so. Dunno why not, it all was."

"Can you get the engines started?"

"Yep, I reckon I can. Just not too sure about the fuel tank switches."

"Ah!" I had a think about that. "Right, I'll tell you what. You get the engines on line, and we'll start running them ahead, to lessen the weight on the quay. Meanwhile I'll have a look at the bridge. Then we test the steering gear, then the anchor winches. Then, when the engines are up to temperature and we're sure they're running OK, we'll see. Have you got a bow-thruster?"

He shook his head at this last. Pity! That might have helped.

"I'll give you a hand with the engines," volunteered Shergar, and the two of them disappeared up the gangway.

Followed by the rest of my interested crowd, which had now grown by the addition of a port policeman and an ordinary policeman, I explored my way up to the bridge. On arrival, the first problem I identified… in my calm, professional manner… was the complete lack of a steering wheel!

If the lack of any apparent means of steering was set aside, the bridge appeared otherwise well-equipped. I quickly found the other bits I needed in the short term… standard Teleflex-type engine controls, a rudder-position indicator, VHF radios and voltage-metres which seemed to indicate good current available. A large captain's chair and a smaller engineer's one faced a compact and crowded instrument panel where I noted two large switches labelled 'steering gear', which I left alone for the moment… even if I could find out how to steer, I didn't know if the generator was large enough to take the load.

I found a trap door into the space below and opened it, wondering if the steering position was below the bridge as in some other warships, but unfortunately it appeared that this was an access to the captain's cabin, and the captain apparently had a mate, who was in the process of dressing. I closed it again with a quick apology.

A phone buzzed, and Les informed me that I could start the port engine using the key on the bridge. It came up second time, and I set it at one thousand RPM, out of gear, to watch the temperatures. Then I asked Simos to go and check that the port propeller was clear of ropes or obstructions. When he said it was, I gently put the engine in gear and increased power a little to try to reduce the contact with the quay.

The phone buzzed again, but the starboard engine resolutely refused to start. I asked Les to come up on the bridge.

"Can I start the steering gear?" I asked. He shrugged again, a deep, comprehensive gesture which eloquently said "Only one way to find out!" and pressed the button. The light flickered on. He pressed the second button, which also lit up.

"And now, how do you steer her?" I asked.

For a reply, he lifted a piece of varnished plywood revealing the shaft where the wheel should have fitted, and a chrome plated lever which was obviously a non-follow-up steering backup system.

"We took the wheel off to varnish it," he announced, "an' then we never put it back. We didn't use it much, see, an' the instrument panel is too slopey to put the beer on."

"Have you got the wheel?" I asked. He shrugged again.

"Probably." He looked vaguely around. "Haven't used it fer ages."

I sighed and tried the lever. It seemed to work.

The port police chief was back on the quay, shouting through the whipping wind to know if we wanted the lines letting go. I went down to talk to him.

"I only have one engine," I told him, "and I don't know how the ship will handle in so much wind. The safest thing to do is slack the anchors, and let her come alongside."

This was translated by Simos again, but before he was halfway done the port police chief was becoming agitated. Simos said, "He wants you to go, now. There is a ferry coming, he needs this space.

I looked at it. True enough, there was no way to get a ferry onto the quay with *Swan* angled across it. I desperately wanted to help out... as I have said before, I like helping anyway, and I especially liked helping this guy, who could probably have me run out of town if the mind took him... yet I also didn't want to end up being held responsible for wrecking the *Swan* by taking her out in a strong wind without all her equipment working, even in an emergency.

"Les, do you have an official logbook?" I asked.

From the now familiar heave of his shoulders and pout of his lips, I inferred that I might as well have asked for world peace and disarmament.

"OK, are you the owner?"

He grinned like a Cheshire tiger, delighted at last to be able to answer a question in the affirmative.

"And is the vessel fully insured?"

Again, he was happy to please me with a positive answer.

"Right, then I need a witnessed letter from you saying that the situation is an emergency..." I pointed at the damage already sustained by the *Swan's* port quarter... "and asking me to put the ship in a safe position."

Les nodded and went off to do this without demur. He was a very obliging chap when it lay within his power. I had a rather different response for the port police chief when I turned to him, however.

Explaining to him, with Simos's help, that I was willing to help but needed to be indemnified in case of a problem, I asked for a letter to confirm that I had been asked to remove the vessel by the port authority. If I had asked for the sole rights to his favourite daughter, I couldn't have had a more negative reaction.

I hadn't yet been long in Greece, and my knowledge of the country was, of course, nowhere near as complete as I conceited myself it was; otherwise, I would have known that getting a Greek official to put a signature on anything, even something mundane and routine, is like asking him to stop a train with his head.

He said he couldn't; I said that, in that case, I couldn't too. He said he was ordering me too; I said he couldn't, I didn't work on that ship. He asked me as a favour, as a fellow seaman, to do it; I, expressing the profoundest regret, in parallel with my esteem for his person and position, declined.

Finally I knew we were getting somewhere when he looked at his watch, cast a haunted look up the bay to see if the ferry was yet in sight, and said he would prepare the letter immediately, and give it to me after I had moved the *Swan*. Well, there was a lot I still had to learn about Greece, but I was ahead of that move at least. I told him that I would try to get the starboard engine working, and wait for the paper, and as soon as it came on board I would move off the quay.

To my amazement, some fifteen minutes later, a port policeman came trotting along the quay bearing a typewritten letter with a big stamp on the bottom. I couldn't read a word of it… I had begun to make some elementary steps in reading Greek, but lower case typewriter script is still difficult a quarter of a century later. So I handed it to Simos.

"What does it say?" He shrugged. It was turning out to be a very shruggy sort of day.

"I think it is very good. You will like."

Just at that moment, Shergar announced that he had cleared a blockage in the starboard fuel filter, and the starboard engine was running. Fair enough, I thought. Let's do it. I scribbled quickly on the letter what I understood it to be, got Les to witness it, and made for the bridge.

Les went to the anchor winch, and confirmed that the hydraulics were running, both cables were in gear and all was ready to heave-up the anchors. Simos and Yiorgaki took a walkie-talkie and went aft to let go the lines. Shergar stayed in the engine room to keep an eye on things down there. One port policeman, Gina, Andrea, Miss Iceland and the captain's mate took up interested positions on the bridge, until I shooed them out onto the wings. Half of the Poros waterfront congregated to watch the fun, and the wind, sensing the theatrical qualities of the moment, began to gust over forty knots according to the anemometer on my instrument panel. Everyone, including the *Meltemi,* appeared to be ready.

When we were down to a single rope aft, a rope which quivered with tension and threatened a lethal backlash if it parted, I got the port policeman to keep spectators clear and told Simos to cut the line with a long knife. He recognised the danger, and kept well out of the way, using a bread knife* lashed to a broom-handle. The line parted with a twang, and we were off.

Increasing the port engine speed, I signalled Les to start heaving and put the tiller hard-to-starboard. *Swan* sprang away from the quay, and began to swing her stern very rapidly into the channel between Poros and Galatas. The windlass began to clank as the chain cable started to come in. And then a hydraulic hose detached itself from the windlass, reared vertically into the sky, and shot a jet of hydraulic oil high over the bridge, and all over my window.

I said a naughty word.

With the windlass disabled, and two anchors down on a long scope, I was somewhat trapped. *Swan* was driven this way and that by the wind, which blattered across the bay from Kalavria, hitting the ship now from one side, now from t'other; and as she swung one way her stern narrowly missed the ferry quay, whilst on the opposite swing she came perilously close to boats anchored in the excellent mud near the channel. As Les and Yiorgaki plummeted into the bowels of the ship to try to find a new hydraulic hose, I grimly manoeuvred the engines and rudders to try to limit our swing, but I was also aware that the anchors were still dragging slowly. I was moving gradually astern towards the shallows off Galatas, where many boats anchor. It was a lovely, clear day... A feature of the *Meltemi* is that it blows under clear, open skies... and the growing crowd in Poros had an excellent view of the proceedings.

I was gratified by the remarkable speed with which Les reappeared, triumphantly brandishing a new hose and a spanner. I was even more

---

* I have elsewhere extolled the invaluable qualities of bread knives when cutting ropes. Never, ever sail without a bread knife, even if you are gluten intolerant with a wheat allergy.

impressed by the very workmanlike manner in which he set about changing it. He was about as nautical as a giraffe on a pogo-stick, but he did appear to be a practical chap.

I was not quite so impressed with the port engine, which now decided to have an afternoon nap. Shergar appeared briefly on the bridge to inform me that this looked like another clogged filter, and estimated twenty minutes at least to clear it... it didn't look pretty, he confided. By way of a reply, I took him out on the bridge wing and showed him the church in Galatas, which was getting steadily nearer, and didn't look very pretty either. He took my point, and submerged again like a cormorant after a fish.

As I tried to manage the meandering of my crippled charge across the narrow, wind-whipped waters between Poros and the mainland, my mind began to dwell somewhat on the number of ferries which passed through here every day, linking the islands of Hydra and Spetses, the ports of Ermioni and Porto Xeli, to Piraeus. I also caught a glimpse of the clock tower, which, if it was correct... it sometimes was... showed that it was about one hour since I had been sitting without a care in the world at George's Cafe; one single hour in which I had gone from being a blameless innocent in the early stages of getting pleasantly inebriated to the man with the potential to cut off half the Peloponnese from Piraeus at the height of the holiday season.

Well aware that things were not going well, but powerless to help, the port police on board tried to get Simos to ask me what was going on. Beyond a polite 'we're working on it', I was too concentrated to reply, and Simos was too sensible of the situation to press me. Then, evidently unaware of the situation, another port policeman arrived in an inflatable boat and shouted up at Les.

"You can't anchor here!"

Les was preoccupied with his repairs, and in any case was not a natural diplomat even by marine standards, but he initially maintained his cool to reply politely that we were not anchoring.

"Then what are you doing here?" demanded the port policeman.

Les's patience expired at this point, and his reply was delivered so forcefully that, even in the teeth of the gale, it reverberated back from the very walls of Galatas.

"We're having a fuckin' picnic, ya butt-head!"

I assumed, from the lack of resentment with which this was received, that the port policeman was not *au fait* with colloquial English.

The windlass hammered and banged a bit as it was restarted, but quickly settled down, and Les resumed heaving the anchors. At last, inch by inch, *Swan's* stern began to edge further from the anchored boats in the channel. My heartbeat slowed to that of a mere machine-gun, and I even found the time to quickly explain to the port policeman that we were moving away now. And, even as I made this fatefully premature pronouncement, the rudders jammed hard-a-starboard.

I was feeling that I was beginning to run out of options now. Only one engine, neither anchor holding, no steering, and the wind battering me left-right-left like a heavyweight boxer moving in on a beaten opponent. I sent Simos down to appraise Shergar of the steering problem, and watched in glum silence as *Swan's* high bow started to swing broadside to the wind.

I had one shot left in the locker. The theory of ship handling says that, when the engine is operated astern, the stern of the ship will 'seek the weather'; that is to say, she will stabilise with her stern pointing into the wind.

The scientific reasoning for this is that a vessel turns about a 'pivot-point', which is normally about a third of her length from the stem when moving ahead; but when she goes astern this pivot-point moves to a position near the propeller. The result is that the whole area of the ship forward of this pivot-point is acted upon by the prevailing wind and behaves like a lever, swinging the bow away from the weather. It is a theory one rarely gets the chance to test, so what the chances were of it working at any time I wasn't sure; when applied to a vessel with a large box on her after deck and designed to be twin-screw, I had no idea what the theory said, but as I found myself broadside on to Galatas with a plethora of small boats in an anchorage between me and the shore, I decided that beggars could not be choosers and I put my last remaining engine full astern. Then, having nothing else to do, I explained what I was doing to my audience. I don't know how much of it they followed, but it was damn good occupational therapy for me.

Considering that we were still trailing two anchors on short scope, I was hardly surprised that it didn't immediately work, but we did progress backwards out of the channel a little, and I began to hope that I could ground the ship clear of most of the boats at anchor. But finally the port anchor broke the surface, and Les put it out of gear. The stern came a little closer to the wind. Les began to recover the last of the starboard cable. As I came closer to the yachts in the muddier water near the point, I risked coming ahead on the engine as much as I could, the starboard engine acting on the rudder to send us reasonably straight back into the channel. Then, as Les roared with triumph and the starboard anchor broke the surface, I came astern again and the *Swan* gently brought her back end up into the pulsing wind.

Ever so slowly she swung, but she kept her gentle parabola, and looking aft from the bridge wing I thought she might just clear the shallower water. I risked one more quick kick ahead, but her stern started to fall off again so I came back astern, shutting my eyes as I saw the clouds of mud now blooming in the back-wash of her starboard prop.

The phone buzzed. I didn't answer it, because I had seen the port engine tachometer leap into life. With the greatest self-control I had ever exerted, I resisted the temptation to ram it full open, but gently increased the revolutions ahead until I felt the stern just start to swing; then I left it strictly alone.

The port screw, acting ahead on the rudder, now started to swing my stern away from the mud-bank whilst the starboard prop continued to edge me to windward into deeper water.

Les appeared on the bridge, wiping oil from his face and forearms, and laconically said "Good deal, Man!" as though everything had gone exactly to some plan I was entirely unaware of. Then Shergar arrived, equally bespattered and wiping his specs.

"Anything you can do with the steering?" I asked tersely.

"Try it now," he replied, "…I just called, but you didn't answer the phone."

I opened my mouth, shut it, centred the tiller, and saw the rudder indicator judder unsteadily back to 'amidships'.

"It's still not too clever. Don't go full over." Shergar advised me.

"What happened?"

"I think it jammed at hard-over. Probably a worn pivot on the linkage, or a bad bearing. I stuck a crowbar under the rudder-heads and lifted 'em a bit. It felt like they came free."

What an utter genius the man was. I could have kissed him.

I reversed *Swan* almost as far as the Poros hotel before swinging her gingerly to starboard and laying as much anchor and cable as I dared in the mouth of Russian Bay. Les brought everyone a cold beer, and then pointed at the aluminium motorboat on the forecastle.

Let's have a cold one, an' then I'll run y'ashore. I reckon I owe ya lunch when this wind goes down." he said, matter-o-factly.

I was in a sort of a daze as we sped back across the bay. It all seemed more like a story I had read in a book rather than something I had participated in myself. The sense of unreality was heightened by the absolute calm with which everyone took it. I had finished the manoeuvre… if such farcical, *force-majeur* antics can be graced with so elegant a title… in a muck-sweat, unable to bend my knees in case they folded under me. Even after anchoring, I had to press my beer can against my lips to prevent it shaking when I drank.

Everyone else, on the contrary, appeared at complete ease and chatted happily. I gathered that they were all quite content with the procedure.

Stepping out of the aluminium 'tinny' at the dock, I saw the clock again. Just two hours after we had left George's Cafe, we resumed our seats and George replenished our beers. As I sat down I felt a crinkling in my pocket, and pulled out the letter from the port police chief. I handed it to Simos.

"What does this *really* say?" I asked him.

He grinned, and added another shrug to the daily total.

"Ah… it is a recipe for *melitzanosalata*… aubergine salad!" he admitted guiltily, and then added, by way of mitigation, "A very *good* recipe!"

We later found out that all our efforts had all been for nothing. The ferry never arrived, having sunk after a collision in Aegina harbour!

* * *

The day after the affair of the *Swan*, Kyria Fotini informed me that I had a telephone call from Petros to go to the cafe. I trotted down through the first cooling of evening and emerged from the maze of lanes behind the cafe. Petros pointed nonchalantly to a table by the statue in the middle of the square where sat a middle-aged couple.

"They wants to see you," he explained economically.

I twisted my hands outwards in the gesture which indicates that a Greek wants to know 'what is it about?', and he replied with the less-than-helpful tut which indicates that a Greek doesn't know and cares less.

They were a couple of the best dressed scruffs I had ever seen; he in faded shirt, threadbare cords and a sun bleached cravat, she in a blouse, skirt and a necklace made apparently of old rope. As I manoeuvred round the front and introduced myself, he rose and removed his hat... a folding panama which looked like it had once belonged to an origami research establishment... in a reflexively gentlemanly manner and introduced them as Sylvia and Gerald. The voices were plum jam with extra plum... fruity, and as far-back as a dinosaur's tail.

"I hyar you are not averse to a Gin-and-Tonic?" enquired Gerald as he motioned me to a seat. Petros had one ready, it seemed, so I didn't bother asking where he had 'hyar'ed it.

"You have been recommended to us," he continued, "...as someone who could porssibly hyelp us ayt. We have to get to an archaeological dig on an island nyar hyar, and we would like to spend the night there; but one does like a modicum of comfort, donch'yer know? Seemed like a boat might be just the ticket."

"Which island?" I asked.

"It is called Dokos, I b'lieve."

An uninhabited island outside Ermioni, about seventeen miles from Poros; but I wasn't aware of any activity there.

"Oh, it's quate new, I b'lieve. Started last week. Diving, an old harbour they've fyound, 'parently."

"Ah! And are you archaeologists?" I enquired

Sylvia said, "May fault, Ay'm afraid. Complete amateur, naturally, but fascinating stuff, fascinating. We've been invited by the professor leading the dig."

"Old school-chum of mine," added Gerald. Yup, he probably would be, I thought. Along with most of the cabinet, and half of the House of Lords.

A couple of drinks, and all was concluded. I phoned Spiros and he did a deal to let me take *Molto Alegro* for two nights... not much of a sailor, but probably the best boat to take if 'a modicum of comfort' was required by the clients in prospect.

"Now," concluded Gerald, "…if you could recommend a decent restaurant, could we porssibly orffer you dinnar?"

Certainly they could. I took them off to The Snail, where we regaled ourselves on his peerless roast pork and fruity, fresh wine… for which beverage they showed an unexpected and endearingly proletarian appreciation. They were excellent company, Sylvia being very knowledgeable about the ancient history of the area and Gerald having done a good bit of sailing in earlier days. I found myself looking forward to the trip, and only a bit sorry that it wasn't longer.

Towards the end of the meal, Gerald suddenly smiled at his glass, and said, "Now, listen hyar, old chap. I'm afraid we haven't been quite above board with you. You've been ambushed, I'm afraid. Not our fault, only actin' under orders, what? But we will have one other passenger tomorrow too."

A finger tickled my ear-lobe.

"Hello, Skip!" said a soft voice behind me. "I see you're ingratiating yourself with the family."

It was Clemmie.

* * *

"I didn't know if I should have come back or not," she mused as she ran a finger around the rim of her glass. "You can tell me to bugger orf again, if you like. But it seemed rather… oh, I don't know… providential, I suppose, this dig coming up just here, just now."

"Couldn't be more delighted!" I assured her.

She cocked an eye mischievously at me.

"Ryally? One hyars such lurid stories… out-of-work actresses haunting the docks, Swedish tour operators, naked bathing on catamarans…"

"Well, if you have done your homework that well, you'll know that the Swedes were lesbians and the catamaran was full of Swiss Nuns. I am clean in soul!" I protested. She laughed.

"As well as in body."

"Oh, no, never that… I'm still a grubby oik!" I protested.

"Well, so you say. So you say. But one hyars of entire communities fed on pig. One hyars other tales too. Tales of derring-do… saving fishermen, and minesweepers, battling the elements? Isn't there some reprehensible pretension of nobility here?"

"Absolutely not. Hadn't a clue what I was doing, got into scrapes by accident and got out of 'em by the luck of my heathen God and the skin of my discoloured NHS false teeth. You know me... as far as I am concerned, *noblesse oblige* means a helpful eunuch."

"One hyars," she continued, "...that on this minesweeper, the 'English captain was very cool, didn't say a word'."

"The English captain had run out of things to say," I assured her. "If the English captain had opened his mouth, he would have screamed for his mum."

"One hyars that the English captain was exceedingly firm with the local authorities. No nonsense from Johnny Foreigner, sort of thing."

"Now that is entirely true!" I agreed, "...and as a consequence, the English captain now knows how to make an exceedingly fine aubergine salad!"

* * *

Sunset over the Peloponnese. The *Meltemi* had subsided, and the *Bouka Doura* was declining gently as the sun sank into the promontory of Akra Mouzaki. *Molto Alegro* lay at anchor in Skindos Bay on the island of Dokos, and we were all invited to share the evening meal of the archaeological team, to which I had contributed a pile of home-made *bifteki* made on *Molto's* charcoal grill. The clatter of chatter sounded behind us as Clemmie and I sat on the end of the promontory and sipped wine in companionable silence.

It was still summer, with all of autumn to come. I had almost two months of fairly steady charter work lined up for me by Rory Carteret, and Clemmie was going to be working at Dokos until she went back to Uni in October. I was extremely comfortable in Poros, and had access to boats to take me down to Dokos pretty much any time I was free.

That sausage in Piraeus, I thought, was taking some time to digest!

At this point, I must repeat the disclaimer made in Adjacent to the Argonauts.

My old friend Pandelis is still the ex-officio master of Hydra Harbour, and my even older friend Petros still runs his cafe in Poros. One new character, The Snail, continues to delight his Poros public with both his cuisine and his humour. As previously stated, there are some people whom it is impossible to describe even remotely accurately without disclosing their identity, and so I have made no attempt to disguise these larger-than-life characters.

I have also indulged myself by mentioning two most excellent teachers from my school days, together with my very good friend Joe Burke, sadly no longer with us. This I have done purely out of an impulse to record a modest tribute to these fine gentlemen.

With those exceptions, however, the identities of all persons in this story have again been compounded from various experiences. The reader is assured that, although the inspiration for the characters and occurrences in this book is genuine, I do not describe any actual person or event apart from the exceptions mentioned.

The cover for this book has been painted by the talented and charming Pats Van Dam, who knows her subject as she has been rash enough to sail with me. Take a look at her work on www.patsvandam.com. Old shipmates Dave Baboulene and Roger Sarginson have been refreshingly unsentimental critics, and cruising buddy Aad Wijt has made valuable analyses from the cockpit of Sahlamara. *To these friends, and to many others who have offered encouragement during the writing of* The Trojan Walrus, *my earnest thanks.*

Once again, my most sincere gratitude to Greece and its people for providing a canvas upon which even a blind man cannot help but paint a glowing picture.

GLOSSARY

This glossary is an updated version of the one published in Adjacent to the Argonauts. *New entries are in italic script.*

Anchor   Intended as a means of finding your boat where you left it, this useful item is primarily a conversation piece. If you have three yachties in a room, you have five opinions on anchors. Some people favour the sorts which are light and easy to lift- these people are dangerous lunatics who should be confined for their own good. What you need is a behemoth with lots of teeth and attitude.

Anchor chain   Attaches the anchor to the boat. In the Mediterranean, you want lots of it, and none of this nonsense about rope being just as good, as the bottom of the Med is mostly made of razor-blades.

Anchor winch   *See Windlass*

Back-stay   A wire which is attached to a very strong point at the back of the yacht and runs up to the top of the mast. It supports the mast from behind, and is an essential safety feature when urinating over the stern.

Beating / Beat   *A vessel is said to be 'beating' or 'on a beat' when she is as close to the wind as she can sail. When doing this into stiff wind and*

237

weather, she is said to 'on a hard beat'. I suspect these terms originate from what the crew feel like afterwards!

Bitter-end	The very last link of the anchor chain. The one you *really* don't want to let go of.

Boom	A spar which attaches to the mast with a hinge. Its purpose is to extend the mainsail aft from the mast, to control the angle of the sail to the wind, and to tension the foot of the sail; its perverse delight is to batter the unwary about the bonce.

Bow-sprit	Devilish device on more traditional boats- a large spike sticking out of the front to extend head-sails, stays and anchor-leads. Fine at sea, but a liability in small harbours.

Bow-thruster	*A propeller fitted on the bow of a boat, sometimes in a tunnel through the hull and sometimes on a telescopic leg, which faces across the vessel and is used to push the bow left or right when manoeuvring. Driven by hydraulics, electric or their own engine, most of them make more noise than thrust. They don't often get you out of trouble, but they do make sure that everyone else knows and can come and have a laugh at your expense.*

Cap-shroud	A wire which is attached to a very strong point on the deck and runs up the side of the mast to the top. Half way up it passes over the end of a small spar called the spreader. Its purpose is to support the mast from the side, and other vital uses are as a hand-hold when entering the boat from the side in a state of impaired equilibrium or a support for a sun-awning.

Companionway	The main entrance and exit of the cabin to the cockpit. This is usually a steep climb down 2 or 3 steps to the cabin floor, and the steps commonly form the cover of the

engine compartment. It is protected from the elements by a sliding hatch cover over the top and by wooden hatch boards which slot in to the vertical side. Effectively, the yacht's front door.

Cruising chute	*A large sail which is somewhere between a genoa and a spinnaker, used when moderate wind is coming from the side or behind. The material and colour are like a spinnaker, but the tack it is fastened to the bow of the boat and there is no pole. It is not as powerful as a spinnaker, but then, it is not as homicidal either.*
Echo sounder	A gadget which sends a sonic signal out of the bottom of the boat and times how long it takes to come back. By a simple sum allowing for the speed of sound in water it takes an educated guess at the depth under the boat. Often complicated by the fact that a signal leaves and takes so long to come back that it returns just after the next signal has been sent... resulting in indications of shoal water where none should be and subsequent myocardial dysfunction. Works equally well on dolphins, fish, and air-bubbles, with the same result.
Engine	A contrivance which works on the principle of squeeze-bang-blow to convert money via fossil fuel into approximately equal portions of noise, smoke and forward motion. The clever little thing also makes something called 'amps', which are the preferred bed-time snack of batteries. Variously referred to as The Iron Top-sail, The Beast In The Bilge, and That Bloody Monstrosity, it is more properly referred to as an infernal construction engine.
Fender	A sort of strong balloon on a rope which is hung over the side to prevent hull to hull contact with adjacent boats or quaysides. Frequently wrongly tied on, and consequently lost.

Foot	The bottom edge of any sail.
Forecastle	The forward part of a ship or yacht, scene of derring-do with ropes and anchors
Fore-sail (or Head-sail)	Any sail which sets forward of the mast, supported on its forward side by the fore-stay.
Fore-stay	A wire which is attached to a very strong point at the front of the yacht and runs up to the top of the mast. It supports the mast from forward and is used to set the genoa or jib. It also acts as a shoulder-rest for urinating off the bow, and supports hammocks excellently.
Furling line	*A rope which wraps around a drum at the bottom of any roller-furling device, particularly genoa roller-furling. When pulled in the cockpit, it rolls the sail away; when released it allows the sail to roll out. Quite often.*
Galley	Sailorese for 'kitchen'. Outwardly simply jargon, but there is in fact a distinct delineation between galleys and kitchens. Food which would never be acceptable from a kitchen is commonly highly esteemed when created in a galley. Examples are sardines in condensed milk, sautéed corned beef in onion brulée and the eight-day curry.
Gang plank	*What you get when you don't have a passerelle. For a more accurate description, simply omit the word 'gang'.*
Genoa	A species of fore-sail commonly fitted to modern yachts. It is attached at the luff to the fore-stay, and extends aft of the mast. Very powerful. Often abbreviated to 'Genny'.
Genoa sheet	Rope which extends from the free corner of the genoa to the cockpit and controls the angle and shape of the genoa.

Due to the power of the genoa, it requires a winch to adjust it. Often abbreviated to 'genny-sheet'.

Genoa track A sort of railway and car with a pulley through which the genoa sheet passes on its way to the winch. There is one on each side of the boat. It is used to alter the shape of the genoa to suit the wind, and to keep curious crew busy when the skipper needs a few minutes to think.

Gin palace Large motor boat of the opulent variety. Much loathed by sailors for running generators in idyllic bays, occupying large chunks of harbours, creating huge washes which spill one's curry, and costing a lot of money.

Gooseneck The hinge at the front of the boom.

Gybe The act of turning the stern of the boat through the wind, so that the sails change from one side to the other, the principle feature being a rapid movement of the boom across the top of the cockpit. Divided into two categories, 'intentional' and 'unintentional'. Both categories are further subdivided into 'controlled' and 'uncontrolled'. An intentional, controlled gybe is much appreciated by sailors; an unintentional, uncontrolled gybe is much appreciated by mast salesmen and, occasionally, undertakers.

Gypsy A sort of gear-wheel in the windlass or anchor winch which grips the chain.

Halyard *Any rope which pulls a sail up the mast and tensions the luff of the sail. (Compare with 'sheet' and 'tack'.) The name originates from the days of square-rig, when the 'yards' were 'hauled-up' to tension the sides of the sail; thus, 'haul-yard', which elided to 'halyard'. Main halyard for the main sail, genoa halyard for the genoa. Something logical at least.*

Hatch	An opening Perspex window in an aluminium frame set in the deck of the boat to allow light and ventilation in and scared yachtsmen out.
Heads	Sailorese for 'toilet'. Derives its name from the 'catheads' - a place up by the anchors on old sailing ships which was designated for the purpose of letting it all hang out. Due to the size and complexity of plumbing in yacht toilets, this old tradition is undergoing an enthusiastic revival.
Helm	*Generic term for whatever means of steering is provided on a boat, whether it be tiller, wheel or oar.*
Helming	*A word coined to allow sailors to mysticise and en-noble the prosaic and often boring task of steering.*
Hook	*Slang for Anchor, which see:*
In irons	See Tacking
Jib	A fore-sail smaller than a genoa. Most charter yachts have only a storm-jib, a very strong, small sail for extreme conditions... and no way of setting it due to the existence of the roller-furling!
Kedge	An anchor which is dropped from the stern of the boat, instead of the bow. Used when mooring bow-first, or when desperately trying to stop, it is also sometimes transferred forward and used to make an open moor... this is defiance of the rule that if a yacht can't lie safely to one anchor, then elsewhere is the place to be!
Keel	Lump of hopefully aqua-dynamic iron attached to the bottom of the boat to a) minimise leeway and b) keep said boat sunny-side up.

Ketch	A sailing boat with two masts, the aft one being shorter than the forward one. The aft one must be positioned forward of the rudder-stock, otherwise she is a yawl. A good, seaworthy rig whose smaller sails making balancing the boat simpler and are easier to handle... but at the cost of a lot more wires and obstructions.
Kicking-strap (or Kicker)	A rope pulley which tensions the boom downwards. It is used to control the shape of the main sail, and to keep idle hands busy when they might otherwise be peacefully employed denigrating the skipper. Known to Americans, for reasons no doubt clear to them, as a 'boom-vang'.
Lazy-line	A thin rope, frequently covered in marine growth, which connects a permanent anchor to the quay, so that a visiting yachtsman doesn't need to drop his own; he simply backs-in and pulls the lazy-line up until he has attached his boat to a large ground-chain and in the process covered himself in slime, slashed his fingers to the bones on barnacles, murdered a large chunk of the eco-system and transformed his gleaming yacht into a kelp-bed.
Leach	The trailing edge of any sail.
Life lines	A sort of fence around the sides of the boat to stop the inhabitants falling off. It is made of wires stretched tightly between the pulpit and the pushpit, supported at intervals by posts called stanchions. Also serves to attach fenders to. Sometimes called hand-rails, guard rails or a bloody liability.
Log	Gadget which measures distance travelled through the water, and calculates speed.
Luff	A) The forward or leading edge of any sail. B) The act of coming closer to the wind until the front of the sail collapses. If persisted in it will lead to a 'tack'. When done

deliberately, a recognised way of slowing down or moving upwind; when done accidentally, a recognised way of annoying the hell out of the skipper.

Main hatch	The sliding hatch over the companionway.

Main sail
: The sail which sets aft of the mast. In a conventional rig it is attached to the mast by the forward edge or 'luff' and to the boom by the 'foot'.

Main sheet
: The system of blocks and line which controls the angle at which the boom lies to the mast. In gybes it can rocket across the cockpit, and since it is close to the crew it can become highly importunate.

Mud-weight
: Substitute for an anchor used almost exclusively on the Norfolk and Suffolk Broads- just a big weight, like the ones Tom always drops on Jerry, attached to a rope.

Open moor
: Dropping two anchors a little way apart in order to give support to the bow from two sides. Very secure mooring, but it requires skill to execute and skill *and* luck to recover afterwards. Usually only attempted in the Mediterranean by the most desperate of skippers, due to the unbelievable amount of ironmongery in Mediterranean harbours.

Outhaul
: *Line which tensions the foot of the main sail along the boom.*

Parallel rulers
: *Navigating instruments... two rulers connected by two movable arms so that they can be walked over a chart whilst remaining always parallel to each other. Used for transferring course-lines and bearings on a chart. Until the skill of directing them is developed, they are harder to control than an orbital floor polisher and the inexperienced navigator can find the 'parallels'*

progressing directly away from where he intends them to go. They also go uncontrollably sideways until they get jammed against the side of the table. Then, as one tries to get them back on track, they hit the dividers or stick on a fold in the chart, jerk out of line, and one has to start all over again.

Passerelle	A neat little gang way, frequently with a tidy rope handrail and sometimes boasting lights and even a door-bell, which extends from the stern, or sometimes bows, of a yacht to allow the crew to walk ashore.
Pawl	A sort of tooth on the windlass or anchor winch which only allows the winch to turn one way, to stop the chain running out again when heaving up. To drop the anchor it has to be lifted up.
Pick	*Slang for anchor, which see:*
Pipe cot	*A temporary bed made of a piece of canvas with a pipe through the edge which pulls out and slots into locking holes. A sort of a cross between a hammock and a stretcher, nice to sleep in at sea, as you don't roll around. They are a bit restricting at other times, and thoroughly reliable as contraceptives.*
Pulpit	A tubular frame, usually stainless steel, which wraps about the forward side of the yacht as a means of projecting the life lines round a person working on front of the boat. Named because of its resemblance to a pulpit.
Pushpit	The same as a pulpit, but at the other end of the boat. So if one is called a pull-pit, the other must logically be…
Reefing	The act of reducing the area of one or more sails in order to stay alive when the wind gets stronger.

Riding-turn   *A condition where a winch is immobilised by a tangle. The load-bearing end of the rope being winched rises over the turns on the drum, trapping them so that the winch cannot be turned and the load cannot be heaved further or released. Difficult to clear, as it requires the loaded part of the line to be de-tensioned. In light weather, a knowing tug upwards may do it; but in strong winds, it is potentially dangerous and takes time and skill to clear. Sometimes it may be necessary to cut the line.*

Roller-furling   A nifty device which rolls a sail up somewhat like a cafe awning, making it easy to set, reef or douse the genoa. A sort of tube which fits around the fore-stay with a reel at the bottom, it winds in a 'furling line' as the sail is rolled out and when the furling line is pulled back out it winds the sail back in again. Most of the time.

Rope-clutch   A devilish enticement… a lever attached to a toothed jaw which holds a rope under tension. The more the tension, the tighter it holds, so it is very easy to apply, and very hard to release when you really, really need to!

Sacrificial anode   *See Zincs*

Sacrificial strip   A strip of material sewn on the leach and foot of the genoa to protect it from ultra-violet damage from the sun when rolled up.

Sheet   *That rope or purchase system which attaches to the free corner at the back of a sail, and which is used to control its angle to the wind. (Compare with 'Halyard' and 'Tack'.) There are, therefore, genoa sheets, main sheets, spinnaker sheets. The expression 'I couldn't give sheet' may mean a crewman cannot release this rope. Honestly, it really could.*

Spinnaker	*A large balloon shaped sail, used to make boats go faster when the wind is not too strong and coming from the side or from behind. Immensely powerful, and can cause a lot of expensive damage if it gets out of control. Unlike other sails, it is not attached along one edge to the boat. The head is attached to the top of the mast or thereabouts;.the windward corner or 'tack' is held out by a pole, and the leeward corner or 'clew' is controlled by a sheet-rope. The ropes controlling these corners are the 'guy' (controls the pole) and the 'sheet' (controls the tack.) The spinnaker is of very light material and usually brightly coloured, it takes skill to use, and even more skill to put up. And once it is up, your troubles have often only just begun... I call mine Gaddafi, because he dressed in bright colours and was suspected of terrorism.*
Stern gland	*Technically, this is the (more or less) water tight seal which fits around the propeller-shaft where it passes through the hull. Metaphorically, it refers to that part of the human anatomy which most closely resembles it in location and purpose. 'Nipping up the stern gland' refers technically to tightening the seal to prevent ingress of water, and figuratively describes a physiological response to a worrying situation.*
Tack	*The side from which the wind is coming and a deciding factor in who is to blame when sailing boats collide. The vessel is on the tack opposite to the side on which the mainsail is. Logical? Just to make things even clearer, 'tack' also refers to that free corner of any sail at which the 'sheet' is attached to control the sail's position relative to the wind. Or, again, it may refer to the rope or purchase system used to act upon that point of the sail. Look, I didn't make this stuff up, I'm just passing it on!*
Tacking	The act of turning the boat so that her bows pass through the wind so as to change from one tack to the other. This is another opportunity for the boom to have a go at the crew. If this is done accidentally with the genoa still

secured on the other side, the boat will be 'taken aback', an ungainly position wherein the skipper's gin and the crew's blood are likely to be spilled. If the boat is not going fast enough she stalls head-to-wind, when she is said to be 'in irons'.

Taken aback   See Tacking

Tiller   A glorified lever which steers the boat by transmitting the helmsman's errors to the rudder. The arcane nature of sailing makes it inevitable that to go left, one has to push it to the right.

Topping-lift   Rope leading down from the mast head to the outer end of the boom which supports the free end of the boom when the mainsail is lowered.

Toe-rail   The railing, usually aluminium, which runs around the outer edge of the deck. It is called a toe-rail because it breaks them, and is carefully designed to be just low enough to fail to stop any dropped object from going over the side.

Traveller   A device fitted close to the helmsman consisting of a sort of railway and car which adjusts the position of the lower end of the main sheet. In the hands of the expert, a powerful tool for trimming the main sail; in the hands of the inexpert, a finger-guillotine.

Trotter-box   *When a seat is too short to be used as a bed, a box just wide enough for the feet is often fitted to extend it into an adjacent compartment. A berth with a deep trotter-box is called a 'coffin berth', for obvious reasons.*

Up & down	Another manifestation of arcane sailing jargon. On a sailing boat, everything reverses itself depending which side the wind is on. 'Up' is used to mean 'towards the side the wind is coming from', and 'down' the opposite. Also, as the tiller goes the opposite way to the rudder, one must put the helm up to make the boat go down, and vice-versa. When the boat changes tack, up becomes down. Sometimes the wind is dead astern, so it doesn't work at all. To further clarify the matter, people also use 'up' and 'down' to mean heave-in or slack-out on various thingamabobs. One may also hear both 'up and down' used together when heaving up the anchor, to indicate that the anchor chain is vertical so the anchor is directly under the boat and about to break out. I hope this has cleared up any confusion.
VHF	Very High Frequency radio… a piece of electronic equipment which develops one's vocabulary and self-confidence. Users instantly begin to use terms which are never normally spoken aloud… words such as 'affirmative' and 'negative', or phrases like 'please advise your location' instead of the sadly proletarian 'where are you?' They are also instantly able to confidently use words they don't understand, such as 'roger' 'radio-check' and 'wilco'. The speaker experiences an embarrassment bypass event, as they cannot see their audience. An indispensable aid to confusion.
Wet	*A term used to describe a boat which readily throws spray or waves onto the deck, particularly in the area of the cockpit where the crew are cowering. Most boats are 'wettest' when going against the wind. In British use, this is almost invariably expressed in understatement – 'a bit wet' means that full waterproofs will be required: 'Wet' means snorkels or aqualungs. 'Really quite wet' is usually reserved for U-boats.*

Winch	A thing like a barrel with gears inside powered by a removable handle inserted in the top. You wrap a rope three times round it and wind the handle, which gives you sufficient mechanical advantage to pull in sails, mooring ropes, very large fish, etcetera… an indispensable device which has made sailing accessible to the indolent.
Windlass (or anchor winch)	A winch mounted on the foredeck for the sole purpose of releasing and recovering the anchor. Love and cherish this machine… its wellbeing is utterly crucial to the success of your Mediterranean holiday!
Yawl	A two masted rig where the aft mast is shorter than the forward one, and is positioned aft of the rudder-stock. The aft sail is used for balancing the rig more than driving the boat. Sweet to look at, but makes the stern of the boat rather complicated.
Zephyr	*Very light wind, especially one just starting.*
Zincs.	*Zinc anodes, sacrificial soft-metal ingots attached below the waterline to draw galvanic corrosion away from more important bits of metal. If a boat is 'showing her zincs' or 'rolling her zincs out' she is either heeled or moving excessively, so that the anodes can be seen above the waterline (Actually I was just chuffed to get a couple of 'Z's' into the glossary! J)*